I'm Glad You Asked

I'M GLAD YOU ASKED

How to Talk With Your Friends About
Their Objections to Christian Faith

Ken Boa & Larry Moody

I'M GLAD YOU ASKED

Copyright © 1982 by Ken Boa and Larry Moody

Revised Edition © 2018 by Ken Boa and Larry Moody

ISBN: 978-0-9899096-0-0

Published by:

Search Ministries

4330 W. Vickery Blvd., Suite 150

Fort Worth, TX 76107

searchnational.org

800.617.3272

4th Printing of Revised Version

To our wives, Karen and Ruth
"...a woman who fears the Lord, she shall be praised."
Proverbs 31:30

Contents

Acknowledgments

Our first acknowledgment must go to Matthew S. Prince. Matt taught us the significance of answering honestly and objectively the skeptical questions of our non-Christian friends. A special thanks to Bill Kraftson, who has faithfully sought to answer these objections through the course of his ministry and whose illustrations and sayings are sprinkled throughout this work. To Dave Krueger for his constant encouragement and insights into the charts and material. And to James Duncan, a layman who loves Christ and unbelievers, for his original suggestion to put these questions into a flow chart form.

We want to offer our particular thanks and gratitude to Joshua Moody who spearheaded and developed this new edition of *I'm Glad You Asked*. His work led to a profound improvement over the original in content, format, and aesthetics, and apart from his diligent and creative work, this would not have come to pass.

— Ken Boa and Larry Moody

The Second Edition

Prior to the first publication of *I'm Glad You Asked*, Ken Boa and Larry Moody, along with a few dozen of their colleagues, spent a decade moderating thousands of discussions where adults would come and wrestle with their questions about God and life. As these discussions took place in houses and workplaces all across the country, a few patterns quickly emerged: (1) Educated adults needed to feel like their questions and objections received a fair hearing before they were willing to consider another perspective. (2) Over thousands of conversations, no one raised an objection for which there was no reasonable response.

In 1982, Ken and Larry wrote *I'm Glad You Asked* and captured the logical, rigorous, accessible, and illustrative approach to apologetics that had made their Open Forum discussion series and follow-up so engaging for so long. Thirty years and 150,000 copies later, this approach still resonates with many.

This revision is both long overdue and surprisingly minor in many places. Ken and Larry were at the front of many cultural, academic, and scientific discussions when they first wrote the book. Thirty years later, only a few paragraphs in the original book needed to be excised because they were now demonstrably untrue. However, over the past three decades, we have seen a shift in the emphasis of a few of these questions, such that the original approach no longer addressed the heart of the current objection.

Every chapter has been updated for content, context, and style. Rob Bowman substantially rewrote the entire chapter on Question 4 regarding the reliability of the Bible. Both the nature of the objections to the Bible and the best approaches for response have changed significantly since 1982.

We've included many new illustrations that we've found helpful, including a number from Bill Kraftson's *Search for Meaning* audio series. We pray that this revised edition will serve a new generation, helping them help their friends think through questions about the Christian faith.

— Joshua Moody, *Editor*

HOW TO USE THIS BOOK

Introduction

Have you ever been overwhelmed by an onslaught of tough objections as you attempted to communicate the message of Christianity to a friend? Or have you ever chosen not to talk about God out of a paralyzing fear that you won't be able to handle their objections?

There are many honest questions that require thoughtful answers, but few Christians are capable of successfully fielding all of them. This book is designed to help you think through the issues involved, so that you can become more effective in your defense of the faith.

Christian apologetics—the rational defense of the Christian faith—really has a twofold purpose. Outwardly, it helps critics and seekers overcome their intellectual barriers to Christianity. Inwardly, it strengthens the faith of believers by showing that their faith rests upon a firm foundation. We wrote this book with both purposes in mind. The objections we deal with are derived from repeated experience, not theoretical speculation. Hundreds of hours of conversation with non-Christian friends led us to the conclusion that the same basic objections keep surfacing in individual and group discussions. Our experience has led us to group these into three types of questions.

Some people ask about the theological quandaries of Christianity—the mysteries surrounding the nature and actions of God. These questions are related to some aspect of God's infinite nature and appear to be paradoxes from our finite point of view. We can provide illustrations and analogies that make it easier to fall sleep at night, but we cannot resolve the tension or fully comprehend the doctrine on this side of eternity.

The second type of questions are what we have come to think of as stereotype-confirming questions or credibility-busters. These questions may include things like our attitude toward science and evolution, or social and political issues like sexuality, gender, abortion, healthcare, and immigration policy. When an outsider asks one of these questions, they are rarely looking to engage in a thoughtful, reasoned debate. Rather, they are expecting to hear us confirm that we belong in the box where they have mentally placed us—ignorant, uneducated, bigoted and narrow-minded.

All of these issues are *impacted by* the Gospel, but are not *central to* the Gospel. We need to formulate a thoughtful, comfortable response that doesn't burn bridges or impact our integrity, but lets us move past the issue towards the heart of the Christian message. Although they are important conversations at the right time and in the right place, if we camp here we risk becoming an irrelevant pariah who is no longer invited to spiritual conversations. Not every battle ought to be fought, winnable or not.

The third type of questions are the legitimate barriers to faith. These are the objections that, if not resolved, make the message of the Gospel incomprehensible. **We have found that the primary objections to personal faith in Jesus Christ can be boiled down to variations and combinations of the twelve questions addressed in this book.**

"Be Ready"

Many Christians shy away from defending their beliefs or resort to a "just take it by faith" attitude. They think that the burden of apologetics is too great to be shouldered by laymen. But Peter exhorts us to be ready to make a defense when we are asked to do so: "Sanctify Christ as Lord in your hearts, always being ready to make a defense to every one who asks you to give an account for the hope that is in you, yet with gentleness and reverence" (1 Peter 3:15).

It is encouraging to discover that practically the entire range of intellectual objections to the Christian Gospel can be conveniently reduced to a set of one dozen basic questions. Furthermore, every one of these objections is actually a golden opportunity—an opportunity to lead up to a natural presentation of the Gospel. This is why our development in this book of each of these twelve objections leads to a confrontation with the claims of Christ.

Keep in mind that people can ask these three types of questions in three different ways. They can be raised as obstacles intended to defeat the Christian position. They can be asked by people who want to show off in a group. Or they can be asked out of a real desire to find the answer, if there is one. A sensitivity to a person's degree of openness will affect the way you handle his or her question.

Questions 1-12 can be read in any order. In one sense, they stand on their own. But in another way, they all are interdependent, referring to one another for support. The two pillars upon which most answers rest are the authority of the Bible and the historical resurrection of Jesus Christ. These are developed in Question 4 and in Question 2 respectively, and the rest of the book often refers to these two key chapters.

The 12 questions are arranged from general to specific. The first three are general objections to religion, the next five are objections to Christianity in particular, and the final four are questions specifically related to salvation.

The flow charts that appear throughout these chapters will help you visualize the basic options to each question and the logical progression from one option to another. They have been provided as conceptual guidelines, not straitjackets. It is not necessary or advisable to take a person through all the steps in one of these flow charts when he raises one of these objections. Doing so could be disastrous. Instead, a knowledge of these diagrams (you may want to memorize the basic flow of each chart) can enable you to pinpoint the real issues that need to be addressed. The charts are not designed to bog you down, but to give you freedom in creatively dealing with these questions.

Some of the flow charts include optional material. This will be represented by boxes that are set off to one side.

In the sample chart in the sidebar, you can proceed directly from *a* to *c* to *f*, because the material in boxes *b*, *d*, and *e* is supplementary. If you find it necessary to deal with issue *d*, you will then have to go to *e* before continuing with *f*.

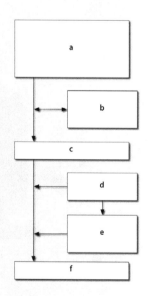

This book includes more detail than you will need on most occasions. Use only what is necessary, and don't try to prove too much. It would be unwise, for example, to discuss the existence of God or to plunge into the problem of evil if a person is ready to personally consider the claims of Christ. Your object is to remove barriers to the Gospel as quickly and effectively as possible, not to exhaustively explore them.

What's In This Book

Throughout the book, we have provided a variety of illustrations to assist you in answering these questions. Illustrations can serve as windows of truth that illuminate concepts by means of analogy. Use the ones you feel comfortable with or create your own. Never underestimate the power of using a benign secular illustration to explain an uncomfortable spiritual concept.

The material in these twelve chapters is limited to fairly brief treatments of these questions. *I'm Glad You Asked* aims to provide a solid overview

Is there really a God?

Why believe in miracles?

Is religion just a psychological crutch?

General Objections to Religion

Is the Bible reliable?

Does God make sense in a world full of suffering?

Is Christ the only way to God?

Will God judge those who have never heard about Christ?

If Christianity is true, then why are there so many hypocrites?

Specific Objections to Christianity

Will my good works get me to heaven?

Isn't salvation by faith too easy?

What does the Bible mean by believe?

Can anyone be sure of their salvation?

Clarification of Christianity

of the issues and the arguments, information, and illustrations that we've found to be most helpful in personal conversations. Of course, entire books and, sometimes, libraries of content have been published on each one of these twelve questions. We can't possibly cover every nuanced position or internet argument in a volume of this size, so at the end of every chapter or section, we've included a "Supplemental Reading" list for further study. Questions 1, 2, & 4 are noticeably more in-depth, as the breadth of issues involved in those questions is far wider than most others.

We hope *I'm Glad You Asked* will strengthen your confidence in the trustworthiness of God and His Word and further equip you to give an account for the hope that is in you.

How to Use the Information In This Book

Your object is to remove barriers to the Gospel as quickly and effectively as possible, and not to exhaustively explore them.

Just knowing the answers to questions that people ask and objections they raise about faith does not guarantee results. Many Christians have made the mistake of dropping answers on people who question Christianity, expecting them to immediately see the light. Little wonder that the Bible uses an agricultural motif to illustrate how people are brought into God's family. There is a period of time between the sowing of the seed (the Gospel) and the harvest of people. But it's unthinkable to sow seed without proper soil preparation, and cultivation must come before the harvest. Much emphasis in evangelism is placed simply on sowing and reaping. The following steps add the very important dimension of preparation and cultivation.

One of the key ways of "cultivating the soil" is *prayer*. Scripture contains many references which describe prayer as essential, but prayer is often ignored in evangelism. Time and time again, we have seen that where there was more prayer, there were more results for Christ.

In Colossians 4:2-6, Paul explains how the Christian should relate to the non-Christian. As we lay the groundwork through prayer, there are three things the Apostle Paul tells us to do. First, we should **devote ourselves to prayer**, making it a priority, because this is where the battle is won or lost.

Second, **we must keep alert as we pray**. After we have asked God for specific things, we need to watch and see what He will do for us. This means that once we have asked God to open doors to reach others for Christ, we must be alert to these opportunities when they come along.

Third, **we are to have a thankful attitude**. This implies expectancy. We can be thankful because we expect God to respond to our prayers. "Without faith it is impossible to please him" (Hebrews 11:6).

After giving us three characteristics of prayer, Paul gives us three requests, for which we are to pray. First, **we need to pray for each other**. Many times as Christians, we forget that we are in a war and that we need to uplift one another in prayer. Even the Apostle Paul recognized his own need for prayer.

The second thing that Paul asks us to pray for is **an open door with non-Christians**. It is unnecessary to beat the fruit off the tree and risk "bruising the fruit" if we have prepared it adequately in prayer. Paul said that we are to pray that the Holy Spirit would go before us and open the door, so that the non-Christian will be receptive to what we have to offer. This takes all the pressure off us and puts it on God. It also prevents us from forcing a conversation and turning someone off. We can pray diligently that God will give us an open door or natural opportunity to talk with someone and then simply wait on God's timing.

The third thing we are to pray for is **the grace to present the message clearly** when the opportunity presents itself.

After we have bathed our actions and attitudes in prayer, how else can we cultivate the soil? When Aristotle instructed his pupils on how to win others to their perspective, he noted that they were not to begin by trying to prove that their philosophical view was correct. Rather, they would first have to **prove themselves trustworthy**. After they won the trust of others, these young philosophers were to **consider the problems facing the people they sought to reach**. Once they accomplished both of these objectives, the students could then show how their philosophy fulfilled the practical needs of their friends. This principle is also valid in transmitting the message of Christ.

Sometimes Christians Share Christ for the Wrong Reasons

As we share Christ with others, it is important to demonstrate a genuine love for them. J. I. Packer stressed this in his book, *Evangelism and the Sovereignty of God* (InterVarsity):

> It must never be forgotten that the enterprise required of us in evangelism is the enterprise of love: an enterprise that springs from a genuine interest in those whom we seek to win, and a genuine care for their well-being, and expresses itself in a genuine respect for them and a genuine friendliness towards them (pp. 79-80).

Christ called us to have an unconditional love for our non-Christian friends. **Friendships are fragile and require as much care in handling as any other fragile and precious thing. A person must trust you before he will be willing to examine your product**. Abraham Lincoln once said:

> If you would win a man to your cause, first convince him that you are his true friend. Therein is a drop of honey which will catch his heart-which, say what you will, is the greater high road to

his reason. When you have once gained his heart, you have little trouble convincing his judgment of the justices of your cause, if indeed that cause is really just.

Once a person recognizes your sincere concern for them and realizes that what you offer stems from a heart of love, they will respond far more readily. **But not only must we love people, we must also listen to what they have to say**. Someone once said, "Christ is the answer; now what's your question?" That doesn't tend to go over well. Having listened to someone's objections, you can more easily expose them to the reality of Christ.

When seeking to explain the message of Christ, it is important to **communicate clearly**. The Good News should be expressed clearly, so listeners will appreciate it, picturesquely, so they will remember it, and above all, accurately, so they will be guided by its light.

God has called us to sow, cultivate, and reap. But it is not an instantaneous process. With some people, we may only sow or cultivate or reap. What we must keep before us is the commission of Christ to be faithful to the task no matter what stage of the cycle we are in.

Finally, our confidence must never be in the answers we offer, but in the convicting ministry of the Holy Spirit (John 16:8-11). We must walk in conscious dependence on his power working through us, or our efforts will be worthless. People often raise these objections as excuses to avoid a confrontation with Christ. Even if we successfully overcome their objections, they will not come to Christ unless they are drawn by the Spirit.

Putting It into Practice

Many people can argue, but not many converse. We want this book to make you more conversant rather than more argumentative. There are occasions where we have all seen a Christian bombard a non-Christian with information in an antagonistic way. We should never be rude, for rudeness is a weak man's imitation of strength. With the message of Christ, we do not have to be defensive and hostile; the claims of Christ can withstand the onslaught of the skeptic's investigation.

Love and listen. Learn to be a friend to those you seek to reach. A woman who had been sharing answers with someone received a letter from that person shortly afterward. The letter read:

> If you want to be a missionary, please accept this advice; be more humane. I mean more alive; cry, laugh, make mistakes, otherwise you will be just like a recorded tape saying good and right things mechanically but in an extremely cold manner. People want to find first of all a friend, a companion, and then a missionary.

What a statement! How many people have we spoken to that could have written us the same letter? It may take minutes, days, months, or years before some people are ready to accept Christ. So we must continue to love them during whatever time frame it takes, and this will demonstrate whether or not we have become genuine friends.

Not only is our approach and attitude important, but so is our ability to answer the objections. It is curious how often people think we are geniuses just because we are the first ones able to help them in their struggle. Alexander Hamilton wrote:

> Men give me some credit for genius. All the genius I have lies in this: when I have a subject at hand, I study it profoundly. Day and night it is before me. I explore it in all its bearings. My mind becomes pervaded with it. Then the efforts that I make are what people are pleased to call the fruits of genius. It is the fruit of labor and thought!

We pray that we will all respond to the call of Christ to be ready to give an answer for the hope that is in us—an answer that will bring people to the reality of Christ. But never place your confidence in your answers. Throughout the entire process, you must walk in dependence on the power and convicting ministry of the Holy Spirit. He, not you, must convict of sin, righteousness, and judgment (John 16:8-11). Apart from his work, your words will be void and fruitless.

Finally, remember to be persistent in the cultivation process and be glad someone asked you to answer their questions. **Every objection is really an opportunity to see people come to Christ**.

But you, beloved, building yourselves up on your most holy faith; praying in the Holy Spirit; keep yourselves in the love of God, waiting anxiously for the mercy of our Lord Jesus Christ to eternal life. And have mercy on some, who are doubting; save others, snatching them out of the fire; and on some have mercy with fear, hating even the garment polluted by the flesh.

Now to Him who is able to keep you from stumbling and to make you stand in the presence of His glory blameless with great joy, to the only God our Savior, through Jesus Christ our Lord, be glory, majesty, dominion and authority, before all time and now and forever Amen.

(Jude 20-25)

QUESTION 1: DOES GOD EXIST?

Often-Asked Questions:

- Can you actually prove that God exists?

- Since God's existence cannot be proved, isn't agnosticism the most reasonable position?

- Hasn't science demonstrated that the idea of a god is unnecessary?

- Why postulate a god when science explains the origin of life and man?

The options are simple—one must believe that God does *not* exist (atheism), God *may* exist (agnosticism), or God *does* exist. There is a growing climate of opinion that modern science has filled in the gaps that were previously occupied by God, thus rendering the existence of God unnecessary. In some circles, atheism and agnosticism have been elevated to the status of an intellectual virtue.

There has been a great deal of debate over the value of theistic arguments, but it is clear that a person intellectually or spiritually closed to the question of God will not respond to the evidence. It has been said that "a man persuaded against his will is of the same opinion still." But a person willing to consider the case for God's existence will find that the evidence consistently points to the conclusion *Yes*.

In this chapter, we'll address these three options. To address the first option, atheism, we will discuss the difficulties of dispproving God and of living in a world without him. To address the second option, agnosticism, we will discuss evidence for the existence of a god. Eventually the conversation must come around to "What kind of god exists?" An impersonal force? Or something more like the infinite, personal, and ethical God of the Bible? We address this in the third option.

First Option: God Does Not Exist, or The Difficulty of Atheism

Even with a perfect memory and a lifetime of study, any single person's knowledge would be paltry when compared to all that could be known. It is simply unreasonable to claim, "I *know* that God does not exist." A person would have to know everything before that statement could be confirmed.

This concept can be illustrated by the 'Circle of Knowledge' or the 'Boy in the Wood' illustrations. Explorers have had difficulty describing ice to natives in equatorial regions. The more they talked about cubes of water or water that became so solid that people could easily walk on it, the harder the natives laughed. Ice was outside their sphere of knowledge, but this did not jeopardize its existence. Similarly, a person may deny the existence of God, but he must be omniscient to logically do so. Ironically, one would have to be God to be sure that God does not exist. In Romans 1, Paul writes that those who deny God are repressing the awareness God has given them.

There have been a few attempts in recent years to recast the atheist position in a less drastic light. Sometimes they play with the order of the words—"I believe God doesn't exist" becomes "I don't believe in God." The common claim is that this shift of emphasis pushes the burden of proof back onto the theist as the atheist is no longer affirming a negative statement, only noting his lack of acknowledgment in a positive statement. This is a clever conversational tactic, but when examined, the atheist hasn't

Circle of Knowledge

Imagine this circle represents all the knowledge in the universe. How much of that knowledge do you feel that you have a handle on? Is it possible that evidence for God exists in the universe in areas of the circle that you haven't yet seen? I believe that there is some good evidence that heavily points in the direction of God–could we look at it together sometime?

Boy in the Woods

Imagine we are camping at a state park, when a man comes into our campsite.

"Please help me with my son! He wandered into the woods several hours ago and hasn't returned!"

We make a plan and start canvasing the hills and valleys. After hours of fruitless searching, we turn back toward the campsite, thinking that perhaps the boy was somewhere else, or the "dad" just made up the story. Just then, a friend emerges from the woods claiming that she saw a backpack matching the dad's description a half mile in the opposite direction. Do we go look for the boy in the new area based on the testimony of another? Or do we retire to the campfire, unconvinced that there is a boy in the woods?

really changed anything. At the risk of inviting comparisons to imaginary creatures, the fallacy inherent in this claim becomes obvious when 'fairies' are substituted for 'God'. "I don't believe in fairies" expresses the same thought as "I believe fairies don't exist."

Key Illustration: One Less God

Another common move is to observe that Christians and atheists are not all that different—the atheist just believes in one less god than the Christian. Even the Christian is an "atheist" in respect to the Greek god Zeus. In fact, the Christian has chosen *not* to worship a whole bunch of gods; the atheist has simply chosen one less god than the Christian. Almost as if gods and religions are like collectible things, whether you have a few or many doesn't make much difference. The unstated assumption in this analogy is that religious ideas are just subjective opinions that accomplish no necessary function. Al Serrato in his piece "Having One Less God Than a Believer" says:

> In the abstract, the difference between one and zero might not seem to amount to much. But it all depends on what "it" is. For marbles or other collectibles, not much perhaps. But to things that do work – like cars or medicines or worldviews – having the one right one can make all the difference in the world... or more importantly, in the world to come.

Verdicts in courts of law are based on legal evidence, not scientific proof. In civil cases, the verdict is reached on the basis of a preponderance of the credible evidence. In criminal cases, the jury must be convinced of guilt "beyond a reasonable doubt" before reaching the verdict of guilty. The phrase is not "beyond the shadow of a doubt" because one-hundred percent proof is not reasonable. If complete proof were required before making legal verdicts or personal decisions, nothing would be accomplished.

The God you pick, or don't pick, can have profound consequences. It's hardly just a matter of preference. We expand on the idea of Christianity as just one option among many in Question 6.

It is good to think through the implications of a universe with no God. The human heart cries out for meaning, value, and purpose, but these are precisely the things that are denied in an atheistic cosmos. The universe is expanding and left to itself, the galaxies will grow farther apart, and the stars will eventually burn out. All will be cold, dark, and lifeless. In the scale of cosmic time, the human race (let alone the life of a man) flashes into existence for the briefest moment before passing into oblivion. From an ultimate standpoint, all that we do will be rendered meaningless—no one will be left to remember in the endless cosmic night.

God's existence cannot be demonstrated to someone with the kind of certainty that forces them to believe.

Also, without God we have no robust basis for *morality*, meaning that values such as right and wrong or good and bad are totally relative and have no absolute mooring. If humanity is the product of an accidental combination of molecules in an ultimately impersonal universe, human values such as honesty, brotherhood, love, and equality have no more cosmic significance than treachery, selfishness, hatred, and prejudice. People *can* do moral good without God. We are saying that there is simply no objective basis for that morality.

Man is also stripped of *purpose* in a godless reality. An impersonal universe is bereft of purpose and plan; in the final analysis, it moves only toward decay, disorder, and death. It is *Macbeth*'s "tale told by an idiot, full of sound and fury, signifying nothing." In such a pointless existence, human aspirations are mocked by silence.

Not many people have come to grips with these logical implications of atheism, and no one can live consistently with them. All of us *act* as though human existence has meaning, as though moral values are real, and as though human life has purpose and dignity. But all these things presuppose an infinite-personal Creator, so if God is dead, man is also as good as dead.

Second Option: God May Exist

As we look at the second option, we overcome some misconceptions about the extent and limitation of evidence, argument and proof. Some people wrongly demand scientific proof for the reality of God, as though he could somehow be found at the end of a repeatable and controlled experiment. Russian cosmonaut Yuri Gagarin, the first man to enter outer space, illustrated this mentality when he returned from orbiting the earth and said, "I didn't see any God out there." This is somewhat like scraping the paint off a portrait to find the artist inside. The painting points to the artist, just as the cosmos points to a creator, but in both cases the creation and the creator are not the same.

The scientific method of controlled and repeatable experimentation is useful for achieving a great deal of knowledge. But *complete proof* is rarely attainable in *any* field, including science, with the exception of pure mathematics. Courtroom verdicts, major life choices, and even significant purchases are based on a process of making the best decision based on the available information.

The danger of demanding absolute proof is that people become immune to the evidence already before them. "If they do not listen to Moses and the Prophets, neither will they be persuaded if someone rises from the dead" (Luke 16:31). **God's existence cannot be demonstrated to someone with the kind of certainty that *forces* them to believe.** The evidence may be powerful, but one must choose to respond. This is where faith comes in—not against the evidence, but as a response to it. Belief in God is never meant to be a leap into the dark, but a step into the light.

A decision must be based on sufficient evidence, not exhaustive evidence. But what constitutes sufficient evidence for the existence of God? Because God is not perceived by our five senses, we must rely upon the indirect evidence of *cause and effect*. We depend on this kind of inferential reasoning every day, and this is the kind of reasoning that will point us in the

Modern Models of the Origin of the Universe

Throughout the 19th century and into the 20th, the prevailing opinion among scientists was that while stars and planets may come and go, the universe pretty well held steady with no necessary beginning nor foreseeable end. In the 1920s, Georges LeMaître proposed that Einstein's theory of general relativity didn't allow for a steady universe, but established that it must be either contracting or, more probably, expanding. Though Einstein didn't like the implications, he and many other astrophysicists were won over to the expanding universe model over the next few decades. Edwin Hubble observed the staggering speed that all observable galaxies were receding from ours. George Gamow and others synthesized these ideas into what became the "Big Bang Theory." Fred Hoyle, the chief opponent and the longest-lived advocate of the opposing steady-state theory, dismissively coined the term, but it stuck and captured imaginations. Gamow's associates predicted that we should be able to detect a faint echo in the form of cosmic microwave background radiation. When a couple of Bell Labs radio astronomers accidentally discovered this predicted omnidirectional background radiation in 1965, the evidence and the scientific opinion began tilting to the side of the Big Bang. Between 1989 and 2013, the COBE, WMAP, and Planck satellites cemented the reputation of the Big Bang Theory and firmly established the age of the universe in the neighborhood of 14 billion years.

Over the years, many solutions have been proposed that avoid a universe with a definite beginning and its inevitable theological complications. The "steady-state" model, with its continuously regenerating universe, didn't fade out until the 1970s. Several forms of an oscillating universe have been proposed, where the universe continuously alternates between an expansion phase and a contraction phase. These models generally fall apart as they succumb to three problems. First, these proposals lack a compelling mechanism for the "bounce" part of the cycle. Second, those with a plausible bounce mechanism retain entropy across the cycles. Simply put, there is less useful energy available for every cycle, and this inevitably leads to a distant but unavoidable beginning. Third, the best empirical data we have on the mass, density, and expansion rate of the universe we inhabit predicts an unending expansion—no crunch, no bounce.

Today's other popular cosmological models feature variations on a multi-verse. There are many proposals that envision our inhabited universe as just one of many. Some models employ a few other universes, others postulate an infinite supply. Some models envision a branching universe, where every possible outcome of an event spawns and branches into a new universe. Others focus on mechanisms

Continued on following page...

direction of God as well. A sufficient *cause* must exist to account for the *effects* of the natural universe, order and design within the universe, personal beings, and the phenomenon of morality.

The philosophers Leibniz and Sartre argued that the most basic philosophical question is, "**Why is there something rather than nothing?**" Why does anything exist at all? There are only four possible answers to this question, and our purpose in taking an agnostic through these options is to help him see that the universe is contingent—it depends on something else for its existence.

If Anything Now Exists, Then Either Something Came from Nothing or Something is Eternal.

Here are the four alternatives we must examine: (1) The universe is an illusion, (2) The universe is eternal, (3) The universe emerged from nothing, or (4) Something eternal created the universe.

(1) *The universe is an illusion.* This is a self-defeating position, equivalent to saying, "It is an objective fact that there are no objective facts." The claim that all things are unreal lacks logical consistency because the claim itself would also be unreal. The following sentence falls into the same category: "This sentence is incorrect." The sentence is self-defeating, because it must be false in order to be true.

Not only does this option lack rational coherence, it also lacks factual correspondence. To entertain it, a person would have to reject every shred of evidence from his five senses. If it is an illusion, the universe is a very powerful, relentless, and consistent fantasy. We are constantly being bombarded by sensory data that can be used to make reliable predictions (tides, planetary orbits, etc.). Furthermore, no human being can live consistently with the implications of this viewpoint for even a day. Even the full-blown skeptic looks both ways before crossing the street. And every human relationship calls illusionism a lie. This option is explored further in Question 5, under the section "Evil Doesn't Exist."

(2) *The universe is eternal.* When we first wrote *I'm Glad You Asked*, the demise of the steady-state theory was still fresh among astronomers and not well known across the general population. In the years since the first edition, the basics of the Big Bang theory have become almost universally accepted in the scientific world. Nearly 100% of scientific data points to a universe that is about 14 billion years old. Even modern young Earth scientists acknowledge that the universe and the Earth *appear* to have this age. Regardless on your personal position on the age of the universe, we've found that it is better to use the generally accepted assumptions of science to establish *that* the universe began, rather than getting bogged down in a distracting discussion on *when* it happened. Whether the universe is 10,000 years old or 14 billion years old or 100 trillion years old, the prior event still lacks a naturalistic explanation.

Every year, new theories are put forth to describe a natural cause for the universe. *All of the data we have* points to a universe with a beginning, and we have not been able see past its borders. When trying to show evidence of a creator to someone who doesn't yet believe in God, we want to use the evidence most likely to be granted and understood. Modern young Earth creationists acknowledge the appearance of an old Earth but explain that appearance through theories of accelerated aging. These theories assume God's existence and require his miraculous intervention, and we have not found them helpful in *this* conversation. The Big Bang is virtually unchallenged among scientists, and we find it useful to demonstrate a non-eternal universe.

There are also philosophical reasons why there cannot have been an actually infinite series of events in time, but the scientific reasons should be sufficient for most conversations. The philosophical arguments against a universe with no beginning center around the impossibilities and absurdities that result when one tries to convert theoretical infinities to actual events. Both J. P. Moreland and William Lane Craig address

Continued from previous page...

for launching new universes from their beginnings, beyond the limits of our observation.

Part of the appeal of the multiverse models is that they seem to nullify two of the most significant arguments for the existence of God: the origin of the universe and its structure that appears finely-tuned to allow for our existence. As far as the fine-tuning arguments go, an infinite number of alternate universes would seem to diminish the significance of ours being "just so." Many people are under the impression that a multiverse reinstates the possibility of an infinite past. This would avoid a key contention of the cosmological argument: the universe/multiverse has an origin that needs explaining. So far that hasn't been the case, and every model yet proposed still runs up against a finite past boundary (Borde, Guth, and Vilenkin, "Inflationary spacetimes are not past-complete," revised 2003).

We can't say for certain that theoretical cosmologists won't come up with a model next year or in ten years that replaces the standard Big Bang model and avoids the implications of a beginning of space and time, but no theory in the past 50 years has successfully done so. A universe that begins to exist requires an agent external to space-time to bring it into existence.

If you'd like to dig deeper into these ideas, William Lane Craig and James D. Sinclair have written a number of resources in the past few years.

In Chapter 2 of Craig's *Reasonable Faith*, he walks through all of the major proposed models up through its 2008 publication date.

James Sinclair wrote the essay "At Home in the Multiverse? Critiquing the Many Worlds Hypothesis" in the book *Contending with Christianity's Critics*, edited by Craig and Paul Copan 2009.

Craig and Sinclair jointly authored the article "The Kalam Cosmological Argument" in *The Blackwell Companion to Natural Theology*. This is a very long and technical treatment of these ideas.

For an explanation of entropy and the second law of thermodynamics see the appendix at the end of this chapter.

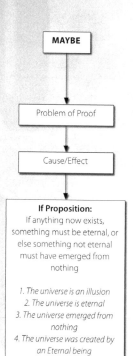

MAYBE

Problem of Proof

Cause/Effect

If Proposition:
If anything now exists,
something must be eternal, or
else something not eternal
must have emerged from
nothing

1. The universe is an illusion
2. The universe is eternal
3. The universe emerged from
nothing
4. The universe was created by
an Eternal being

Who caused God?

these arguments in several of their books. (See the Supplemental Reading section at the end of this chapter.)

(3) *The universe emerged from nothing.* Usually, little needs to be said about the absurdity of this position. All reason and observations tell us that nothing produces nothing. To say that an effect can exist without a cause is to deny the whole basis of scientific investigation and rational thought. No one would seriously maintain that a house, planet, star, or galaxy simply popped into existence without a cause. Yet some are willing to strain at these gnats while swallowing the camel that the entire universe came into an uncaused existence out of nothing.

There have been a number of theories posited over the past few decades that *on the surface* appear to offer a scientific mechanism for the universe to emerge from nothing, based on the peculiar properties of quantum mechanics and quantum field theory. In the subatomic world of quarks, electrons, neutrinos, and other exotic particles, the physics of Newton break down and quantum physics takes over. At this level, the boundaries between matter and energy fade and are crossed easily. Fluctuations in the energy field of a vacuum spontaneously spawn "virtual particles," always as a particle-antiparticle pair. Most of the time, these particles instantly annihilate each other, but sometimes they split, interact with other matter, and remain in existence. The paradigm-shattering possibility of these events often clouds the fact that *none of these theories provide a mechanism consistent with the requirement of creation out of nothing.* Virtual particles are spontaneously created out of *space* characterized by the quantum energy field, and *space* is something, *not nothing.* There are no currently viable theories that void the ancient pillar of scientific reasoning, "out of nothing, nothing comes."

(4) *Something eternal created the universe.* This is the only option left if the universe is real, not eternal, and caused. The universe is an effect, contingent on a cause that is beyond it. The only sufficient cause is an eternal and necessary being—someone or something incapable of not being, whether or not anything else exists. Otherwise, there would be the problem of an infinite regression of causes and effects. People still trot out the old question, "Who caused God?" But once you understand the "If..." proposition that started this section, then you can communicate that there are no other viable options. *If anything now exists, than something came from nothing or something must be eternal. If the universe we inhabit isn't the thing that is eternal, then something outside the universe must be eternal and uncaused.* It is true that every effect must have a cause, but God is *not* an effect because he was never created. God is eternal and self-existent. The concept of self-existence is not the same as self-creation. Nothing could create itself because it would have to exist prior to its existence to do so! So we are left with an eternal being as

the only viable solution.

Third Option: God Does Exist

What kind of God? So far we have used cause-and-effect reasoning to conclude that the natural universe points beyond itself to an eternal being for the cause of its existence. This *cosmological argument* for the existence of God is based on evidence from the existence of the whole cosmos. But this argument is limited; it does not prove that this eternal being is the personal God revealed in the Bible.

When a person is willing to admit the existence of some kind of eternal "being" or God, the next question is whether this is an impersonal force or energy source or a personal being with its own will. To answer this question, we need to narrow our focus. What cause is sufficient to explain the effects of order and design in the universe, the personality of man, and the moral consciousness of man?

Before looking at the argument from design, note that even the cosmological argument favors a personal over an impersonal cause of the cosmos. If an impersonal cause always existed, why did the universe come into existence only a finite time ago? What kept the cause from producing the effect (the universe) an eternity ago? It certainly couldn't be an act of the will. Only a personal being could make the choice to create the universe a limited time ago.

Our universe appears engineered for life. Now we are ready to look beyond the *fact* of the temporal universe to the *form* of the universe. We live in a universe of order, complexity, and symmetry, not a jumble of chaos and confusion. The whole scientific enterprise is built upon the assumption that the universe is orderly and predictable enough to be described and understood.

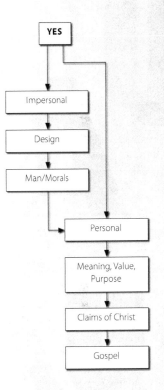

We can find thousands of examples of order and purpose in the world, especially in living systems. This is the argument from design, also known as the *teleological argument* from the Greek word *telos*, meaning "end" or "goal."

If we examined a radio, we would find that its component parts are all designed to work together to accomplish a specific function. The more we understand the principles of electronics and how components, such as transistors, capacitors, resistors, and transformers work in accordance with those principles, the more we can appreciate the purposeful intelligence and creative design required to make a radio. Yet a radio is only child's play when compared to the enormous complexity and subtlety of a living cell. We are only beginning to realize how profound living systems really are, and the more we learn, the more astoundingly complex they appear.

A few words about evolution may be helpful, as there is tremendous misunderstanding on all sides of this issue. There are three terms that are often used interchangeably—but wrongly—by Christians. Evolution, the Big Bang, and atheism.

Atheism, or naturalism, is a system for understanding the world where God does not exist or interfere.

The Big Bang has to do with the structure and form of the early universe, how the galaxies and stars came to be in the formation as we see today.

Evolution usually refers to a combination of the following three ideas:

- Animals look alike because of *common descent*—a shared ancestor—not just common design.
- The populations drifted over time due to *natural selection*.
- The engine for change is *random mutation*.

These three primary terms are neither synonymous nor interchangeable. The Big Bang is not the same as evolution, and Evolutionists are not the same as Atheists.

While there is widespread (though not universal) Christian adoption of the Big Bang story of the beginning of the universe, Christians are sharply divided over how much of the evolutionary story they can accept. From our perspective, belief in evolution *can be* compatible with belief in God and to argue this point is often unhelpful in coversation. We find the best topic of conversation revolves around the engine for change in the universe. Is random mutation a sufficient engine to create the depth of order and breadth of diversity that we see in living systems today? Or does the astounding precision and complexity of living things point to purposeful planning? For our purposes here, in looking for evidence that points to God, it does not matter when and where this purposeful planning took place. Whether it happened in ages past and God "set the table" of the universe to bring forth life, or whether God intervened at intervals during the process is beside the question. We would rather talk about whether unguided chance alone is enough to bring about the world we inhabit, including ourselves. We find that further conversations beyond this one often devolve into "your scientist verses mine" and do not help us get closer to the question we really want to address: "Has the architect of the universe revealed himself to mankind?"

An even stronger evidence for the personality of the Creator is the personality of man. Personality refers to man's intellect, emotion, and will. The basic issue in this *anthropological argument* is, once again, cause and effect: The impersonal has no ability to think, feel, or choose and is, therefore, vastly inferior to that which is personal. How, then, can an impersonal agent cause conscious, personal beings? We can strengthen this argument by looking in more detail at the three basic areas of personality.

The three qualities of intellect, feeling, and will form the basis for the arguments from thought, aesthetics, and morality.

The *argument from thought* shows that the human mind cannot be the product of an impersonal process. It is self-defeating to argue that the mind is merely the physical brain, an organic electrochemical mechanism, which evolved as a result of irrational causes. To do so would be to use human reasoning to question the validity of human reasoning. This is like trying to prove that there are no proofs.

Human thought transcends the brain and the material world as it reflects upon abstract concepts like justice, wisdom, and spirit. We can not only think about the future, but we can also think about the process of thinking about the future.

The *argument from aesthetics* appeals to a personal God as the only adequate explanation of the universal aesthetic experience in man. While there are differences in taste, there is, nevertheless, an amazing amount of consensus concerning beauty and greatness in art, literature, music, architecture, and so forth. This awareness and appreciation of what is beautiful cannot be reduced to a mechanical response to sensory input. The aesthetic capacity transcends the material world, and an impersonal force is insufficient to create this transcendent quality.

The *argument from morality* holds that man's moral consciousness requires a personal God to have ultimate meaning. Like aesthetic experience, moral experience is a universal human phenomenon. There are variations, but in all ages and countries, qualities like honesty, wisdom, courage, and fairness are regarded as virtues. Even if a person claims that moral notions are the subjective products of cultural conditioning or evolutionary artifacts, he betrays himself every time he criticizes or praises. If a skeptic says, "How could you be so selfish?" he is really appealing to an objective moral standard: consideration for the needs of others. Otherwise, his criticism has no weight. For moral experience to be valid (and all of us *live* as though it is), it must be based on more than individual or group preferences. Groups and societies can pursue paths as evil as those followed by any individual. The only absolute foundation for morality is the changeless character of the personal creator of the universe. Righteousness, love, justice, and mercy find their true basis in the personality of God. These qualities have no ultimate significance if the universe is the product of impersonal causes.

Putting all these arguments together, we are left with an eternal, personal, and ethical God as the only sufficient cause of the universe, order and design within the universe, and the personality of man. We saw earlier that no one can live consistently with a philosophy that rules out meaning, value, and purpose in life. We long for these things because we were made to

The argument from thought has recently been explored further by Thomas Nagel in *Mind and Cosmos.*

A deeper question raised by this debate is the fundamental nature of good and evil. Does morality actually have any foundation? To be consistent, a committed atheist, who argues that evolution can fully account for all aspects of human nature, must also argue that the human urge toward altruism, including its most radical and self-sacrificial forms, is a purely evolutionary artifact. This forces the conclusion that the concepts of good and evil have no real foundation and that we have been hoodwinked by evolution into thinking that morality provides meaningful standards of judgment. Few atheists seem willing to own up to this disturbing and depressing consequence of their worldview.

–Francis Collins. *Belief: Readings on the Reason for Faith.* HarperCollins, 2010.

Illustration: "Says who?"

If right and wrong are determined on an individual basis, then there is no room to criticize Charles Manson or Ted Bundy. They just acted according to what was true for them. If a societal group can determine truth for itself, then we have no room to criticize the actions of inner city gangs or the Ku Klux Klan. They simply acted according to what they had determined to be truth. If truth can be determined by larger groups, like nations and kingdoms, then we have no room to criticize Hitler's Germany, Europe's Crusades, or Stalin's USSR. Only if truth is an objective standard outside of individuals, groups, or nations can we rightfully condemn the horrific actions of these people and regimes.

find them all in the infinite-personal God who makes them real. We are not merely biological entities; we are spiritual creatures, made in the image of God and designed to receive and display his life.

Again, these arguments do not provide the kind of absolute proof that will overwhelm a person who chooses to reject God. But they can help a nonmilitant agnostic recognize the reasonableness of faith in God. They can also make him aware of the danger of straddling the fence between rejecting and accepting God.

Suppose a doctor told you that you were afflicted with a disease that would take your life if left untreated. You have a 50-50 chance if he operates. Shaken up, you seek two other opinions, and they both concur. Now the choice is up to you, but you can only defer your decision for so long. You would no doubt choose the operation, because a possible solution is better than no solution at all.

Non-decision agnosticism is even more foolish than an indefinite postponement of the operation, because the chances are greater and the stakes are higher. If God exists, agnosticism is eternally unwise. The agnostic gains nothing and loses everything.

From a biblical perspective, agnosticism is not simply an intellectual process of reserving judgment. It is really a suppression of the truth that God has implanted within the human heart: "For the wrath of God is revealed from heaven against all ungodliness and unrighteousness of men, who suppress the truth in unrighteousness, because that which is known about God is evident within them; for God made it evident to them" (Romans 1:18-19). This is a *moral*, not merely intellectual, issue. The evidence is not only internal, but as we have been arguing, it is also external: "For since the creation of the world His invisible attributes, His eternal power and divine nature, have been clearly seen, being understood through what has been made, so that they are without excuse. For even though they knew God, they did not honor Him as God, or give thanks; but they became futile in their speculations, and their foolish heart was darkened" (Romans 1:20-21).

The arguments in this chapter will not be effective unless the Holy Spirit overcomes the natural rebellion in the unbeliever's heart. The non-Christian's responsibility is to respond with faith to the convicting ministry of the Holy Spirit. "And without faith it is impossible to please him, for he who comes to God must believe that he is, and that he is a rewarder of those who seek him" (Hebrews 11:6).

When a person acknowledges the existence of the infinite and personal God, he must then come to know this God in a personal way. At this point, he needs to be confronted with the claims and credentials of Jesus Christ (see Question 6).

Jesus is the Creator of the cosmos, the divine Word who became flesh and came to Earth in the likeness of men. "No man has seen God at any time; the only begotten God, who is in the bosom of the Father. He has explained him" (John 1:18). By looking at the person and work of Jesus Christ, we see the person and the character of God.

The presentation of the claims and credentials of Christ should be followed by an explanation of the Gospel and what it means to believe in Christ (see chap. 13).

Summary

Atheism is unreasonable because a person would have to be omniscient to know that God does not exist. In addition, if there were no God, human life would be stripped of ultimate meaning, value, and purpose. Agnosticism is not as unreasonable, but the agnostic needs to realize that the weight of the evidence is in favor of theism. No absolute proof can be offered which will force the skeptic to believe against his will, but a strong case can be built by applying cause and effect reasoning to the universe, the order and design in the universe, and the personality of man (thought, aesthetics, and morality). The argument from the universe is designed to show that the universe is not eternal and is, therefore, contingent on an eternal being for its existence. This being must be personal, because an impersonal creating agent could not account for human thought and morality. Those who question God's existence must suppress the internal and external testimony that their Creator has given them (Romans 1:18-21). The clearest manifestation of God in human history was the incarnation of Jesus Christ, who is the Mediator between God and men.

Supplemental Reading

These accessible books provide a wide overview of the key arguments for the existence of God. In each of them, the first sections explore classical arguments for the existence of God, and the later chapters deal with Jesus and the Bible.

Boa, Kenneth, and Robert M. Bowman, Jr. *20 Compelling Evidences that God Exists: Discover Why Believing in God Makes So Much Sense.* RiverOak Publishing, 2002 (I).

Dembski, William A. and Michael R. Licona, eds. *Evidence for God: 50 Arguments for Faith from the Bible, History, Philosophy, and Science.* Baker Books, 2010.

Strobel, Lee. *The Case for a Creator: A Journalist Investigates Scientific Evidence That Points Toward God.* Zondervan, 2004.

Keller, Timothy. *The Reason for God: Belief in an Age of Skepticism.* Dutton, 2008.

Lewis, C. S. *Mere Christianity.* Collier/Macmillan, 1952 (I).

Appendix on Thermodynamics

Apart from the Big Bang, the most significant argument that the universe had a beginning is the second law of thermodynamics. The first law of thermodynamics is the law of conservation of mass and energy. Mass and energy are interchangeable, but they cannot be created or destroyed. The energy equivalence of mass can be found by using Einstein's equation $E=mc^2$. We will call this mass equivalence. Graphically, the first law looks like the chart below.

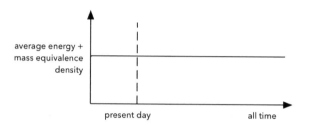

"Density" is added to show that these laws would be true even if the universe were infinite. Regardless of time, the quantity of energy and mass equivalence in the universe is a constant. But the second law says that the quality of energy in the universe is constantly declining.

"Entropy" refers to the amount of useless or random energy in any closed system. As entropy increases, the amount of useful energy decreases. For example, when a chair is pushed across a floor, the work energy turns into heat energy and heats the floor molecules slightly due to friction. This heat energy in the floor cannot be reorganized to perform work (i.e., move the chair again) and becomes lost. Energy did not disappear, but it became more random and incapable of being used again.

Entropy can also be seen as a measure of disorder, because anything left to itself (a closed system) moves toward a state of equilibrium and randomness. The universe as a whole can be viewed as an immense closed system. (Don't confuse this with a closed universe, i.e., a universe that will eventually stop expanding and begin to contract.) As time increases, universal entropy increases (see chart below).

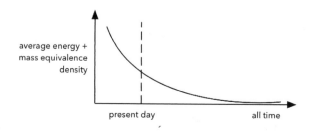

The area below the curved line (an exponential decay curve) is useful energy. As time increases, this useful energy approaches zero. Ultimately, a state of equilibrium will be approached, often called the "heat death" of the universe. The stars will have burned out and there will not be enough gas in the steadily expanding galaxies to form new stars. In effect, the universe will have run down like a clock with no one to wind it back up. All will be coldness, darkness, and disorder. (This process is irreversible apart from the intervention of a supernatural agent—God. Romans 8:20-22 describes the future redemption of nature when God sets it free from its "slavery to corruption.")

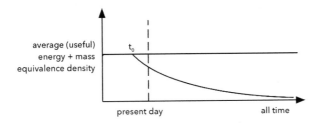

In the above chart, point t_o represents the time when the curved line (second law) intersected the horizontal line (first law). The curved line is absent before that time because there cannot be more useful energy than total energy. It is clear that the universe cannot be infinitely old because it has not yet worn down. The only other viable option is to say that the universe existed prior to point t_o. But for this to be true, the universe prior to that point had to be perfectly sustained with no increase in entropy. This would require an omnipresent agent that continually removed useless energy and disorder and replaced it with useful energy and order on a cosmic scale. In short, it would require God himself.

Appendix on the Origin of Life

Everyone who believes the Bible accepts the fact that God is the Creator of the universe. But while evangelicals agree on the *who*, they do not all agree on the *how* of creation. Some believe that this is a young Earth and that the six days of creation in Genesis 1 are 24-hour days. Others believe that these days are figurative and that God directly used the long evolutionary process. Many theologians fall somewhere between these two extremes.

The question here is not who is right, but how to deal with the issue of evolution when the non-Christian raises it as an objection to the existence of God or the reliability of the Genesis creation account. You should deal with this question as quickly as possible so that it will not become a barrier to the discussion about God or the Bible. Resist the temptation of trying to prove too much. You may believe the earth is young, but the more basic issue is non-theistic evolution versus creation by God (regardless of the method and time he used).

The non-theistic evolutionary model assumes that nonliving systems generated life by means of time plus chance. The philosophical problem with this model is that it makes the effects (complexity, life, intelligence, personality) greater than the causes (disorder, non-life, random interactions and mutations, and impersonal events).

The biggest problem with the atheistic evolution as an origin story is that it offers no workable mechanism that will account for the first living cell. The following paragraphs will be very technical, but we wanted to give you an idea of how staggeringly complex even the simplest life forms are.

The chemical production of a first living cell would have to follow this sequence: (1) Random atoms must be formed into amino acids. (2) These amino acids must link together to form chains (polypeptides). (3) These chains must become long (hundreds of amino acids), and they must form in an ordered sequence, since there are 20 kinds of amino acids. This will produce a simple protein molecule. (4) More complex proteins must be produced. (5) Very long and highly ordered molecular chains known as DNA must be formed and maintained. (6) An enormously complex chemical factory must be produced, complete with special protein formations, enzymes, DNA, RNA, ribosomes, a cell wall, etc. This single cell must be able to reproduce itself and carry on all the functions of life.

Without a rational ordering agent, every step but the first would require nothing short of a statistical miracle, even under the most ideal circumstances.

Many people argue that, given enough time, even the most improbable events become probable. This sounds reasonable only until specific numbers are used. Let's consider George Bernard Shaw's argument that if a million monkeys constantly typed on a million typewriters for a long enough time, one of them would eventually pound out a Shakespearean play. Assume a million monkeys typing 24 hours a day at 100 words a minute on typewriters with 40 keys. If each word of the play contained four letters, the first word would be typed by one of the monkeys in about 12 seconds. However, it would require about five days to get the first two words (eight letters) on one of the typewriters. How long would it take to get the first four words? About 100 billion years! No one could imagine the amount of time which would be required to produce the first scene.

Beginning with the first step, many assume a primordial earthly atmosphere with no oxygen so that amino acids could be formed. However, the very atmosphere that could produce them would immediately lead to their destruction (due to ultraviolet light penetrating this oxygen-free atmosphere) unless they were protected. Unfounded assumptions must be multiplied to overcome this problem.

On the next level, let us assume an ideal environment with a primordial soup full of amino acids and the proper catalysts with just the right temperature and moisture. Some estimate that under these favorable conditions the chances of achieving dipeptides (two amino acids bonded) would be about 1 in 100. But the chances of dipeptide formation would be about 1 in 10,000. To get a polypeptide of only 10 amino acids, the probability would be 1 chance in 100,000,000,000,000,000,000 (100 quintillion). Yet the proteins in the simplest living things have chains of at least 400 amino acids on the average.

To make matters worse, all proteins are built of amino acids that are exclusively "left-handed" in their molecular orientation. Left-handed and right-handed amino acids are mirror images of each other, and their chances of formation are about the same. Although both kinds can link with each other, the first living systems must have been built with left-handed components only. Some scientists *have* evoked natural selection here, but this only applies to systems that can already reproduce themselves. Without an intelligent ordering agent, we have only chance to explain this amazing phenomenon. For a chain of 400 left-handed amino acids, the odds would be roughly equivalent to tossing an ordinary coin and coming up with tails 400 times in a row. The chances for that would be approximately 1 in 10^{120} (a 1 followed by 120 zeros). All this for one protein molecule, and hundreds of similar molecules would be needed in the first living system.

None of this accounts for the fact that the 20 kinds of amino acids operate like letters in an alphabet, and they must link in a meaningful sequence to form a usable protein. A random sequence of amino acids would be utterly useless.

DNA is far more complex than any of this, and it too is built out of a highly organized alphabet. The letters are molecules called nucleotides. A cell contains a chain of about 3 billion pairs of these nucleotides (each gene has about 1,200 nucleotide pairs). The order of these nucleotides or bases is crucial because every triplet of bases along this immense chain is a word. Each word stands for one of the 20 kinds of amino acids. Using these words, the DNA can literally create any kind of protein that the cell needs. The amount of time required to synthesize even one gene (a paragraph of these words) has been calculated by some scientists using absurdly generous assumptions. Using a variation on a well-known illustration, suppose a bird came once every billion years and removed only one atom from a stone the size of the solar system. The amount of time required for the stone to be worn to nothing would be negligible compared to the time needed to create a useful gene by chance, even accounting for chemical affinities and an ideal environment. Shaw's monkeys would long since have pounded out the words of Shakespeare!

But none of this can compare to the *far greater* complexity of a living cell. Even the simplest living system would require elaborately coded information, growth, reproduction, stability, adaptability, environmental response, and metabolism. Yet atheists demand spontaneous generation of life through chemical interaction because they think the only other option would be a miracle. In reality, a miracle cannot be avoided. The only question is whether life appeared out of the primordial soup or by the living God.

In addition, none of the above considers the fact that every chemical reaction along the way from amino acids to life is reversible. This means that whenever a higher point of complexity is reached, it is unstable compared to its environment and may break down into its components. A polypeptide bond of four amino acids can easily break down into four separate amino acids.

We mentioned the second law of thermodynamics in connection with the age of the universe. This same fundamental law tells us that all natural processes cause a net increase in entropy (disorder) and a net loss of useful energy. Any system left to itself will decay and degenerate. Free energy from the sun can cause slight increases in complexity, but the breakdown rate soon matches the buildup rate. The only way to build structures as complex as protein is to have an already existing machine that can translate raw energy into a more highly organized form. Solar energy may be plentiful, but it is useless for building complex systems unless such systems already exist. Life comes only from life, complexity only from complexity. Faith in an original, spontaneous generation of life goes against all experience and evidence.

It has been said that "teleology is a lady without whom no biologist can exist; yet he is ashamed to be seen with her in public." Design requires a designer, and this is precisely what is lacking in non-theistic evolution.

All we are trying to do in relation to the question about God's existence is show that the impersonal mechanism of undirected evolution will not by itself produce personality from non-living particles. Whether or not God superintended any kind of evolutionary process is an entirely different issue and need not be raised to answer this question.

Study Guide for Does God Exist?

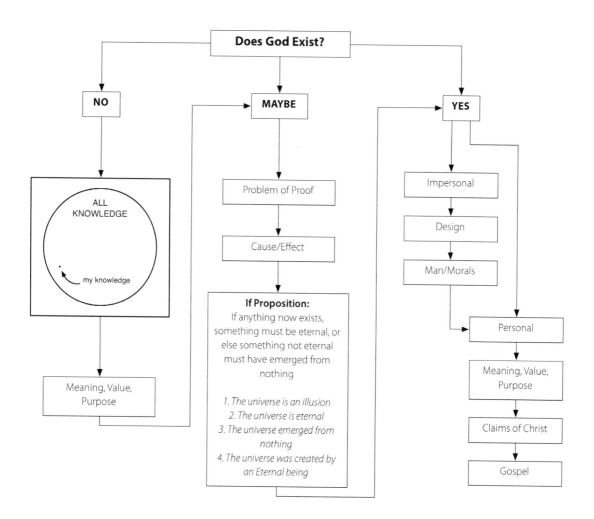

Key Illustrations

Illustration: "Says who?"

If right and wrong are determined on an individual basis, then there is no room to criticize Charles Manson or Ted Bundy. They just acted according to what was true for them. If a societal group can determine truth for itself, then we have no room to criticize the actions of inner city gangs or the Ku Klux Klan. They simply acted according to what they had determined to be truth. If truth can be determined by larger groups, like nations and kingdoms, then we have no room to criticize Hitler's Germany, Europe's crusades, or Stalin's USSR. Only if truth is an objective standard outside of individuals, groups, or nations can we rightfully condemn the horrific actions of these people and regimes.

Circle of Knowledge

Imagine this circle represents all the knowledge in the universe. How much of that knowledge do you feel that you have a handle on? (The smarter they are, the smaller the dot.) Is it possible that evidence for God exists in the universe in areas of the circle that you haven't yet seen? I believe that there is some good evidence that heavily points in the direction of God; could we look at it together sometime?

Boy in the Woods

Imagine we are camping at a state park, when a man comes into our campsite.

"Please help me with my son! He wandered into the woods several hours ago and hasn't returned!"

We make a plan and start canvasing the hills and valleys. After hours of fruitless searching, we turn back toward the campsite, thinking that perhaps the boy was somewhere else, or the "dad" just made up the story. Just then, a friend emerges from the woods claiming that she saw a backpack matching the dad's description a half mile in the opposite direction. Do we go look for the boy in the new area based on the testimony of another? Or do we retire to the campfire, unconvinced that there is a boy in the woods?

Key Verses

In establishing the existence of God, there aren't any key verses outside of the Bible's claim that God created the universe.

Genesis 1:1-3–In the beginning, God created the heavens and the earth. The Earth was empty, a formless mass cloaked in darkness... Then God said, "Let there be light," and there was light.

Study Questions

1. What illustration might help a person move from atheism to a more open agnosticism?

2. How would you respond to the following statement: "It takes a tremendous leap of faith to believe in God. Belief in God is something that simply can't be proven."

3. Give a brief overview of the "If Proposition" as you understand it and the alternatives it presents.

4. Name several "cause and effect" arguments for the existence of God and give a sentence of explanation for each.

5. "So what? What real difference does it make whether or not someone believes in God?" (How does the existence of God affect one's view of the meaning, value, and purpose of life?)

Notes

QUESTION 2: WHY BELIEVE IN MIRACLES?

Often-Asked Questions:

- How can a rational person today accept the stories of miracles in the Bible?

- Aren't miracles contrary to the laws of modern science?

- There is no historical basis for the miracles in the Bible—aren't they simply myths and legends designed to create religious faith?

- If there were miracles then, why doesn't God perform miracles today?

One of the unique features of Christianity is that its teachings are built directly upon God's miraculous acts on behalf of his people. Contrary to popular belief, most other religions record very few accounts of miracles, and even those are veiled in mythology or irrelevant to the core of the religion. Miracles are more prominent in the scriptures of Hinduism, yet even Hinduism does not crumble if its miracles are removed. But the miracles of the Bible are firmly embedded in space-time history, and the truth of Christianity stands or falls with the historicity of the Resurrection.

Three Options to the Question "Have Miracles Occurred?"

No: The first option flatly denies even the possibility of miracles. A *philosophical* assumption is made that miracles *cannot* and therefore *do not* take place. Following these assumptions leads to the conclusion that *no* evidence will ever be sufficient to verify a miraculous event.

Maybe (but unlikely): The second option grants that God *could* perform miracles but questions whether there is any *historical* evidence that he *has* done so. Either there is no evidence sufficient to settle the issue, or it is unreasonable to expect that Almighty God would stoop to the use of miracles to cause people to believe in him. We will look at the evidence for the Resurrection in this section.

Yes: The third option is that God has intervened in history in miraculous ways to accomplish his purposes.

First Option: Miracles Are Not Possible

Those who hold this position claim that miracles like those described in the Bible cannot occur for philosophical or scientific reasons. They start with the assertion that the physical universe operates according to the uniformity of natural law. This idea states that, according to our observation, our universe always behaves in a constant way. For example, the factors that determine how gravity affects a thrown football have *always* worked the same way, *everywhere* in the universe. The conclusion drawn from this observation is that, since our universe has always operated as it does, it is impossible for any force outside of nature (the supernatural) to exist and intervene in the cosmos. This is called the philosophy of naturalism and was eloquently described by Carl Sagan at the start of his *Cosmos* broadcast, where he asserts that the physical universe "is all that is or ever was or ever will be" (Carl Sagan, *Cosmos*).

The problem with this conclusion is that naturalists have stepped from the realm of science into the realm of metaphysics (philosophy). Overwhelmed by the unparalleled power that science has provided to understand, describe, harness, and change the physical world, many make the inappropriate conclusion that *only* science has the power to describe truth and ultimate

---

Passages that underscore the centrality of miracles to the truth claims of Christianity:

John 10:25 Jesus answered them, "I told you, and you do not believe. The works that I do in my Father's name bear witness about me..."

John 14:11 Believe me that I am in the Father and the Father is in me, or else believe on account of the works themselves.

John 15:24 If I had not done among them the works that no one else did, they would not be guilty of sin, but now they have seen and hated both me and my Father.

1 Corinthians 15:12-19 [12]Now if Christ is proclaimed as raised from the dead, how can some of you say that there is no resurrection of the dead? [13]But if there is no resurrection of the dead, then not even Christ has been raised. [14]And if Christ has not been raised, then our preaching is in vain and your faith is in vain. [15]We are even found to be misrepresenting God, because we testified about God that he raised Christ, whom he did not raise if it is true that the dead are not raised. [16]For if the dead are not raised, not even Christ has been raised. [17]And if Christ has not been raised, your faith is futile and you are still in your sins. [18]Then those also who have fallen asleep in Christ have perished. [19]If in Christ we have hope in this life only, we are of all people most to be pitied.

Scientific laws are descriptive, not prescriptive. They describe what we see, they don't determine what can be.

reality, therefore that which science cannot explain, cannot happen! We must remember that though the scientific method is very useful in gaining a great deal of knowledge, science is limited in its scope to the study of natural phenomena, that which is observable and repeatable. Scientific laws are *descriptive*, not *prescriptive*; they describe how nature operates, but they do not enforce that nature operates a certain way. They do not limit reality. It's a presupposition that God either does not exist or cannot directly intrude into the historical process. The problem is, this shows a misunderstanding of the nature of miracles and the God of the Bible.

Miracles are, by definition, empowered by something higher than nature. They do not violate our natural laws because those laws simply describe how the universe operates; they do not dictate how the universe operates. Miracles simply supersede these described laws in the way a stronger force can supersede a weaker force. If you took a flying leap off the edge of a sheer cliff, the force we know as gravity would surely bring you to an untimely end. But if you leaped off the same cliff in a hang glider, the results would (hopefully!) be quite different. The acceleration of air over the glider's wing creates a force of lift that overcomes the pull of gravity as long as the glider is in the air. In a similar way, the occurrence of a miracle means that a higher (supernatural) principle has superseded a lower (natural) principle for the duration of the miracle. To claim that miracles violate or contradict natural laws is just as improper as to say that the principle of aerodynamics violates the law of gravity.

Key Illustration: The Law of the Traffic Signal

Perhaps a better analogy of this interaction is the Illustration of the Traffic Signal. Imagine that aliens came from another galaxy to observe life on this planet. They deployed teams to investigate various aspects of life in the city. One little group was instructed to unravel the mystery of the intersection. In other words, how do all these vehicles come from all these different directions and yet, for the most part, manage to navigate the intersection without accident?

As the alien observation team began to take in data, they recognized the connection between a traffic light that was in the middle of the intersection and the flow of traffic. When the traffic light was red in one direction, it was green or yellow in the other. Green or yellow meant you could go, red that you had to stop. So they took in data from thousands of cars using sophisticated computers and were kind of patting themselves on the back. They had cracked the code. They now knew the law of the intersection. Traffic was controlled by a traffic light.

Just about that time, a vehicle with a loud, wavy noise and a red, flashing light on top approached the intersection. Vehicles stopped in all four directions while this vehicle drove right through the red light. The aliens were dismayed. They felt like the law that they had discovered had been violated and maybe wasn't true in spite of all the data. One of the aliens, as it turned out, followed the vehicle and discovered that there was a fire and that lives were saved as result of the vehicle that went through the red light.

As they began to put the information together with all the data that they had compiled before, they realized that the law of the intersection was valid. It's just that the law could be superseded at certain times for important reasons.

Just like the alien's law of the intersection, the laws of nature are descriptive, rather than legislative—they describe what we see, they don't determine what can be. Rather than thinking of miracles as "violations" of the laws of nature, they could be seen simply as superseding those laws at certain times and for certain reasons.

If there is a God who can act, acts of God are possible.

Another piece of the objection to miracles is that they destroy the regularity of nature. The scientific method is built on the assumption that we live in an orderly universe. If the universe could change on a dime, anything we learn about the universe could suddenly be wrong. Imagine how chaotic your commute would be if gravity could suddenly reverse? Many argue this is exactly what happens if divine interventions can take place: order is replaced by confusion. However, the opposite is true. An orderly universe is *crucial* for miracles. If our world was chaotic, full of seemingly miraculous events, God's miracles would have no impact and would cease to be such. A miracle, by its very nature, must be a unique event that stands out against the background of ordinary and regular occurrences. The Bible affirms that this is an orderly universe because it has been created and sustained by an orderly God. God set up the laws of nature, but he is not bound by them. He rarely chooses to supersede them, only doing so to reveal something about himself to men.

Do miracles destroy the orderly universe?

An examination of the Bible shows that these sovereign interventions are unusual, not commonplace events. Significantly, the miracles of the Bible are actually clustered around three relatively brief periods associated with the giving of new revelation by God: the times of Moses and Joshua, Elijah and Elisha, and Christ and the apostles. These miracles were irrefutable signs from God that were designed to authenticate God's revealed Word (the Law, the Prophets, and the New Testament). These three periods were separated by centuries in which only a very few miracles are recorded. The gap between Joshua and Elijah was about 540 years, and the gap between Elisha and Christ was about 830 years. The Bible is not a record of one miracle after another; its miracles were singular events that produced a profound response in some of those who were privileged to observe them.

The three major periods of miraculous events in the Bible:
Moses, Joshua and the Law
1500-1300 BCE
Elijah and Elisha and the Prophets
800-600 BCE
Christ, the apostles and the NT
30-100 CE

The key issue behind this whole question is whether God exists. If God

Focus on David Hume

A word must be said about Scottish philosopher and British empiricist David Hume (1711-1776). The tenth chapter "Of Miracles" of his 1748 book, *An Enquiry Concerning Human Understanding*, laid out the primary argument against the existence of miracles used for the past two and a half centuries. Even today, most of the arguments against miracles are based on or informed by Hume's basic idea that no amount of evidence could ever establish that a miracle has occurred. This, he argued, is because of the uniformity of natural law (the idea that the laws of nature are unchanging). The uniformity of natural law is in turn supported by the uniform experience of men against the occurrence of miracles. But what about the documented reports of miracles? They must be false, because they violate the uniformity of natural law! This is arguing in a circle, because it assumes the very thing that must be proven. It is not reasonable to define miracles as impossible and then conclude from the definition that there is no evidence for them. This is a case of determining the verdict before openly examining the evidence on its own merits.

Hume would also say that when evaluating claims of the miraculous we must weigh the chances of a miracle against the chances that the witness is lying. He concludes that it is always more likely that the witness is lying, because in all of human experience no credible report of a miracle has ever emerged. He illustrates his point with this: "It is no miracle that a man, seemingly in good health, should die on a sudden [sic]: because such a kind of death, though more unusual than any other, has yet been frequently observed to happen. But it is a miracle, that a dead man should come to life; because that has never been observed in any age or country." But if Hume had written 300 years earlier, before the first circumnavigation of the earth, this might have been the illustration: "It is no miracle that a man, seemingly a competent sailor, should disappear over the western horizon, never to be seen again. Though more unusual than a successful return from the same horizon, the sea has been known to claim good sailors. But it is a miracle, that a sailor that sailed west should return from the east, because that has never been observed in any age or country."

In 2011, Craig Keener published his two-volume work, *Miracles*. In it, he challenges Hume's assumption that uniform human experience is devoid of encounters with the miraculous or that in cases where miracles are claimed, they are devoid of trustworthy eyewitnesses. "Contrary to what appeared to be the case to many Western intellectuals one or two centuries ago, history does not support a linear evolution of all cultures to [the modernist assumption that genuine miracles are impossible]."

created the universe, there is a supernatural dimension to reality, and this means that miracles *are* possible. To put it another way, ***if there is a God who can act, acts of God are possible***. If the questioner challenges the existence of God, it may be necessary to deal with this more basic issue (see Question 1) before moving further into the miracles question. On the other hand, developing the historical case for the Resurrection of Jesus Christ may be a more direct argument for the existence of God than some of the strategies offered in Question 1.

If a person acknowledges the existence of God, he cannot flatly deny the possibility that miracles have occurred. Now the question is not one of philosophy but of history. Miracles are possible, but is there enough evidence to show that any have happened?

Second Option: Miracles Could Happen

Once we can get past the philosophical objection to miracles, we still need to answer the question of whether or not miracles have actually occurred. It's not enough to know *that* God can act, we need to know *if* he has acted in history.

First, let's be clear on the definitions and goals. A miracle, as defined by Dr. Richard Purtill, is "an event in which God temporarily makes an exception to the natural order of things, to show that God is acting" (Purtill, "Defining Miracles", *In Defense of Miracles*, 1997). Songwriters and poets often use the word "miracle" to describe unexpected or wonder-inducing moments. Flowers in springtime and the birth of a child point to the wonderful handiwork of God, but it is not really correct to call these miracles. An amazing touchdown pass as time expires can be inspiring and unexpected, but it hardly counts as divine. When "miracle" is used this way, the concept of the miraculous dilutes to the point of uselessness. What we mean and what most people who raise this question mean by the term "miracle" is a phenomenon that occurs in space-time history that is so radically different from the ordinary operations of nature that its observers are justified in attributing it to the direct intervention of a supernatural agent.

As far as our goals, we must remember that it is better to use the miracles of Christ and the Resurrection in particular to answer this question than to appeal to contemporary examples. Amazing stories of personal miracles or answers to prayer have their place, but our faith is not based on these experiences. Christianity stands or falls solely on the words and works (miracles) of Jesus, and he himself pointed to the Resurrection as the only sign that mattered (Matthew 12:39-40).

The historical evidence for the Resurrection is very strong, and because of its significant personal implications, this is the miracle to use when answering the question, "Why believe in miracles?" If the abundant evidence convinces a person that the Resurrection took place, the miracles question must be answered in the affirmative.

The Resurrection

The New Testament makes it clear that the bodily resurrection of Jesus Christ is the pillar that supports the Christian faith. The preaching of the apostles in Acts revolved around the hub of the historical Resurrection. Paul told the Corinthians in the mid-50s: "If Christ has not been raised, your faith is worthless; you are still in your sins. Then those also who have fallen asleep in Christ have perished. If we have hoped in Christ in this life only, we are of all men most to be pitied" (1 Corinthians 15:17-19). Without the Resurrection of Christ, Christianity is not worth defending. So the question is, "Is the Resurrection of Christ defensible?"

First, we will look at what we consider "historically knowable" about the events surrounding Christ's death. Then, we will examine the supposed explanations for these facts and how adequately they explain what happened. Finally, we will look at some circumstantial, yet still intriguing, evidence that fits a Resurrection narrative better than any other solution.

Historical Facts

The passion story is full of details that have been useful when building a case for the Resurrection. There is the Roman guard at the tomb, the difficulty in moving the stone, the weight of the burial wraps, etc. However, these details are only useful when talking to people who are willing to read the Biblical accounts as mostly factual history or those who have missed the bulk of the critical attacks on the Gospel accounts the past few decades. Many skeptics won't grant those details as reliable; they assume the Biblical accounts are error-prone or fictional.

When weighing the truth of any claim, and especially one as debated as the Resurrection of Christ, the first question is, "What do we *know*?"

*While modern historians often differ in the amount of weight they put behind certain criteria, there is general agreement on what factors help establish "historical verification." Among these are **multiple attestation** across sources and genres and the criterion of embarrassment- that is, if the author couldn't find a way to express a fact that didn't undermine his pride or position, then the story is probably accurate.

What historical facts do we know?

(1) Jesus suffered death by crucifixion under Pontius Pilate in 30 or 33 CE.

(2) Friends placed Jesus' body in a tomb.

(3) Jesus' friend, Mary Magdalene, and other followers found the tomb empty on the third day.

(4) The disciples had real experiences that they thought were appearances of the risen Jesus.

(5) Among the earliest converts to Christianity were Paul of Tarsus, who was persecuting the early church, and James, who was raised as a brother to Jesus.

What are the facts generally accepted by people on both sides of the debate? The following are five of the most important "generally accepted historical facts" that pass the current tests for historical verification.*

(1) **Jesus suffered death by crucifixion under Pontius Pilate in 30 or 33 CE.** Following a series of religious and civil trials, he was scourged by many lashes from the mutilating Roman whips. After a tortuous walk to the execution site, Roman soldiers drove iron nails through his wrists and feet to secure him to the cross. He would have spent several hours suspended from his hands where he would struggle to breathe, using his nailed feet to push himself up enough to inhale. Eventually, he would lose too much blood and energy to push up and inhale, and he would asphyxiate to death. Once he no longer appeared to be breathing, he may have had a spear thrust into his side to verify death. Then, a Roman centurion would have pronounced him dead.

On what basis do we consider this a "fact?" This is confirmed by all four Gospels, the early Jewish historian Josephus (Antiquities 18:3), Tacitus (Annals 15:44), Lucian (The Death of Peregrine 11-13), Mara bar Serapian (from a letter at the British Museum), and even the Talmud. There are virtually no serious religious scholars of any persuasion—from atheist to skeptical theist to conservative Christian—who deny that Jesus died of crucifixion in either 30 or 33 CE.

(2) **Friends placed Jesus' body in a tomb.** Why do we think this? When looking at historical sources for Jesus's life, death, and resurrection, it's important to understand that "the Bible" doesn't count for only one source. Biblical scholarship has spent the past century peeling back the layers of the 27 books and letters that make up the New Testament. They've been able to identify a number of places where the authors wrote while looking at somebody else's notes and where they've brought their own sources or perspectives to the story. So, when we are looking for "multiple attestation" of a fact or plot point in the Jesus story, we don't need to go outside of the Bible to get it. Many significant pieces of information can be found attested in the multiple layers and source documents of the New Testament. For example, in the passion accounts (from the Triumphal Entry to Easter Sunday), Joseph of Arimathea appears as a key figure in all four Gospels (and nowhere else in the story!). The four Gospel writers appear to have drawn from different sources or strands of tradition for their passion accounts, so these references to Joseph count as four different attestations to his historicity. The Gnostic *Gospel of Peter*, though composed at least a hundred years later, captures another strand of tradition about Joseph, that he was a friend of Pilate, as well as a disciple of Jesus.

(3) **Jesus' friend, Mary Magdalene, and other followers found the tomb empty on the third day.** This fact was disputed in the past, but recent

studies even by critical theologians have led to a growing scholarly consensus that the tomb was found empty first by the women. The reason this idea has gained significant acceptance today is because of how embarrassing it was to have the women be the first witnesses. In their culture women could not be trusted; their testimony was not admissible in court. But the women weren't the only ones who said the tomb was empty. This was clearly admitted, even by Jesus' enemies. The chief priests and elders bribed the guard to say that the body was stolen by his disciples (Matthew 28:11-15). Certainly, if the tomb was still occupied when the word about his resurrection began to spread, the authorities would have exhumed the body and put it on public display to quell the insidious rumors. Of course, these rumors would never have started to spread in the first place if the tomb was not empty. The first Christians began preaching a resurrected Jesus *in Jerusalem*, right where Jesus was crucified and buried. The people could easily have walked out to the tomb and looked for themselves. But no body was ever produced, and the empty tomb was never denied.

(4) **The disciples had real experiences that they thought were appearances of the risen Jesus.** As a result, the disciples were completely transformed, even to the point of being willing to die for their faith. How do we know this? Paul, in his letters (50-62 CE), reminds readers of the message that Peter, James, John, and himself all teach—Christ resurrected from the dead. Creeds found in 1 Corinthians 15 and sermons recorded in Acts confirm that it was the professed belief of the early church that many witnessed Christ risen from the dead (32-50 CE). Finally, all four Gospel authors claimed to believe Christ resurrected (50-100 CE), and early church fathers such as Clement of Rome (95 CE) and Polycarp (110 CE) confirmed this belief. This belief by the disciples that they witnessed Christ risen was so strong that it lead to their eventual martyrdom, as recorded by Luke (60-70 CE), Clement of Rome (95 CE), Ignatius, Polycarp (110 CE), Dionysus of Corinth, Tertullian, Origen, and others.

(5) **Among the earliest converts to Christianity were Paul of Tarsus and James, who was raised as a brother to Jesus**.

Paul, an ambitious young man and a devout Pharisee, left his hometown for Jerusalem to pursue an education under Gamaliel, one of the brightest minds of his day. While there, he established himself as a great enemy of the early church. Convinced that the followers of Jesus were heretics, he sought to wipe them out by imprisoning and killing all he could find.

James grew up with Jesus as his brother. Imagine being asked to believe that your brother is God on Earth, the promised messiah, and the savior of the world. John 7:5 makes it clear that none of Jesus' brothers believed in him during his earthly ministry. What evidence would *you* need in order to

A number of thinkers who sought to disprove the Resurrection and thus invalidate Christianity found themselves confronted instead by such a weight of evidence in favor of the Resurrection that it forced them to bend their knees before the living Christ.

1880: General Lew Wallace decided to create a historical novel about a Jewish contemporary of Jesus. Something quite unexpected took place, however, as he researched the background for the book. The historical evidence for the Resurrection overwhelmed him, and he wrote *Ben Hur* as a new believer in Christ.

1920s: Albert Henry Ross planned to write a book that would lay the myth of the Resurrection to rest. But his research compelled him to embrace the empty tomb as established history. He published *Who Moved the Stone?* under the pseudonym Frank Morison to lay out the evidence he encountered for the empty tomb and Resurrection.

1930s: C. S. Lewis recorded his reluctant trek from atheism to Christianity in his autobiography, *Surprised by Joy*. He did not want to meet Christ, but the evidence brought him "kicking and screaming" into the kingdom.

1960s: Malcolm Muggeridge, a former editor of *Punch* magazine and a provoking analyst of modern culture, was a late convert to Christianity. He traced his journey from skepticism to faith in *Jesus Rediscovered and Chronicles of Wasted Time*.

1980s: Lee Strobel set out to show his wife that her new faith couldn't stand up to the scrutiny of a modern investigative journalist. Within a decade, he published *The Case for Christ*, a substantial work that shows, through interviews with expert scholars, how each aspect of the Jesus's life, death, and resurrection can be reasonably believed.

stake your life on the claim that your sibling is divine?

Fast-forward about 15-20 years, and an amazing scene unfolds. Paul and James, two of the most unlikely candidates for conversion, have become two of the main voices at the first major church council (Acts 15). James has become the leading voice of the church in Jerusalem. When he writes, he refers to himself not as Jesus's brother, but as "a servant of God and the Lord Jesus Christ." He is stoned to death for this belief in 62 CE. Meanwhile, Paul changed from being the church's powerful adversary into its most passionate advocate.

Historians and theologians cannot ignore these five facts, but they can and have interpreted these facts in various ways to avoid the conclusion that Jesus rose from the dead. Several naturalistic theories regarding the tomb and the appearances have been proposed, but all of these fail to explain the historical data. Furthermore, there is a quantity of circumstantial evidence that supplements this data and makes the case for the Resurrection even stronger.

Explanations Regarding the Tomb

The tomb of Jesus was either occupied or empty on the first day of the week. We will first consider three theories that claim that the tomb was still occupied. Then, we will examine four naturalistic theories that attempt to explain why the tomb was empty.

The first option is that the tomb was still *occupied*:

(1) The location of the tomb was unknown, or Jesus wasn't buried in a tomb at all. The common practice to dispose of crucified criminals was to throw them in a mass grave or in the dump outside of town. This theory is completely unacceptable because all four Gospels state that Joseph of Arimathea obtained permission from Pilate to bury the body of Jesus in his newly hewn tomb near the crucifixion site. Certainly he knew the location of his own private garden tomb. The accounts also make it clear that the women and disciples had no trouble finding the tomb, and the guard certainly knew the location as well. A variation of this theory holds that Jesus's body was thrown into a common pit for the executed. This view can only be maintained by an outright denial of all four burial accounts, and there is not a shred of evidence for doing so.

(2) The women and disciples went to the wrong tomb. This theory requires the absurd conclusion that Peter and John, eventually Joseph of Arimathea, the guards, and the Jewish and Roman authorities *all* went to the wrong tomb and that the correct tomb was never found. We aren't aware of any current proponents of this idea.

(3) Jesus was resurrected spiritually, not bodily. This "pious" compromise rejects the physical resurrection of Jesus but holds that he is alive. His appearances to the disciples were genuine, but they misinterpreted the nature of his resurrection. Like the other theories, this one does a severe injustice to the Gospel accounts. In the post-Resurrection narratives, Jesus placed special emphasis on the fact that his body was resurrected: "See My hands and My feet, that it is I Myself; touch Me and see, for a spirit does not have flesh and bones as you see that I have" (Luke 24:39). The disciples took hold of his feet (Matthew 28:9), Mary clung to him (John 20:17), and he ate a piece of broiled fish before the disciples (Luke 24:42-43).

Jesus stressed his physical resurrection because a mere spiritual resurrection (with his body rotting in the tomb) would have been unacceptable to the Jews; first-century Judaism awaited the restoration of the whole person, including the body. This can be clearly seen in 2 Maccabees, a Jewish text about the Jewish revolt from the Greek empire in 160 BCE. The story about the gruesome death of seven brothers for their faith graphically illustrates their expectation of a physical resurrection. While Catholics and Protestants disagree on the authoritative nature of this and other Jewish apocrypha, they agree that the book captures the Jewish beliefs of its day.

The remaining option is that the tomb was *empty*:

(1) One or more of Jesus' friends stole his body. This was the original explanation for the empty tomb (see Matthew 28:11-15), and it remained the primary alternative a hundred years later when church father Justin Martyr composed his Jewish polemic, *Against Trypho*. If the Gospel accounts are taken seriously, a number of problems appear. How did the disciples get past the Roman soldiers? If the soldiers were asleep, how could they know that the disciples were responsible? A Roman guard found sleeping would be put to death, so it is unthinkable that a whole group fell asleep through the theft of the body.

In addition to these problems, neither Joseph of Arimathea nor the disciples would have had any real motive to steal the body. They did not expect the Resurrection to take place, and they had nothing to gain and everything to lose by perpetrating a deliberate fraud. The disciples endured

Explanations Regarding the Tomb

If the tomb was occupied:

(1) Among the earliest converts to Christianity were Paul of Tarsus and James, who was raised as a brother to Jesus.

(2) The women and disciples went to the wrong tomb.

(3) Jesus was resurrected spiritually, not bodily.

If the tomb was empty:

(1) One or more of Jesus' friends stole his body.

(2) The enemies of Jesus stole the body.

(3) Jesus "swooned" on the cross and appeared to be dead.

great suffering because of their testimony about the resurrected Lord, most to the point of death. Such behavior would have been absurd if they knew it was all a lie. True, people die for ideas that turn out to be wrong, but does anyone die for a lie that they know to be false? This kind of deception is also inconsistent with the high moral character exhibited in their New Testament epistles.

This idea also vastly underestimates the impact "growing up Jewish" would have had on the disciples. Had they knowingly perpetrated the lie that Jesus was the resurrected "Son of God," they would have been guilty of blasphemy (and the judgment of God) themselves.

Finally, it's very difficult to imagine that a hoax like this could have persuaded Paul or James to proclaim Jesus as a risen savior.

(2) The enemies of Jesus stole the body. This theory is also plagued by the problem of motive. Why would the Jewish or Roman authorities want to steal the body when this is precisely the thing they sought to avoid? Even if they did remove the body for security purposes, they would have made such a claim and displayed the body, if necessary, to put an end to the rumors of the Resurrection that were circulating in Jerusalem. The complete silence on the part of the Jewish and Roman authorities loudly proclaimed their acknowledgment that the body was inexplicably gone.

(3) Jesus "swooned" on the cross and only appeared to be dead. The cool air of the tomb then resuscitated him, and his disciples were convinced he rose from the dead. This eighteenth-century rationalistic theory, when analyzed, requires as great a miracle as the Resurrection itself. It means that Jesus endured being whipped to the point of disfigurement, nailed to a cross and left to hang for hours, before being pierced with a spear by professional executioners, who examined and declared him dead. His body was then wrapped in linen, along with one hundred pounds of spices. In spite of great loss of blood and many hours in the cold tomb without food, water, or assistance, he revived. Then, he managed to escape from the grave clothes and spices, replace them neatly in the tomb, roll the huge stone up an incline away from the opening, overcome the armed guards, walk miles on pierced feet, and convince his disciples that he had conquered death as the resurrected author of life. This ludicrous theory would also have us believe that Jesus lived on after all this and died a natural death in obscurity.

(4) Other conspiracy theories. From *The Passover Plot* to *The DaVinci Code*, there have been no shortage of creative attempts to re-imagine the events of first century Palestine and the dawn of the church.

None of these theories even comes close to accounting for the historical facts associated with the empty tomb, the appearances of the resurrected Christ, the radical changes in the lives of the disciples, and the emergence of James and Paul as early church leaders. They distort the clear evidence without any basis and require more faith to believe than the Resurrection itself. It is ironic that the chief priests and the Pharisees made such an effort to have the tomb secured, because had they not done so, the case for the Resurrection would not have been as strong.

Explanations of the Appearances

(1) **The disciples all lied about seeing the resurrected Jesus.** The first problem with this view is that it contradicts the historical accounts. It also means that all of the disciples who claimed to have seen the Lord (including the five hundred people mentioned by Paul) were liars. To make matters worse, these people had nothing to gain by perpetuating such a falsehood, and many of them suffered for this testimony, even to the point of violent deaths. Would this many people willingly give up their lives for the sake of a fraud? They were also giving up more than their lives, but also their standing before God. Having "grown up Jewish," the disciples knew falsely claiming Christ as the resurrected "Son of God" was blasphemy, a very serious offense in the Jewish religion.

The strongest example of this is Paul and James. What would have caused such a radical transformation of such unlikely candidates for Christianity? The only adequate explanation is a personal encounter with the resurrected Jesus. Paul's testimony is particularly compelling because he was an enemy of the church when he claimed to have seen the risen Christ. His metamorphosis was so complete that he spent the rest of his days preaching the Gospel and suffering for it, ultimately losing his life for his belief in Christ's resurrection.

(2) **The post-Resurrection appearances of Christ were merely hallucinations in the minds of the disciples.** There are a number of reasons why the hallucination theory does not fit the facts: (a) Hallucinations are private, not publicly shared experiences. But according to the accounts, Jesus appeared several times to groups of people. Paul includes a reference to an appearance to a crowd of five hundred in 1 Corinthians 15, though unless this is the ascension story in Acts 1, it isn't recorded in the Gospels. (b) Hallucinations are generally restricted to favorable places and times of day, but Christ appeared in a variety of locations and times. There was no pattern in his appearances. (c) Only certain kinds of people (e.g., people with schizoid tendencies, ascetics, those who use hallucinogenic drugs) are subject to hallucinatory experiences, but the appearances of Christ involved a great range of personalities. (d) After Christ appeared to people over a forty-day period, his appearances suddenly ceased. Hallucinations, on the other hand, generally recur over a long period of time and do not abruptly stop.

Explanations of the Appearances

(1) The disciples all lied about seeing the resurrected Jesus.

(2) The post-resurrection appearances of Christ were merely hallucinations in the minds of the disciples.

(3) The whole story of the resurrected Jesus, including the appearances, is simply an elaborate legend created by the early church.

(e) Hallucinations are stimulated by expectation, but the disciples had no hope at all of Christ's Resurrection. They were very skeptical about the earliest reports. (f) The disciples touched, talked, and ate with the Lord at various times, and this is certainly not characteristic of hallucinations.

(3) The whole story of the resurrected Jesus, including the appearances, is simply an elaborate legend created by the early church. To answer this objection, it may be necessary to look at the question concerning the reliability of the Bible (see Question 4). These accounts were backed up by eyewitness testimonies and widely circulated without being challenged by the friends or enemies of Jesus. Peter firmly declared, "We did not follow cleverly devised tales when we made known to you the power and coming of our Lord Jesus Christ, but we were eyewitnesses of his majesty" (2 Peter 1:16). The dating of the New Testament documents also precludes the development of such a legend because there was not enough time. With every passing year, additional archaeological discoveries continue to vindicate the historical reliability of the scriptures.

Circumstantial Evidence

(1) Christ predicted his own resurrection on the third day and announced that this would be the most significant sign for the affirmation of his truth claims (e.g., Mark 8:31; 10:33-34; Matthew 12:38-40). It is unlikely that these predictions would be included in the material circulating so early about the teachings of Jesus; if the church tacked on the Resurrection story much later.

(2) The entire crucifixion saga came about because the Jewish leadership wanted to end the Jesus movement. If there was a body to be found or some other clear refutation of the Christian claim, they would have shouted it from the rooftops. But the silence of the Jewish leaders about the Resurrection eloquently testified that they knew the basic facts were undeniable.

(3) Before the Resurrection, the disciples were fearful men whose faith was weak, and all abandoned Jesus after his arrest. But by the Day of Pentecost, seven weeks later, they were boldly proclaiming Christ to the multitudes in Jerusalem. This transformation was complete, permanent, and unanimous. According to early church tradition, all of them suffered for the sake of the message of the resurrected Lord, and almost all died as martyrs. A solid case can be made for certainty of the martyrdom of Peter, Paul, James the brother of John, and James the brother of Jesus. It is clear that they were totally convinced of the truth of the Resurrection, and they were certainly in a position to know whether the Resurrection had indeed taken place.

(4) The success of the early Christian church in spite of fierce opposition is another evidence for the Resurrection. During the height of his popularity,

Jesus drew crowds that numbered in the thousands, but by the time of his death, his followers had dwindled to, at most, a few hundred. Then, something happened, and what we now know as Christianity exploded into history. At the end of the first century Christians could be found in every major city in the Roman Empire. At least a few major attempts to quash this new religion (under Emperors Nero, Domitian, and Diocletian) failed, along with countless attempts on the local level. East to west across the Empire, from the slave quarters to the palace of the Emperor, people were worshiping Jesus Christ as Lord. With no military campaign, no "incubation" period, and no charismatic and unifying leader walking the earth, by 300 CE the church had grown from a few hundred to a population in the millions. The church began right in Jerusalem, the city of the empty tomb, and the apostles' preaching centered on the resurrected Savior. Without the Resurrection, the church would not have come into existence.

(5) The shift from Saturday to Sunday as the day of worship for the early Jewish Christians (cf. Acts 20:7; 1 Corinthians 16:1-2) was a radical act that would never have taken place if Christ had not been raised on the first day of the week (Matthew 28:1; Luke 24:1).

(6) The sacraments of baptism and communion are both related to the Resurrection, and would have been senseless in the early church apart from the historical reality of the Resurrection.

The Verdict

All the attempts to find naturalistic explanations for the historical facts related to the Resurrection have failed. The direct evidence concerning the tomb and the appearances, combined with the circumstantial evidences establish beyond a reasonable doubt the bodily resurrection of Jesus Christ. He conquered the grave, and he offers resurrection life to those who place their trust in him.

Third Option: Miracles Are Possible

Even if a person admits that the Resurrection and other miraculous events in the Bible took place, this is not enough. Many believe these things and still refuse to place their trust in Christ. The miracles in the Bible were signs that authenticated God's message and messengers, but those who saw them didn't always respond with faith.

The scriptures make it clear that the heart of an unregenerate person is at enmity with God and refuses to bow to his revelation and authority. This is why the Council of Sanhedrin sought to suppress the message about the resurrected Christ, even though they could not deny the Resurrection or Peter's healing of the man who had been lame from birth (Acts 4:16-17; cf. Luke 16:31; John 12:10-11). Only the Holy Spirit's work of convicting

Estimates vary widely on the number of Christians in the world by the end of the first century, but it is generally agreed upon that the church had spread across the entire geographic and socio-economic range of the Roman empire. By the year 300 CE, scholarly consensus estimates that despite periodic persecution Christians made up 10% of the Roman Empire, or about 6 million of the estimated 60 million people that made up the Empire. The last major Roman persecution of Christians occurred in 303 CE, under Emperor Diocletian. It officially ended when Constantine declared Christianity the religion of Rome in 313 CE.

Some have compared the explosive growth of Christianity in the first three centuries to the growth of other religions. The difficulty with this comparison lies in the radically different cultures, environments, and methods of growth. Christianity grew in a population of only millions that was declining demographically at the time, and the church was often under severe persecution during its early years. To join the Christian church was to risk disownment, exile, torture, or even death. Islam spread in the absence of powerful empires, through a coercive military campaign. To refuse Islam was to risk torture or death. Mormonism saw its early growth in an unpopulated corner of a far more populous planet, and, later, in cultures that preach religious tolerance.

unbelievers of "sin, and righteousness, and judgment" (John 16:8) can break through the spiritual blindness of non-Christians.

Some object that God's revelation is too remote. If he wants people to believe, he should reveal himself in a more direct way. In effect, the objector wants God to clobber him into the Kingdom by forcing him to believe. What would it take—a cloud formation spelling out John 3:16? A glowing angel hovering above his bed at 3 A.M.? Perhaps a fulfillment of Philip's modest request would do: "Lord, show us the Father, and it is enough for us" (John 14:8). God, however, has already done more than enough. When Jesus Christ returns to Earth, he will not come to offer salvation but to judge those who have already rejected God's offer of salvation through faith in his finished work.

Miracles cannot create faith, but they can be used by the Holy Spirit as catalysts to faith, especially when a person begins to consider the claims and credentials of Christ (see Question 6). Christ's miracles (especially the Resurrection) demonstrate the validity of his claims, and if his claims are true, they have profound implications for the eternal destiny of every human being. This naturally leads into a presentation of the Gospel and the biblical meaning of belief in Jesus Christ (see Question 11).

Summary

Those who object to the possibility of miracles usually assume that the natural laws of the universe cannot be overruled by some outside force; it is a closed system. This anti-supernatural assumption has profoundly influenced many scientists who argue that a universe open to miracles would not be orderly. But scientific inquiry is not threatened by the occurrence of miracles, because they are by definition unusual events that involve a very brief suspension of the normal processes of nature by a higher power. The real issue behind this question is whether God exists. If there is a God who can act, then acts of God are possible. How can we know whether God has chosen to intervene in his creation through miraculous works? To answer this we must turn from philosophy to history. According to the Bible, God has chosen to reveal himself in historical ways, and these include divinely empowered miracles. The only sign worth subjecting to historical scrutiny is his Resurrection, and a presentation of the case for the Resurrection is the best way to affirm that miracles have occurred. But belief in the miracles of Christ is no guarantee of saving faith. Many have acknowledged the Resurrection without receiving Christ as their Savior. The unbeliever needs to consider the implications of the claims and credentials of Christ for his life and respond to the convicting work of the Holy Spirit.

Supplemental Reading

Many of the Supplemental Reading books from Question 1 contain chapters addressing the conflict between naturalism and the possibility of supernatural events. The following books focus entirely on the issue:

Geivett, R. Douglas and Gary R. Habermas eds. *In Defense of Miracles*. IVP Academic, 1997.

Lewis , C.S. *Miracles*. HarperOne, 2009. These two books encapsulate Christian thought on the topic of Miracles for the past century.

Twelftree, Graham, H. *The Cambridge Companion to Miracles*. Cambridge University Press, 2011. This book looks at how miracles have been historically and recently viewed in the major religious traditions of the world.

Keener, Craig S. *Miracles: The Credibility of the New Testament Accounts*. Baker Academic, 2011. This substantial two-volume work looks at the perception and critique of miracles throughout history, as well as an extensive evaluation of modern-day miracle claims.

Resurrection: Two short books and two really long books

Strobel, Lee. *The Case for Christ: A Journalist's Personal Investigation of the Evidence for Jesus*. Zondervan, 1998 (I) This book still sets the standard for an introduction to the critical facets of the Resurrection narrative, presented in an interview format with credentialed academics.

Habermas, Gary R. and Michael R. Licona. *The Case for the Resurrection of Jesus*. Kregel Publications, 2004 Nearly every author and speaker on the Resurrection over the past 40 years, including the original version of this book, has been heavily influenced by Gary Habermas's research. In this volume he and Licona give the bare-bones version of his Minimal-Facts approach.

Wright, N.T. *Resurrection of the Son of God*. Fortress Press, 2003. Wright's massive book explores the concept of death and resurrection throughout ancient history leading up to the time of Jesus. He conclusively demonstrates that the concept of Jesus's resurrection as espoused in the New Testament was an entirely new idea, completely without precedent in the ancient world.

Licona, Michael R. *The Resurrection of Jesus: A New Historiographical Approach*. IVP Academic, 2010. Licona's massive book explores the ideas of historical knowledge, and then uses all the available tools of historical inquiry to establish the "historical bedrock" of the life, death, and after-death accounts of Jesus. This book drills down deeper into the "minimal facts" than the one he co-wrote with Habermas.

In this chapter, we reference the historical bedrock of what we know about Jesus, his death, and his Resurrection appearances. If the historicity of Jesus is the issue, the following works all explore the current challenges to the historicity of the biblical account of Jesus:

Habermas, Gary R. *The Historical Jesus: Ancient Evidence for the Life of Christ*. College Press Publishing Company, Inc., 1996.

Bock, Darrell L. *Who Is Jesus?: Linking the Historical Jesus with the Christ of Faith*. Howard Books, 2012. (I)

Eddy, Paul Rhodes and Gregory A. Boyd. *Jesus Legend, The: A Case for the Historical Reliability of the Synoptic Jesus Tradition*. Baker Academic, 2006.

Strobel, Lee. *The Case for the Real Jesus: A Journalist Investigates Current Attacks on the Identity of Christ*. Zondervan, 2006. (I)

Evans, Craig A. *Fabricating Jesus: How Modern Scholars Distort the Gospels*. IVP Books, 2008.

Study Guide for Why Believe in Miracles?

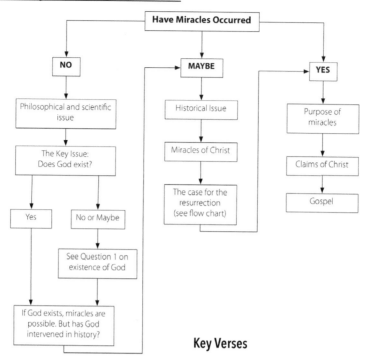

Key Illustrations

The Law of the Traffic Signal

Imagine that aliens came to observe life on this planet, and they had teams to investigate various aspects of life in the city. One little group was instructed to unravel the mystery of the intersection. In other words, how do all these vehicles come from different directions and yet, for the most part, manage to navigate the intersection without accident?

As the alien observation team began to take in data, they recognize the connection between a traffic light that was in the middle of the intersection and the flow of traffic. When the traffic light was red in one direction, it was green or yellow in the other. Green or yellow meant you could go, red that you had to stop. They had taken in data from thousands of cars using sophisticated computers and were kind of patting themselves on the back. They had cracked the code. They now knew the law of the intersection. Traffic was controlled by a traffic light.

Just about that time, a vehicle with a loud, wavy noise and a red, flashing light on top approached the intersection. Vehicles stopped in all four directions while this vehicle drove right through the red light. The aliens were dismayed. They felt like the law that they had discovered had been violated and maybe wasn't true in spite of all the data. One of the aliens, as it turned out, followed the vehicle and that there was a fire and that lives were saved as result of that vehicle that went through the red light.

As they began to put the information together with all the data that they had compiled before, they realized that the law of the intersection was valid. It was just that the law could be superseded at certain times for important reasons.

Key Verses

Purpose of Miracles

John 10:24-25 The Jews gathered around him saying,"How long will you keep us in suspense? If you are the Christ, tell us plainly." Jesus answered,"I did tell you, but you do not believe. The miracles I do in my Father's name speak for me..."

John 20:30-31 Jesus did many other miraculous signs in the presence of his disciples, which are not recorded in this book. But these are written that you may believe that Jesus is the Christ, the Son of God, and that by believing you may have life in his name.

Nicodemus in John 3:2 "No one can do these signs that you do unless God is with him."

The Key Verse for Focusing on the Resurrection:

1 Corinthians 15 [13] For if there is no resurrection of the dead, then Christ has not been raised either. [14] And if Christ was not raised, then all our preaching is useless, and your trust in God is useless.

[15] And we apostles would all be lying about God, for we have said that God raised Christ from the grave, but that can't be true if there is no resurrection of the dead. [16] If there is no resurrection of the dead, then Christ has not been raised. [17] And if Christ has not been raised, then your faith is useless, and you are still under condemnation for your sins. [18] In that case, all who have died believing in Christ have perished! [19] And if we have hope in Christ only for this life, we are the most miserable people in the world.

The Resurrection of Jesus

The *Almost Universally Accepted Facts* of the Resurrection Account
• Jesus suffered death by crucifixion under Pontius Pilate in 30 or 33 CE
• His body was placed in a new tomb, and guarded by Roman Soldiers
• Some women, then some of the disciples found the tomb of Jesus empty.
• All the disciples, and the women, and other groups of people claimed to have seen Jesus alive and well
• These disciples began to proclaim a Physically Risen Jesus Christ to the Jews in Jerusalem within 2 months of His death, and spread this message around the world.
• Among the earliest converts to Christianity were Paul of Tarsus and James, who was raised as a brother to Jesus.

The Obvious Options
Either the tomb is or isn't empty...

Tomb Not Empty
• Wrong Tomb?
• Unknown tomb?
• "Spiritual" Resurrection
• A Look-alike was crucified (Jesus twin...)

Empty Tomb
• Friends stole the body
• Enemies stole the body
• Swoon Theory
• Other conspiracy theories

Not only is the tomb empty, but dozens to hundreds of people claimed to have **seen Jesus alive** after his death!

Explanation of Appearances
• Witnesses Lied
• Hallucinations
• Legend made up by Early Church

Circumstantial Evidence
• Jesus foretold his resurrection
• Changed Lives of Disciples
• Silence of the Jewish leaders
• The existence and explosive growth of the Church
• Sunday Worship
• The Sacraments (Baptism and Lord's Supper highlight Death and Resurrection)

Study Questions

1. What is the key issue being discussed when attempting to help someone determine whether miracles could have ever occurred?

2. Define "miracles" as you understand the term and then address the concerns some have over the way the word is sometimes used.

3. Give an answer and an illustration in response to the following statement: "I'm a scientist and believe in the order of the laws of nature. It seems to me that miracles are, by definition, a violation of those laws."

4. What difference does it make to Christianity if any miracles did occur? Give Scriptural references to support your answer.

5. Assuming that a person is open to consider the Resurrection, what are several lines of evidence to support it?

Notes

QUESTION 3: ISN'T CHRISTIANITY JUST A PSYCHOLOGICAL CRUTCH?

Often-Asked Questions:

- Isn't Christianity, like all religions, just a crutch for emotionally weak people?

- Don't people just create God in order to cope with an uncertain future?

- Why should it matter what you believe as long as you have a sincere faith?

- If you were raised to believe in God, can you ever deny that preconditioning?

- What if I don't need religion?

- Christianity may be true for you, but it's not true for me.

Two Options

The underlying assumption in this question is that religious experience is merely psychological. It exists solely in the mind, so it must be totally subjective, without any objective data to substantiate a conclusion. This objection rarely presents itself so antagonistically, usually appearing far gentler, as in "that may be true for you, but it's not true for me."

Either religion is a subjective experience that has no objective reality, or it is an experience that has an objective basis, and its truth transcends personal preference. While the broader objection often focuses on *all* religion, we'll focus on the case for an objective basis for Christianity (the objection probably holds up against some religions).

We need to remember, a position is not rendered false just because it is completely subjective. This just removes it from the sphere of investigation. If Christianity can be relegated to the state of total *subjectivity*, we will be hard-pressed to prove the validity of our claims. Many critics have found the corner of subjectivity a comfortable one into which they can sweep opposing views when faced with an uncomfortable decision.

First Option: Christianity Is Subjective

For centuries, religion in general and Christianity in particular have been categorized as emotional crutches. The word crutch almost always has negative connotations. It conjures up the image of a clumsy device to help a person lurch through life. It is an awkward help, not a satisfactory solution to the problem. According to this view, a religious person operates strictly from emotion to meet his needs and overcome his weaknesses. The major skeptics of religion have often portrayed religion as something for the emotionally weak, and those who can't cope with the future on their own. Marx saw the problem as economic; religion was the carrot on a stick used by the upper classes to keep the lower classes from revolting. The masses were kept in tow with the promise of a better existence in the next life if they persevered now. Freud and others related religion to the fear that comes from contending with natural forces. According to Freud, man invented God to help him deal with the dangers and unknowns of life. Now that man is more sophisticated and less superstitious, there is little need for God.

In conversation with others, it helps to acknowledge that religion *can* be a crutch. Some people seek solace in religion because they are too insecure to face the future on their own. They invent their own gods to assist them through life's burdens and woes. Christianity is often caricatured as an escape mechanism for emotionally needy people. But the fact that religion *can* be a crutch doesn't actually mean that it *always* is.

There are a number of statements often made to dismiss Christianity

---

Another way to describe the subjective vs. objective issue:

(a) How much money is in your wallet?

(b) What is the best kind of ice cream?

Which category of question does religion fall into? Is it an objective question that can be investigated, evaluated, and has real-world implications like (a)? Or is it just a matter of personal preference like (b)?

Religion can be a crutch, but that does not mean it always is.

that assume a subjective basis for belief. We'll examine three of them.

- People think Christianity is true because they were raised to believe it. They are *preconditioned* for belief by their family and culture.
- People buy into Christianity because of their subjective personal *experience*. They accept it because it works, not necessarily because it is true.
- People think Christianity is true because they *want* it to be true. They have an *emotional* need that it fills.

Preconditioning. Some try to invalidate the Christian's claim to be objective by stating that Christians were preconditioned to believe in Christ by their family and culture. They make two false assumptions:

(1) All Christians were raised in a Christian environment. This is true across large populations, since those born into Christian homes are more likely to be Christian than those born into Hindu or Muslim families and cultures. But the assumption completely falls apart on the individual level. Many Christians came to Christianity out of religiously hostile or neutral environments.

(2) If a person is preconditioned to believe something, his position is not valid. Though preconditioning doesn't make a position true, preconditioning doesn't make it false, either. The question to be asked is: "Does my preconditioning have any correlation to objective reality?" Take this statement out of the realm of religion for a moment. Many of us were brought up to believe in Santa Claus. As we grew up, we realized that Santa was just a nice story to encourage us to be good little boys and girls. Things that we were taught as children are not necessarily true. But most of us were also taught that fire is very hot and would burn us if touched. Things that we were taught as children are not necessarily false, either. Don't allow a person to fall into the trap of rejecting Christianity just because he was preconditioned to believe it as a child. Preconditioning does not validate *or* invalidate a position. An investigation of the validity of Christianity's claims should lead to a search for some kind of objective basis.

Key Illustration: Santa & Fire

Experience. The second objection raised to demonstrate that Christianity is subjective rather than objective is to claim that religious beliefs are based solely on personal experience, and *experience does not determine truth*. "I'm glad it works for you, it just doesn't work for me." The misconception here is that most Christians assume the truth of Christianity on the basis of their experience. Experience *or lack of it* can lead a person to a conclusion, but it remains a subjective conclusion and, therefore, removed from the sphere of investigation (I prayed for God to heal my mom, and he didn't, so he must not be real). An individual's personal experience can corroborate truth, but it doesn't prove it.

An I.Q. test will affirm that a genius is a genius, but the experience of taking the test did not make him a genius. He was a genius, and the test confirmed it. A blind man may never have seen a sunset, but he should not conclude from this that sunsets do not exist.

Key Illustration: The Blind Man & the Sunset

A belief or an experience does not prove a position, nor does a lack of belief or experience disprove a position. Again, the real question is whether there is any objective reality to one's belief or experience. If not, then the Christian position might be a psychological crutch.

Emotions. Critics may raise a third objection: Christians want Christianity to be true because they have an emotional need that it fills, but *belief and emotions do not determine truth*. They assume that Christians declare Christianity to be true on the basis of their own beliefs and emotions. But Christianity is true because of Christ and who he is and not because Christians want to believe in him. One's belief in something does not make it true, and, conversely, one's lack of belief does not make something false.

For example, suppose someone decides to believe that every time he throws a ball up it will come back down. Does it come back down because he believes it will? Does it come back down because he wants it to? No, it comes back down because of gravity and not because of his belief or desire. Suppose another person no longer believes that the law of gravity exists. Would we encourage that person to leap from the tallest building in town? Obviously not, for he would plummet to earth regardless of how much he wanted to fly or believed he could. The law of gravity is valid on the basis of its objective criteria and not on the basis of one's belief or lack of belief.

Key Illustration: Morphine vs. Penicillin

Take the case of a patient with a deadly bacterial infection. When this patient recieves a dose of morphine, the symptoms of her disease are erased because of the numbing effects of the drug. The patient believes she is cured, and she feels much better. But believing she is cured and being cured are two different things. Now suppose the patient receives penicillin instead of morphine. She still has her pain and thus she believes that the medicine is having no effect, but she is actually *being* cured. Her lack of belief does not alter the reality of her cure. We must remember that one's belief is only as valid as the object in which it is placed. The Christian does not attempt to validate Christianity on the basis of his subjective beliefs and emotions. Instead, he turns to the objective data regarding Christ.

It should be noted that all of these criticisms leveled at religion in general and Christianity in particular can also apply to atheism. A growing number of people are being raised without religion, and many spend their formative years in a culture, both online and in the classroom, that preconditions them to believe Christianity is not true. We've met many people who quit believing in God when they encountered life experiences that were incompatible with their perception of God. These are usually related to evil and suffering in the world (see Question 5 for a further exploration of that topic).

As for an emotional basis for atheism? Aldous Huxley on the foundation of his former atheistic views:

> For myself, as, no doubt, for most of my contemporaries, the philosophy of meaninglessness was essentially an instrument of liberation. The liberation we desired was simultaneously liberation from a certain political and economic system and liberation from a certain system of morality. We objected to the morality because it interfered with our sexual freedom; we objected to the political and economic system because it was unjust. The supporters of these systems claimed that in some way they embodied the meaning (a Christian meaning, they insisted) of the world. There was one admirably simple method of confuting these people and at the same time justifying ourselves in our political and erotic revolt: we could deny that the world had any meaning whatsoever. Similar tactics had been adopted during the eighteenth century and for the same reasons. (*Ends and Means*, 1937, p. 273)

It seems that on many occasions it would appeal to men and women not to have to answer to an almighty God. If there is no God, the consequences of one's actions can be minimized. Could it be that the atheist eliminates God so that his own fear of having to face such a being can be reduced? The very character of God is disturbing to men in rebellion against him. He is holy, unchanging, all-powerful, and all-knowing. Ability to dismiss the concept of this kind of God would alleviate a great deal of guilt in people's hearts. Be careful, however, when explaining the psychological reasons for atheism, and don't caricature the viewpoint. The goal is to level the playing field, not to make all atheists look like scoundrels.

Everyone needs meaning in life. That is why every society has religious manifestations. Seeking meaning (through basic questions about life) is not a sign of weakness. It is not a matter of *if* we seek meaning, only a matter of *how*. Someone once said it does not matter what we believe, as long as we believe in something. But faith is only as good as the object in which it is placed.

Take, for example, the story of two men hiking in the Colorado mountains in January. When dusk came upon them quickly, their only hope for getting back to the lodge before dark was to cut across the lake. One of the men was afraid the ice would not support him and hesitated. His friend reminded him that it was the middle of January, the ice had to be several feet thick, and they had no reason to worry. The frightened man had little faith, and so he inched his way back to the lodge. The ice supported him; his faith was small but its object was strong. Later that year, the two men were again hiking and dusk came upon them suddenly. The once fearful man now suggested they cut across the lake. The first man, however, told his now brave friend that it was late May, and the ice was no thicker than a quarter of an inch. But he could not be dissuaded, for his faith was great. So he ventured a few feet from shore and crashed through the ice. His faith was much stronger the second time, but the object of his faith far less sound. Faith is only as good as the object in which it is placed.

Second Option: Christianity Is Objective

While probing for an objective reality, we must decide how much and what kind of evidence and arguments we can use. Because it is not possible to establish historical claims using scientific proofs, we turn instead to a legal and historical approach. See the corresponding section in Question 1 for further explanation.

In our quest to establish an objective basis for Christianity, we must examine the person and work of Christ. The most critical historical event in the connection between Jesus and his works is the Resurrection. The Resurrection is the jugular vein of Christianity—if it is true, so is Christianity. If Jesus did not rise from the dead, then Christianity is a farce, and our faith is in vain (1 Corinthians 15:12-19).

In Question 2, we examined in some detail the evidence and established beyond a reasonable doubt the resurrection of Jesus Christ. The object of faith in Christianity is sound, and, therefore, faith in this object is well-placed. Since Christians do not base their belief on subjective feelings and have an objective reality in which they trust, Christianity has an objective foundation and is not merely a psychological crutch.

"But I don't feel a need for God or religion." The declaration made by Christ in John 14:6, "I am the way, and the truth, and the life; no one comes to the Father but through Me," exposed the need of every man, woman, and child. If Christianity is true, we all have a real need for Christ, even though we may not feel it. Children have a real need for nutritional, well-balanced meals, but they may not feel it. A person may have a severe disease and be in need of medical attention, even though he doesn't feel a need for it.

A "crutch" assumes a problem or need and the supply of aid or assistance. People have a need and a problem—sin, which resulted in death and separation from God (Romans 3:23; 6:23). Christ doesn't offer a *crutch*; he gives us a *cure*. He substituted his life for ours so that we would not have to pay the penalty (Mark 10:45). This substitution was a full payment, a

If the Resurrection of Jesus is true, so is Christianity.

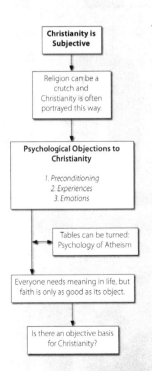

Christianity is Subjective

Religion can be a crutch and Christianity is often portrayed this way.

Psychological Objections to Christianity

1. Preconditioning
2. Experiences
3. Emotions

Tables can be turned: Psychology of Atheism

Everyone needs meaning in life, but faith is only as good as its object.

Is there an objective basis for Christianity?

Christianity is not rejected because it has been examined and found wanting for objective truth; it is often rejected because it hasn't been examined at all.

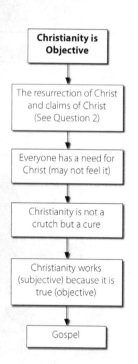

complete restoration. A person on a crutch is hindered and hobbles along with an artificial aid. Christians are not given a crutch for minimal assistance, but they are given a complete cure which provides maximum abundance.

Christians should not claim that Christianity is true simply because they experienced it; rather, they should say that Christianity is true and their experience confirms it. Experience plays a supportive role in substantiating the validity of Christianity. Imagine rising before dawn for a week. You stand on your back porch with a compass in hand and wait for the sun. Each morning as it rises, you position your compass and see that the sun rises in the east. Your getting up each morning with a compass didn't cause the sun to come up in the east. The truth is that the sun rises in the east each morning, and your experience with the compass only verified that truth.

We laid out a detailed analysis of the proofs for the Resurrection and concluded that Christianity was based on a solid foundation of *objectivity* rather than a shifting foundation of subjectivity. Christianity is not rejected because it has been examined and found wanting for objective truth; it is often rejected because it hasn't been examined at all.

If you are talking to an unbeliever, this is an appropriate time to focus on an explanation of the Gospel. Christ is the answer to man's problems, and we have objective verification as to his worthiness. See Question 11 for a presentation of the Gospel and of what it means to believe.

C. S. Lewis and others have turned this argument completely around. Rather than dismissing our desire for the eternal world as a form of escapism or wishful thinking, he argues that our unfulfilled desires, hopes, and longings may be evidence for another world. He notes that every other desire in nature corresponds to a real object that can satisfy that desire:

> Creatures are not born with desires unless satisfaction for those desires exists. A baby feels hunger: well, there is such a thing as food. A duckling wants to swim: well, there is such a thing as water. Men feel sexual desire: well, there is such a thing as sex. If I find in myself a desire which no experience in this world can satisfy, the most probable explanation is that I was made for another world. If none of my earthly pleasures satisfy it, that does not prove that the universe is a fraud. Probably earthly pleasures were never meant to satisfy it, but only to arouse it, to suggest the real thing. (Lewis, Mere Christianity, 1952)

Summary

Although some Christians have been influenced by preconditioning, this does not contradict the reality of Christianity. The real issue is whether there is an objective reality behind it. We also argued that a belief or experience by itself is not ample reason to accept a position as objectively true. The critic of religion states that God has been created out of some emotional need, but the atheist has as much to gain in meeting his own needs if God can be eliminated.

The crux of Christianity's objective reality is Christ and the Resurrection. When we examine the evidence, we must conclude that the Christian faith rests not on subjective mental or emotional experiences, but offers ample objective support for belief.

Supplemental Reading

Williams, Clifford. *Existential Reasons for Belief in God: A Defense of Desires & Emotions for Faith.* IVP Academic, 2011.

Nicholi, Armand M., Jr. *The Question of God: C. S.. Lewis & Sigmund Freud Debate God, Love, Sex, and the Meaning of Life.* The Free Press/Simon & Schuster, 2002.

Vitz, Paul. *Faith of the Fatherless: The Psychology of Atheism.* Spence Publishing Company, 2000. This book is sadly out of print, but it's worth trying to find at your local library.

Puckett, Joe, Jr. *The Apologetics of Joy: A Case for the Existence of God from C. S. Lewis's Argument from Desire.* Wipf & Stock, 2012 (I-A).

Study Guide for Isn't Christianity Just a Psychological Crutch?

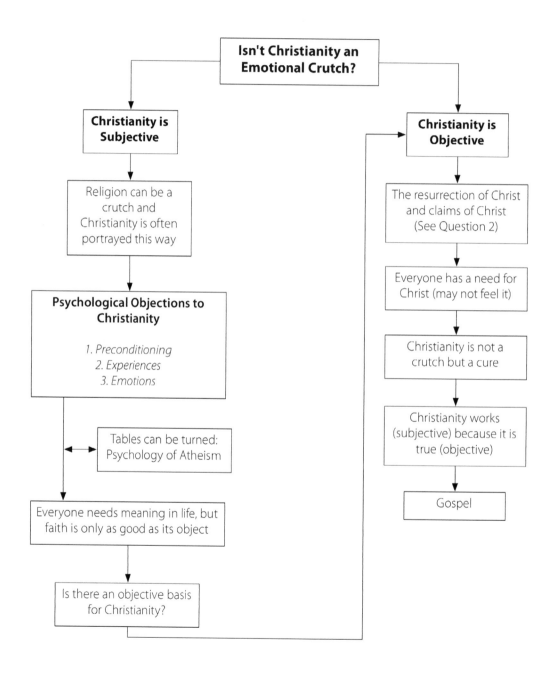

Key Illustrations

Santa & Fire: In Response to "Preconditioning & Truth"

Many of us were brought up to believe in Santa Claus. As we grew up, we realized that Santa was just a nice story to encourage us to be good little boys and girls. Things that we were taught as children are not necessarily true. But most of us were also taught that fire is very hot and would burn us if touched. Things that we were taught as children are not necessarily false, either. Don't allow a person to fall into the trap of rejecting Christianity just because he was preconditioned to believe it as a child. Preconditioning does not validate or invalidate a position.

Penicillin vs. Morphine: In Response to "Belief & Emotion & Truth"

Take the case of a patient with a deadly bacterial infection. When this patient gets a dose of morphine, the symptoms of her disease are erased because of the numbing effects of the drug. The patient believes she is cured, and she feels much better. But believing she is cured and being cured are two different things. Now, suppose the patient receives penicillin instead of morphine. She still has her pain and thus believes that the medicine is having no effect, but she is actually being cured. Her lack of belief does not alter the reality of her cure. We must remember that one's belief is only as valid as the object in which it is placed.

Blind Man & Sunset: In Response to "Experience & Truth"

A man born blind has never experienced a beautiful sunset, but he should not conclude from this that sunsets do not exist.

Hikers & The Ice Lake: To illustrate faith is only as valid as the object in which it is placed.

Take, for example, the story of two men hiking in the Colorado mountains in January. When dusk came upon them quickly, their only hope for getting back to the lodge before dark was to cut across the lake. One of the men was afraid the ice would not support him and hesitated. His friend reminded him that it was the middle of January, the ice had to be at several feet thick, and they had no reason to worry. The frightened man had little faith, and so he inched his way back to the lodge. The ice supported him; his faith was small, but its object was strong.

Later that year, the two men were again hiking and dusk came upon them suddenly. The once fearful man now su,ggested they cut across the lake. The first man, however, told his now brave friend that it was late May and the ice was no thicker than a quarter of an inch. But he could not be dissuaded, for his faith was great. So he ventured a few feet from shore and crashed through the ice. His faith was much stronger the second time, but the object of his faith far less sound. Faith is only as good as the object in which it is placed.

Key Verses

Unique Claims of Christ

- Claimed to be sinless (John 8:46)
- Claimed to fulfill Old Testament messianic prophesies
- Claimed that he would rise from the dead and raise all men
- Claimed to be the exclusive way to salvation (John 3:18, 5:24, 5:40, 8:24, 14:6)
- Indirectly claimed to be God:
    - Claimed to have power to forgive sins (Mark 2:1-12)
    - Claimed eternality (John 17:5)
    - Claimed that he would come again and judge the world (John 5:22, 23, 27)
- Directly claimed equality with God (John 8:58)

Credentials of Christ

- His sinless life (even his enemies had to acknowledge this)
- His power over nature
    - Walking on water (Mark 6:45-52);
    - Calming the storm (Mark 4:35-41);
    - Multiplication of loaves and fishes (Matthew 14:13-21, 15:34-39)
- His power over disease (Matthew 4:23-24)
- His power over demons (Matthew 8:16)
- His power over death (John 11:1-44)
- His unique character and teaching (Matthew 7:28 – "as one with authority")
- His fulfillment of messianic prophecies
- His resurrection from the dead

Christianity is not rejected because it has been examined and found wanting for objective truth; it is often rejected because it hasn't been examined at all.

Study Questions

1. Define what is meant by the terms "psychological" and "crutch" in this chapter.

2. List the three psychological objections to Christianity and give a brief response to each.

3. Give a few examples of psychological reasons for atheism.

4. "Faith is only as good (valid) as the object in which it is placed." Do you agree or disagree? Please explain and give an illustration.

5. Assuming you have now convinced your friend of the objective basis for Christianity, how would you respond to the issue,"But I don't feel any need for Christ"?

Notes

QUESTION 4: IS THE BIBLE RELIABLE?

Often Asked Questions:

- The Bible has been copied and translated so many times—hasn't this process led to errors?

- How can you be sure that the Bible is the same now as when it was written?

- Is there any proof from archaeology that the stories in the Bible happened?

- Is it true that most of the books of the Bible were not written by the people whose names are put on them as authors?

- Isn't the Bible full of contradictions and errors?

- Doesn't the Bible make a number of claims that are scientifically inaccurate?

- Didn't the church arbitrarily decide which books should be included in the Bible and which books should be rejected?

- How can you place your faith in a book that condones genocide and slavery?

- So many people have different interpretations of the Bible—what makes you think that yours is correct?

Is the Bible reliable? The Bible has 66 books and 1,189 chapters in it. Obviously we will not try to mention, let alone defend, the truth of every statement, or even every part, of the Bible in this single chapter. Instead, we will discuss some of the most common objections you will hear to the reliability of the Bible.

In one sense, the question of whether the Bible is reliable has only two possible answers: yes or no. However, the matter is a little more complicated. In this chapter, we will consider three ways in which people often question the reliability of the Bible. First, people question the *textual reliability* of the Bible—what we will call its *authenticity*. The issue here is whether the words of the Bible we are reading reliably express what was originally written in those books. Second, people question the *factual reliability* of the Bible—what we will call its *accuracy*. The issue here is whether the Bible's descriptions of the world and past events reliably match up with the facts. Third, people question the *doctrinal reliability* of the Bible—what we will call its *authority*. The issue here is whether the Bible's teachings about God, Christ, human beings, salvation, and ethical matters reliably represent God's truth. We will consider each of these issues in turn.

FIRST OBJECTION: THE BIBLE IS NOT AUTHENTIC

When we read the books of the Bible, are we reading what those books originally said? To answer this question intelligently, we must know something about the process by which we have the Bible today. That process began with individual books written by hand thousands of years ago. Men wrote the Old Testament books around roughly 1400 to 400 BCE in Hebrew with Aramaic used for portions of Ezra and Daniel. Jesus lived on earth between about 5 BCE and 33 CE, and his followers wrote the New Testament books between about 50 and 100 CE in Greek (with about a dozen words and one short sentence in Aramaic, mostly in sayings of Jesus). Christians who knew how to read and write then copied those books by hand as new copies were needed. Because the materials used in ancient documents were perishable, no original manuscript for any of the books of the Bible has survived.

Beginning in the third century BCE, books of the Old Testament were translated into Greek and, in later centuries, into other languages as well (notably Aramaic and Latin). Likewise, by the second century CE, Christians were translating the books of the New Testament into Latin, Coptic, and Syriac and, as Christianity spread outward, into many other languages as well. By the fourth century, people were producing handmade books called *codices* (singular *codex*) that contained most or all of the books of the Bible. Handwritten copies in the original languages and translation, of both individual books and the Bible as a whole, circulated throughout the

Discern the issue: Each of the sub-categories requires different information and approaches to effectively answer. There is an overwhelming amount of information in this chapter. Breaking it down into these categories is essential for learning how to answer this question.

Authenticity: Is what we have now a fair representation of what was first written?

Accuracy: Is what we have now a fair representation of what actually happened?

Authority: Is what we have now a fair representation of what God wanted to communicate to us?

Accumulation: How do we know the right books were chosen to be in the Bible?

Is what we have now a fair representation of what was first written?

known world for the first fifteen centuries after Christ. When Gutenberg introduced the printing press to Europe in 1450, copies of the Bible were printed in large quantities and made the Bible far more widely available in both the original and many translation languages.

From the dawn of time until the invention of the printing press, all books were written and copied by hand, including the Bible. Because the original documents no longer exist, we are dependent on copies—and, in fact, on copies of copies—of those writings, usually dating centuries after the originals. These copies differ as to the precise wording of the text. That is, when one compares multiple copies of the same document, one finds differences in the way the same sentences are worded. In a few instances, there are even differences as to whether a particular sentence or passage belongs in the text. The combination of these two facts—the loss of the originals and the differences between existing copies—has led many people to be very skeptical about the reliability of the biblical texts. They ask how we can even know what the books originally said in light of these facts about the copies that have come down to us.

To address this objection, we must evaluate the "manuscript evidence" for the Bible the same way we evaluate every other ancient document, by looking at the number of manuscript copies that still exist, the quality and consistency of those copies, and the timespan between the original writing and the oldest remaining copies. We will discuss the Old Testament first and then the New Testament.

The Old Testament Text

As mentioned above, the books of the Old Testament were written primarily in Hebrew between about 1400 and 400 BCE. The "Hebrew Bible" as it came down to us in modern times had an essentially unchanging form that went back well over a thousand years ago. Groups of Jewish scribes called the Masoretes worked between the seventh and eleventh centuries CE carefully preparing complete editions of the Hebrew Bible. These editions contained various kinds of notations to ensure consistent, standardized copying, pronunciation, and oral liturgical use of the texts. During this medieval period, the actual wording of the texts was rarely in question. Jewish scribes going back at least to the time of Christ had taken painstaking measures to ensure that each manuscript was copied with as close to perfection as possible. The Jews called the scribes responsible for this work *sopherim*, or "counters." The word meant that the scribes actually counted every letter of their manuscripts to make sure they had made absolutely no mistakes. Since people can also make mistakes when they are counting, some mistakes still got through, but very few. For this reason, we

The authenticity of today's Bible is determined by evaluating the manuscript evidence.

Quantity: How many ancient manuscripts do we have?

Quality: How careful were the scribes and copyists when they made their copies?

Timespan: How long is the gap between the original writing and oldest remaining copies?

can be sure that the wording of the copies of the Hebrew Bible that survive today goes back centuries earlier. The extraordinary care of the work that the copyists did is obvious from the consistency in the numerous copies they produced. More than six thousand Masoretic manuscripts are extant today, including over 2,700 that have dates written on them. The most important of these medieval Hebrew Bibles are the Cairo Codex (895 CE), the Aleppo Codex (930 CE), and the Leningrad Codex (1008 CE). There are mostly minor verbal differences among these codices, but they are so rare as to be of interest only to textual critics.

Whatever doubts might have lingered about the reliability of the Hebrew Bible that has come down to us were alleviated by discoveries of manuscripts in the Judean Desert. The most famous of these discoveries was the finding of the Dead Sea Scrolls in caves near a place called Qumran, in 1947. The Qumran biblical manuscripts were produced between about 250 BCE and 68 CE, when the community at Qumran fled due to the war between the Jews and the Romans. This means that our earliest manuscripts of the Hebrew Bible were made less than two centuries after the end of the Old Testament era. That closes the gap considerably from when the earliest manuscripts were dated thirteen centuries after the close of the Old Testament era. Yet, as we shall explain, the biblical texts of the Dead Sea Scrolls are not substantially different in wording from the Masoretic Text.

The Significance of Qumran. The religious community at Qumran was a Jewish sect that rejected the Jerusalem religious leadership and was expecting divine judgment. Their biblical manuscripts are from about 210 scrolls, most in fragments. The manuscripts discovered there include parts of every book of the Old Testament except for Esther. The lack of any surviving copy of Esther, a short and less-often cited book in any context, need not imply any disapproval. For example, only one fragment of Chronicles happened to be found at Qumran, and there is even some question as to whether that fragment is from a copy of Chronicles. For most of the Old Testament writings, there are fragments from multiple scrolls of the same book: some two dozen for Genesis, over thirty for Deuteronomy, three dozen for the Psalms, and twenty-one for Isaiah.

The Great Isaiah Scroll is the oldest complete copy of any Old Testament book discovered to date, which is all the more remarkable considering the length of the book. It was probably produced in the late second century BCE, more than a thousand years earlier than the Cairo Codex, the earliest dated Masoretic codex of the Hebrew Bible. There are differences between the Great Isaiah Scroll and the Masoretic Text, but they are minor.

Another scroll containing Isaiah has not survived whole but still contains parts of 46 of the 66 chapters of Isaiah. It is sometimes called the "small"

OT Manuscript Quality: Unparalleled in ancient literature: A+

OT Manuscript Quantity: Better than anything other than the NT: A

OT Manuscript Timespan: Average–with Dead Sea and other Judean desert scrolls, the timespan between writing and earliest copies is now equal or better than most works of antiquity: B or C

Isaiah Scroll. Produced in the first century BCE, scholars have carefully compared this scroll and the Masoretic Text. For example, scholars have cataloged 234 places where the small Isaiah Scroll differs from the Leningrad Codex. However, 107 of these are spelling differences, and most of the remaining differences are extremely minor. For instance, one may use the Hebrew equivalent of the definite article ("the") while the other omits it, or use a noun that is singular instead of plural or vice versa. Only 22 of the differences are at the level of words. The small Isaiah Scroll has a different word in eleven places, lacks a word in five places, and adds a word in six places compared to the Leningrad Codex. That works out to an average of less than one word difference for every two chapters of the book!

Other biblical manuscripts among the Dead Sea Scrolls show even closer agreement with the Masoretic Text. A fragment from a scroll of Genesis, containing Genesis 1:1-4:11, is verbally *identical* to the Leningrad Codex.

As of 2009, archaeologists had found additional manuscripts from about 25 biblical scrolls in the Judean Desert at sites other than Qumran. All of these texts are verbally almost identical to the Leningrad Codex and other Masoretic codices. Some were found at Masada, where Jewish rebels made their last tragic stand in the war with Rome in 66-73 CE. These Masada manuscripts date from between 50 BCE and 30 CE. The others were found at several other sites linked to the Bar Kochba revolt of 132-135 CE and were written between 20 and 115 CE. Thus, all of these manuscripts belonged to people who supported the Jerusalem religious establishment, unlike the sectarian separatists at Qumran. Perhaps not surprisingly, in general the Qumran manuscripts tend to differ from the Masoretic Text somewhat more than the non-Qumran manuscripts. Yet for both Qumran and non-Qumran manuscripts, the differences with the Masoretic Text are amazingly minimal.

The point here is not that there are no textual questions with regard to the Old Testament. There are passages where scholars find significantly different wording in different manuscripts, especially when comparing Hebrew manuscripts with ancient Greek translations of the Old Testament. In some places the scrolls from the Judean Desert have matched the Greek versions rather than the Masoretic Text, which can make for some interesting debates. But the places in the Old Testament where such debates are over theologically significant differences are rare, and no such textual differences legitimately threaten to overturn the dominant teachings of the Bible. We may now be reasonably confident that the text of the Old Testament we have is the same one used by Jews in Jesus's day and even for some centuries earlier.

The New Testament Text

In the case of the Old Testament, until the twentieth century its Hebrew manuscript tradition was extremely uniform but dated 1,300 years or more after the last books of the Old Testament were written. The discoveries of the twentieth century showed that the Hebrew text went through remarkably little change during that long gap. The situation is a little different with the New Testament. It too enjoyed a highly uniform textual tradition but one that, until modern times, could not be traced much earlier than about eight hundred years after the New Testament era. However, manuscript discoveries in the eighteenth and nineteenth centuries revealed that copies of the New Testament writings that were made before about the eighth century had numerous textual differences. Scholars now estimate that there are 300,000 or more of these differences! Critics of the Bible have often cited this multitude of textual differences, or variants, in the New Testament writings as a reason to question the reliability of the Bible.

To address this question it will be helpful to know that scholars divide Greek New Testament manuscripts into four categories. (1) *Papyri* were manuscripts written on papyrus, a writing surface similar to paper but made from reeds. Many of the New Testament papyri are among the earliest manuscripts; they also are the fewest in number. (2) *Uncials* were manuscripts mostly written on parchment and that use the older block-letter script—what we would call "capitals." (The papyri use the same script.) Because they used all "large" letters, these manuscripts are also called majuscules. (3) *Minuscules* were written on parchment or paper in a cursive script with lower-case letters. (4) *Lectionaries* are manuscripts containing set readings from the Bible for use in Christian worship services throughout the year.

In addition to nearly six thousand Greek manuscripts, biblical scholars have an embarrassing wealth of other sources that strengthen and confirm our knowledge of the original wording of the New Testament writings. The New Testament books were translated into many other languages, and we have numerous manuscripts of these other-language texts (called versions). Such versions were produced in Coptic, Syriac, and Latin in the second century, and other languages followed in every century thereafter. There are roughly ten thousand New Testament manuscripts in Latin alone (so many they have never been thoroughly counted!) and thousands more in Coptic, Syriac, and other languages. Another source is the quotations from the New Testament found in the writings of the church fathers—Christian writers from the first through about the sixth centuries. There are so many of these quotations that one can find virtually every verse of the New Testament several times over in the writings of the church fathers. If we had nothing

You can find lists of the papyri, uncials, minuscules and lectionaries in many places, including various textbook editions of the Greek New Testament. The University of Münster in Germany maintains a continuously updated online database of all such manuscripts. The database will tell you where a particular manuscript is kept, when it was written, the kind of writing material used, the size of the document, how many pages it is, and what verses of the New Testament it has. As of 2012 this database cataloged 5,784 Greek New Testament manuscripts—some fragments, some whole books like Mark or Romans, and some complete or near-complete codices of the New Testament. Of these manuscripts, 127 are papyri from the second through the eighth centuries. All of the papyri, though fragmentary, are important to scholars studying the New Testament text. Most of the 322 uncials, especially those that date before the eighth century, are also important for determining the earliest New Testament text. The earliest and most complete uncials are the codices known as Sinaiticus and Vaticanus (fourth century) and Alexandrinus (fifth century), which also include the Old Testament translated into Greek. Comparisons with the papyri from the second and early third centuries show that these great codices reflect a very early form of the New Testament text. The minuscule and lectionaries tend to be of lesser importance, but occasionally they figure in academic studies of a particular text where the other manuscripts may not tell the whole story.

NT Manuscript Quantity:
Unparalleled in ancient literature:
A+

The P52 Scrap

NT Manuscript Timespan:
Excellent. Unparalleled in ancient literature: A

else, we might be able to reconstruct nearly the whole New Testament from those writings alone!

When the King James Version of the Bible was published in 1611, its New Testament was based on a published Greek text that used no more than about six manuscripts, the earliest from the twelfth century. Some earlier manuscripts were known but did not play a significant role in the study of the text at that time. This meant that the gap between the original New Testament books and the earliest copies used was more than a thousand years. The number of manuscripts found and studied grew throughout the next two centuries, but the most dramatic manuscript discoveries came in the nineteenth century. These discoveries included early codices of the New Testament from the fourth century. They also include fragments of papyri from the second and third centuries found in the trash at a site near the Nile River called Oxyrhynchus. The gap between the original compositions and the earliest manuscripts studied by scholars had narrowed to three centuries at most and to one or two centuries for some parts of the New Testament. During the twentieth century the gap has narrowed further for much of the New Testament. An especially famous example is the University of Manchester's John Rylands Library papyrus known as P52, a fragment of the Gospel of John (containing John 18:31-33, 37-38) studied in the 1930s. This fragment is generally dated about 125 CE, within thirty years or so of the traditional date when the Gospel was written. Now about half of the verses in the New Testament are found in manuscripts that were made less than two centuries after the books were originally written.

A gap of a century or two may seem like a lot, but let's put it into perspective. The most popular and frequently copied writings of the ancient Greco-Roman world outside the New Testament were the writings of Homer, especially the *Iliad*. Scholars think the *Iliad* was written in the eighth century BCE, but the earliest manuscripts we have for it are papyri fragments from the third century BCE. The earliest near-complete manuscripts of the *Iliad* were produced in the tenth century CE, some 1,700 years after it was written! And again, the *Iliad* was copied far more than most other books and the existing manuscript evidence for it is better than for most. The typical classical works of literature from the ancient world have come down to us with only a handful of copies each, often only one or two. They typically date a millennium or more after the work was originally written. If we're going to doubt the authenticity of the New Testament, to be consistent we're going to have to throw out the writings of Homer, Plato, Aristotle, Cicero, Josephus, and every other ancient author.

Author	Date Written	Oldest Remaining Fragments	Timespan (In Years)	# of Existing Manuscripts
Homer	900 BCE	400 BCE	500	~2000
Plato	380 BCE	900 CE	1300	7
Aristotle	350 BCE	1100 CE	1400	49
Caesar	60 BCE	900 CE	950	10
Tacitus	100 CE	1100 CE	1000	20
NT	40-100 CE	125 CE	25-50 (John) 50-150 for the majority of NT.	6000+ Greek 24k including translations

Scholars now have a thousand times more manuscripts they can study than were used by the translators of the King James Version. The time gap has narrowed from more than a thousand years to around one to three centuries. As the number of manuscripts of the New Testament has increased and the time gap between the earliest manuscripts and the original compositions has decreased, scholars' knowledge of the Greek text of the New Testament books has been *refined* but not radically revised. With all of the new manuscript discoveries, scholars have identified only about 41 verses, out of 7,957, in the King James Version of the New Testament that were probably not part of the original text. That computes to one-half of one percent of the total verses in the New Testament that need to be weeded out. Of these 41 verses, 24 are in just two passages: the long ending of Mark (16:9-20) and the popular story of the woman caught in the act of adultery (John 7:53-8:11). Another ten are verses in Matthew, Mark, or Luke that the copyists added to those Gospels because the verses were found in a parallel or similar passage somewhere else in the Gospels. In other words, those ten verses were already in the Gospels, just not in those specific places.

Perhaps more surprising is the fact that as scholars have found and studied more and earlier manuscripts, they have found *not even one sentence* that belongs in the New Testament but was missing from the King James Version. The often heard claim that significant material was likely lost from the Bible in the process of copying turns out to be contrary to all the evidence. We can now say confidently that the current text of the Bible has *no* significant omissions. Future manuscript discoveries are not likely to reveal whole sentences or verses that have been missing for centuries from the New Testament. If the traditional versions were radically different from the earliest form of the New Testament, the wealth of earlier manuscripts should have uncovered *something* missing by now. So there is very little chance that anything substantial was lost from the New Testament, or anything added beyond the 41 or so verses that have long been recognized as suspect.

NT Manuscript Quality:

Better than anything other than the OT: A-

Telephone Game

Everyone remembers the telephone game from childhood. One boy whispers a phrase to the girl sitting next to him, and the message is whispered around the circle. The last person says aloud what he thinks the message is, often with hilarious results. Through many transmissions, the message has become grossly distorted. The process of copying the Bible has been compared to this game. But in order to make the comparison fair, we would have to make this adjustment. The first person would say the message out loud to the person sitting next to him and the message would be repeated out loud around the entire circle. If someone deliberately changed the message or got it wrong by accident, anyone who caught the mistake would be able to correct them. The Bible was not copied in secret or through hushed voices, but was conducted openly.

Manuscript Evidence Report Card

	OT	NT
Quantity	A-	A+
Quality	A+	A-
Timespan	B	A

What about those 300,000 or more textual variants in the New Testament? It turns out that the vast majority of these variants are spelling changes. The Jewish scribes responsible for copying the Hebrew Bible were trained and exacting in their work. By contrast, the Gentile Christian scribes who copied the New Testament during the first several centuries of Christianity had no such training or skill. As a result, they made predictable mistakes, mostly spelling errors. They made other kinds of mistakes as well, such as accidentally copying the same word or group of words twice, skipping one or two lines because a later line ends with the same word or letters, or writing a different word that sounds like the word they were copying. (Scribes copying the Hebrew Bible made these same kinds of mistakes, but far less frequently than early copyists of the New Testament.) Most of the time, these kinds of mistakes are easy to spot because the sentence is nonsense or otherwise obviously wrong. If you read a sentence in a copy that says, "And then Peter walked walked on the water," there isn't much question that the repetition of *walked* was a simple copying mistake! Also, although some of the copies will have such mistakes, other copies will not. This means that the scholars' task is to sort through the available options for each text and pick the wording that is most likely to be the earliest reading. The right wording is always there somewhere in the mass of thousands of manuscript copies, and 99 percent of the time there is no difficulty identifying that correct wording.

Admittedly, copyists made deliberate or intentional changes to their copies as well, but most of the changes are of minor importance and again scholars can usually tell. Many such deliberate changes are attempts to correct the spelling or grammar of the text, changes that generally don't affect the meaning at all. Copyists sometimes reworded a text in one of the Gospels to match the way a parallel passage was worded in another Gospel. That's something to notice if we're trying to know each Gospel's exact wording but typically not something of much historical or theological significance. In the book of Acts and in the epistles, copyists often added titles to the name "Jesus" for the sake of piety, writing "Lord Jesus" or "Lord Jesus Christ" instead of just "Jesus." However, not once did they change "Jesus" to "Fred!"

Once we have eliminated all of the obvious mistakes, easily identified deliberate changes, and inconsequential verbal differences, we are left with a very small fraction of those 300,000 or more variants. The number of variants that affect the meaning of the text in a significant way—and it is not obvious which variant is correct—is in the hundreds, or perhaps around a thousand. That's much less than one percent of the variants. Even the most interesting of these significant variants do not call for a radical change in the way we think about God or other major topics of the Bible. A well-known example of such a significant variant is found in a verse about Jesus being asked for healing by a leper (Mark 1:41). Most manuscripts—and most English translations—say that Jesus felt "compassion," but some of the earliest manuscripts say that Jesus felt "anger." This variant definitely makes a difference in the way we understand this particular incident in the ministry of Jesus, but it does not significantly change the way we think about Jesus. After all, in other places in the Gospel of Mark where there are no such variants we are told both that Jesus got angry (Mark 3:5) and that he felt compassion for people (Mark 6:34; 8:2; 9:22).

Notice that it is not necessary to have absolute certainty about the exact wording of every verse of the New Testament in order to understand its teachings. The best scholar's knowledge of the Greek text will always be a little below 100 percent certainty. However, the information available now is sufficient to conclude that we have a New Testament text that is better than 99 percent reliable. In fact, it turns out that even the text used in the King James Version was extremely reliable. What little uncertainty remains does not substantially affect our understanding of what Jesus did and taught.

When you're sharing the Gospel in conversation, keep in mind that your goal should not be to try to explain away all of the textual difficulties or to prove that we can know for sure the exact wording of every verse. Those goals are not realistic even for biblical scholars. Your goal should be to say just enough—if they have doubts or questions about the authenticity of the Bible—to show them that the text of the Bible is a fair representation of what the original authors had to say about Jesus Christ.

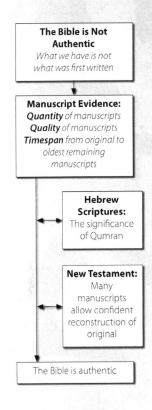

SECOND OBJECTION: THE BIBLE IS NOT ACCURATE

Be careful not to confuse the issues of what we are calling authenticity and accuracy. Proving that we have the actual words of the Gospel of Luke does not prove that what Luke says actually happened. Being able to show that the text of 2 Samuel has been reliably copied over the centuries does not demonstrate that David, the main figure in that book, was a real person or that he did the things recorded there.

Once we have established that the books of the Bible we have today say substantially the same thing as they did thousands of years ago, we are ready to address the issue of whether the things the Bible reports actually happened. This is the question of the Bible's factual reliability, or *accuracy*.

Is what was first written a fair representation of what actually happened?

The Bible: History or Myth?

Although many people regard the Bible as myths, even a cursory reading of the Bible's narratives should dispel that notion. Myths don't claim to be giving historical facts; they have their own style and characteristics that

Internal clues to historicity:

- Real locations
- Geographical notes
- Chronological information
- Citation of sources, oral and written
- Genealogies
- Unflattering incidents

We can't use Bible verses to prove that the Bible is reliable, that would be begging the question. However, we can show that the authors intended the scriptures to be read as history, not just as imaginative stories that illustrate theological concepts. Because they claim to record accurate details of past events, the scriptures can be evaluated by archaeological evidence. The Bible records hundreds of people, places, events, and traditions that overlap with what we know about history from archeology and other ancient historical witnesses.

clearly separate them from history. The Bible, on the other hand, does not read like myth. Its narratives are firmly planted on the ground, located in real places like Jerusalem, the Sea of Galilee, the agora in Athens, and the island of Malta that can be visited firsthand or studied in numerous Bible atlases. The Bible includes geographical notes of various kinds that reflect its real-world concern (e.g., Genesis 13:10; Deuteronomy 1:1-2; Luke 24:13; Acts 17:1). It also contains chronological information that situates its accounts in real times (e.g., 2 Kings 25:1-3; Luke 3:1-2; Galatians 1:18; 2:1). Its books cite earlier written documents as sources to explain where some of their information originated (e.g., 2 Kings 10:34; 24:5; Luke 1:1-2). A fairly prominent feature of its historical narratives is the use of genealogies, including nine chapters of them in 1 Chronicles 1-9 (see also, e.g., Genesis 5; Matthew 1:1-17; Luke 3:23-38). The narratives report incidents that are quite unflattering to the Bible's most respected figures, such as Abraham (Gen. 12:10-20), Moses (Exodus 4:10-13), Peter (Luke 22:54-62), and Paul and Barnabas (Acts 15:37-40). All of these sorts of features mark the biblical narratives as historical in purpose and intent. One might try to argue that the Bible fails in its purpose of reporting fact or that the biblical authors were lying, but it really makes no sense at all to claim that the Bible is a collection of "beautiful myths" that should not be "taken literally" as historical fact.

Given that the Bible claims to present historical facts, is there any evidence from outside the Bible to support its claim? Here again, it is important not to claim too much. It is not realistic to claim that we can prove that every event reported in the Bible is fact. It is also not necessary to do so in order to make a sound case for believing the Gospel of Jesus Christ. We cannot prove that Isaac's wife was named Rebekah (Gen. 24) or that Jesus amazed the adults in the temple when he was twelve (Luke 2:46-47). We don't need to prove such things to show that the Gospel is true. What is important is to be able to respond to questions about the general reliability of the Bible in matters of historical fact. If the Bible were little more than a collection of myths, fables, and legends, then it would not make sense to claim that people should accept the death and resurrection of Jesus Christ as the way that God chose to save people from their sins. On the other hand, if people see that the Bible contains a great deal of historical fact, they will be in a position at the very least to take its message about Jesus seriously.

In examining the evidence for the historical reliability of the Bible, an important point to keep in mind has to do with the great span of time that the Bible covers. Its narratives begin literally with the creation of the universe and move forward through time to the first century CE. Even if we pass over the first several chapters of Genesis, which talk about creation and the earliest history of mankind, the detailed history of the Bible covers a period of over two thousand years. By the very nature of history, the more recent an event happened, the more plentiful the evidence for it. This means that if the Bible is historically reliable we should expect to find more evidence for the period of the Israelite kings than for Abraham, Isaac, and Jacob, and even more evidence for the period of Jesus and the apostles than for anything in the Old Testament. With that in mind, we will begin by taking a look at some of the evidence for the historical reliability of the Old Testament.

The Old Testament as history

The patriarchal era (Gen. 11:27-50:26, ca. 2200-1700 BCE). The earliest sorts of evidence from outside the Bible that might support its historical reliability show up gradually with the development of writing. Practically speaking then, the place to begin looking for potential outside sources to illuminate the Bible is in the narratives in Genesis about the patriarchs—Abraham and his descendants. The usual critical view is that Genesis was a fictional narrative about Israel's origins compiled in the fifth or sixth century BCE from sources originating perhaps in the ninth or eighth centuries. This would mean that even the written sources used in Genesis originated about a thousand years after the patriarchs. Yet there is good evidence that Genesis reflects knowledge about the patriarchs and their culture that writers a thousand years later would be unlikely to know.

Surprisingly, archaeologists appear to have found an ancient reference outside the Bible to Abraham himself. On a wall of the Egyptian temple at Karnak is a list of towns in the Negev, the southern region in the land of Israel. The list, which is dated about 925 BCE, does not include perhaps the most important town in the Negev, Beersheba—at least not by that name. It does, however, refer to one of the towns as "Fort of Abram" (Abraham's original name). Abram, when he went by that name, spent much of his time camped in the Negev and also went into Egypt to escape famine. Years later, he actually founded Beersheba (Gen. 21:31-32). The place name "Fort of Abram" very likely refers to Beersheba by the name of the man whom the Egyptians associated with that place. It isn't proof (since the inscription comes from about nine centuries after Abraham), but it is pretty good evidence that Abraham existed.

We do not have records outside the Bible referring to the other notable figures in Genesis. However, there is some indirect evidence that the names of these individuals in Genesis originate from their time period and not from fictional accounts a thousand years later, as many people think. Several of the names of Abraham's family began with *I-* or *Y-* (often spelled in English with *J-*): Ishmael, Isaac, Jacob, and Joseph. The Mari texts, which date from the eighteenth century, show that such names were very popular during the

In this section we will look at how we establish accuracy during these Biblical ages:

- Patriarchal era
- Exodus and the Conquest
- The Kings of Judah & Israel
- Babylonian Conquest & Exile

patriarchal era. A thousand years later, such names were still used but only rarely.

There are also various kinds of incidental details in the Genesis account that suggest that it is at least based on historical fact. For example, when Joseph's brothers sold him as a slave, they received twenty shekels for him (Gen. 37:28). Yet during the period of the Israelite kings the typical price for a slave was fifty shekels or more, as was the price Menahem paid the Assyrians in the eighth century (2 Kings 15:20).

Although Genesis presents the patriarchs as worshiping the same God as Israel worshiped centuries later, it depicts patriarchal religion very differently from Israelite religion. The patriarchs hear from God directly in visions and dreams, not through prophets like Moses or Elijah. The patriarchs set up altars as they move around from place to place and offer their own sacrifices rather than depending on priests to perform sacrifices for them, as the Israelites did. The way Genesis describes the religion of the patriarchs is appropriate to the early second millennium BCE and does not match Israelite religion in the first millennium BCE.

The exodus and the conquest (Exodus—Joshua, ca. 1600-1300 BCE). We should acknowledge that the question of the historical reliability of the Bible's accounts of the exodus from Egypt under Moses and of the conquest of Canaan under Joshua is very unsettled today. Most historians and archaeologists view the biblical accounts as later legends with little or no anchor in real historical events. Not surprisingly, skeptics are quick to dismiss the dramatic miracles of the ten plagues and the crossing of the Red Sea.

Ironically, the main problem is not a lack of evidence for events matching the biblical narrative. There are ancient accounts from non-Israelite sources that describe events that sound very much like what the Bible reports. There is substantial archaeological evidence for the destruction of Jericho and other cities in Canaan. The main problem is one of *chronology*—of matching these events known from ancient records and archaeological finds with the timing of the events as recorded in the Bible.

Assigning specific dates to events of the distant past depends on literary and inscriptional references that include indicators of the passage of time. The most common such information in very ancient sources is tied to the lengths of various kings' reigns. One can see this easily by reading through 1-2 Kings or 1-2 Chronicles, where the narrative's main dating information pertains to the lengths of the reigns of the kings of Judah and Israel. In order to provide external evidence that decisively connects events reported in the Bible with events recorded by Egyptians or other non-Israelite peoples, the chronological information given in the Bible should be correlated with similar chronological information from outside sources. The most important such information in this context would be tied to the lengths of the reigns of the Pharaohs in Egypt. Unfortunately, correlating biblical chronology with Egyptian chronology has generally been done at the expense of the Bible. Archaeologists tend to privilege the Egyptian dating information over that of the Bible, and then conclude that the major events of the Old Testament never happened.

If we bracket the problem of establishing fixed dates, we can see that there *is* evidence for events matching the Bible's descriptions. For example, consider the document called the Admonitions of Ipuwer, which has been preserved in a papyrus usually dated to the thirteenth century BCE. It describes a series of natural disasters in Egypt that match the Exodus account rather well. Early in its account the Ipuwer papyrus reads, "Blood is everywhere....the River is blood," recalling the first plague of the Nile river turned to blood (Exodus 7:17-25). It goes on to talk about death that came on cattle, whole buildings "consumed by fire," disturbing darkness in the land ("the land is not light"), and death among the Egyptians ("the children of princes are dashed against the walls"), similar to the fifth, seventh, ninth, and tenth plagues (Exodus 9:1-7, 13-35; 10:21-29; 11:1-12:32).

The kings of Judah and Israel (1 Samuel—2 Chronicles; ca. 1100-600 BCE). The Bible contains two extensive, parallel histories of the rise and fall of the Israelite monarchy. The earlier account comes in 1 Samuel through 2 Kings and the later account in 1-2 Chronicles.

Archaeologists have found some evidence pertaining to the period of David and Solomon, the first two Jewish kings to rule from Jerusalem. Inscriptions from the ninth century BCE on the Tel Dan Stele and the Mesha Stele (also known as the Moabite Stone) refer to the southern kingdom as the "House of David," the earliest references outside the Bible to David. A piece of pottery found at Tell es-Safi, known in the Bible as Gath, the home of Goliath, has the names *ALWT* and *WLT* written on it. These are Philistine names related etymologically to the name *Goliath*, suggesting that the name of David's Philistine opponent is not a later legendary creation. Excavations at Hazor, Megiddo, and Gezer have confirmed that these cities were military installations during the time of Solomon (see 1 Kings 9:15-19).

Beginning in the late tenth century BCE, when the northern tribes of Israel had broken away from Judah under their rival kings, archaeology provides the first explicit confirmation of specific events mentioned in the Bible. The wall relief of the Egyptian temple in Karnak mentioned earlier commemorates Pharaoh Sheshonq's defeat of various cities, including some in Israel. The inscription matches well the account in 1 Kings 14:25-26 about "Shishak" (almost certainly the Hebrew name for Sheshonq) invading Israel

I'm Glad You Asked

during the reign of Rehoboam, the first king of Judah after the schism with Israel. The ninth-century BCE Mesha Stele inscription, also mentioned above, announces Mesha's victory over an Israelite king (Jehoram, compare 2 Kings 3:4-27). Another famous ninth-century artifact, the Black Obelisk, records the Assyrian king Shalmaneser forcing the Israelite king "Jehu, son of Omri," to pay tribute to him. (Jehu was not related to Omri; Omri was evidently so powerful a king in Israel that the Assyrians viewed his successors as part of his royal house.) This event is not mentioned in the Bible, but it fits with what the Bible says about the end of Jehu's reign (2 Kings 10:31-33).

One of the key events in biblical history was Assyria's conquest of Israel in 722 BCE (2 Kings 18:9-12). Assyrian royal annals of Sargon II recorded on the Taylor Prism, a clay marker inscribed with Akkadian cuneiform text, refer to the conquest and deportation of Israel and other neighboring nations. These annals also include a detailed account of the Assyrian king Sennacherib's military campaign in Judah in 701 BCE that dovetails in many ways with the biblical account (2 Kings 18:13-19:37; 2 Chronicles 32:1-22). There is also archaeological evidence confirming a notable element of the story found only in the Bible: In response to the threat from Sennacherib, Hezekiah had a tunnel built underground to redirect water into the city and prevent it from supplying the Assyrians (2 Kings 20:20; 2 Chronicles 32:2-4, 30). In 1838 an American scholar named Edward Robinson discovered the tunnel, which runs for a third of a mile. Tourists can still walk through the tunnel from one end to the other. An inscription on the wall describes how the tunnel was built (men started at both ends and dug toward each other using sound to guide them). In this instance we have both an impressive physical structure and a non-Israelite historical record confirming the account given in the Bible.

The Babylonian conquest and exile (2 Kings 24-25; 2 Chronicles 36; Jeremiah; Ezekiel; 609-539 BCE). The climactic events of the Old Testament are the Babylonian conquest of Judah, including the destruction of Solomon's temple, the Jewish exile, and the return of the Jews to their land. We know a great deal from external sources about the world events of which this story is a part, from Nebuchadnezzar's victories over the Assyrians and the Jews (recorded in the Babylonian Chronicles) to Cyrus's conquest of the Babylonians (recorded on the Cyrus Cylinder). The Lachish letters, written on pieces of pottery by a Jewish military officer, describe the last days of the Babylonians' siege of Jerusalem. One of the Babylonian kings mentioned in Daniel, Belshazzar, long thought by skeptics to be unhistorical, is mentioned on the Nabonidus Cylinder discovered in 1881. The basic factual reliability of this part of the biblical history is no longer in serious question.

When will the last witnesses to the 20th century's most memorable events pass from the scene?

Event / Estimated death of last witness

Cubs win the world series / 2013

WWI veterans / 2005*

'29 stock-market crash / 2035

FDR's first inauguration / 2039

Holocaust survivor / 2052

Brown v. Board of Ed. / 2063

JFK assassination / 2074

Woodstock Festival / 2080

Vietnam Veterans / 2062

From Newsweek, Spring 1996

Sources: Social Security Administration, Dept. of Veteran Affairs, Research of Dante Chinni

* Though 2005 was predicted for the passing of the last WWI veterans, the last combat and non-combat vets lived until 2011 & 2012.

The New Testament as History

Whereas Old Testament history (even excluding most of the first eleven chapters of Genesis) covers a period of roughly two thousand years, New Testament history covers only about 75 years (from the birth of Jesus, ca. 6-5 BCE, to the destruction of the Jerusalem temple, 70 CE). Yet within that period fall the events that define Christianity: the death and resurrection of Jesus Christ. The reliability of the historical material in the New Testament, then, is of extreme importance.

The New Testament books that are primarily historical in content are the four Gospels, which deal with the life, death, and resurrection of Jesus, and the Book of Acts, which deals with the first three decades of the Christian movement. We will focus our attention, then, on these books.

Authorship and date. In discussions about the historical reliability of the New Testament, many people focus on the question of who its authors were. It is therefore interesting to note that none of the Gospels (or Acts) identifies its author by name. The titles "Gospel according to Matthew," etc., were not part of the original books, though they appear to have been added very early and may reflect genuine knowledge about the books' origins. The authors did not make themselves the issue.

Let's concentrate on facts accepted by all or virtually all biblical scholars. The authors of the Gospels and Acts all lived and wrote in the first century, composing their books at the latest within about sixty years or less of the death of Jesus. They were not writing hundreds of years later. Furthermore, they used sources that originated earlier than their own writings, as Luke makes explicit (Luke 1:1-4). This means that much if not all of the information in the Gospels comes from sources within the lifetime of people who knew Jesus personally. Everyone also agrees that the Gospels named for Mark and Luke were *not* written by eyewitnesses; they don't claim to be, and Luke, in the same passage just cited, says that he was not. (Luke does, however, claim to have been an eyewitness of some of the events in the Book of Acts.) The Gospel of Matthew says absolutely nothing about its author, so one may accept or reject the view that the apostle Matthew was the author without in any way contradicting what the Gospel says about itself. The Gospel of John, on the other hand, does claim its author as an eyewitness (John 19:35; 21:24), though many modern critics reject that claim.

What we have just said is sufficient to show that it is reasonable to accept the authors of the Gospels, whoever they may have been, as historically reliable sources of information about Jesus. It is not necessary to defend or prove the traditional views of their authorship. That having been said, there is good evidence supporting at least some of the traditional views. As for their dates, most conservative scholars date Matthew, Mark, and Luke in the

JFK Witnesses

Suppose a man wrote a book today claiming that after he was shot in Dallas, John F. Kennedy came back to life, appeared to groups of people around the country for a couple of weeks and then disappeared. How many copies would he sell? Probably quite a few. But could this new view gather a large following? Probably not. There are simply too many eye witnesses to the events of 1963 still alive today to contradict this fiction. The book might garner a few headlines, but it would only be months before its believers could be found only in the fringes of society. And yet the stories of Christ's death and resurrection were circulated immediately in the very place where he died and the first Gospels were written down within 30-40 years. There was simply not enough time for myths to be created and propagate–too many eyewitnesses remained.

60s (within 30-40 years of Jesus' ministry and death) and John in the 90s. Other scholars typically date Mark around 70 CE, Matthew and Luke in the 80s, and John in the 90s.

Genre. Genres are types of writing, such as letters, love songs, poems, allegories, and the like. Myths and legends are also genres. In the case of the Gospels, scholars are increasingly recognizing that they should be categorized as biographies, fitting rather well into the conventions of biographies in the ancient Greco-Roman culture. Unlike modern biographies, those ancient biographies usually did not give a lot of attention to childhood experiences or attempt to develop psychological insights into the subject. Instead they typically focused on the individual's major accomplishments and (for philosophers, teachers, etc.) their sayings. Such biographies also often gave disproportionate attention to the individual's last days and death. This is just what we find in the Gospels. Ancient biographies in Greco-Roman culture were expected to be historical and factual in content. The Book of Acts just as clearly fits the category of ancient historical writing.

As we have already discussed, the New Testament writings do not fit the genres of myths, legends, or fables. The authors repeatedly distance their work from such categories. The apostle Paul warned against accepting myths instead of the truth (2 Timothy 4:3-4). When he told the Galatians about how he saw the risen Jesus and became an apostle, Paul insists, "Now in what I am writing to you, I assure you before God that I am not lying" (Galatians 1:20). The apostle Peter asserted, "For we did not follow cleverly devised tales when we made known to you the power and coming of our Lord Jesus Christ, but we were eyewitnesses of his majesty" (2 Peter 1:16 NASB). Luke stated that he carefully investigated everything and sought to make known the exact truth based on the word of eyewitnesses (Luke 1:1-4). The apostle John emphatically insisted that what he wrote was his own eyewitness testimony and confirmed by Jesus's other disciples (John 19:35; 20:30; 21:24). The point here is not that these statements prove that everything in the Gospels is true, but that one cannot fairly claim that the Gospels were meant to be read as myth or spiritual fiction.

External evidence. Literary sources and archaeological artifacts provide abundant evidence from outside the Bible confirming the accuracy of the Gospels and of Acts. Nearly all of the cities and villages mentioned in these books, if they were not already known, have been discovered by archaeologists. The political figures who appear in the New Testament are well known from ancient Greek and Roman histories and biographies. These include Herod the Great and his sons Archelaus and Herod Antipas, the Roman governor Pontius Pilate, the Roman emperors Augustus, Tiberius, and Claudius, and the high priests Annas and Caiaphas. Archaeologists have

---

Facts about Jesus from ancient Non- or anti-Christian documents

Jesus was a Jewish teacher, he had a brother named James. *Josephus, c. 37-100 CE, Antiquities*

Some people believed he was the Messiah. *Josephus, c. 37-100 CE, Antiquities*

He was crucified under Pontius Pilate during Tiberius' reign. *Tacitus, c. 56-120 CE, Annals*

Despite this, followers believed he was still alive, and they spread. There were a multitude of Christians in Rome by 64 CE. *Tacitus, Josephus.*

Jesus claimed to be God and that he would depart and return. *Rabbi Eliezer, c. 90 CE*

All kinds of people from all walks of life worshiped him as God. *Pliny the Younger, Epistles, c. 120 CE*

found artifacts that pertain to many of these individuals, such as the famous inscription discovered in 1961 referring to Pilate as the "prefect of Judea," but there was never much debate or doubt about such facts.

There is also external evidence for the existence of Jesus as well as John the Baptist and James the Lord's brother. All three are mentioned in the writings of Josephus, the Jewish historian writing in the late first century. Christ is also mentioned in the histories of Tacitus and Seutonius, though neither seems to have had any firsthand information about him. Only the more extreme skeptics question the existence of Jesus. After all, someone had to start the Christian movement. It makes no sense to claim that a group of Jews got together and decided to make up a story about a crucified man that never existed!

A fairly new line of external evidence for the historical credibility of the Gospels focuses on the names that they mention. Modern readers are so familiar with such names as Joseph, Mary, Simon, and John that it generally does not even occur to us to ask whether these names are consistent with the historicity of the Gospels. The discovery and cataloging of numerous burial sites around Jerusalem in the first century as well as the evidence of first-century Jewish literature has made it possible to determine how common specific names were among Jews living in Galilee and Judea in that period. It turns out that Simon and Joseph were the two most popular boys' names, and Judah (Judas), John, and Jesus (Joshua) were also among the top ten names. Mary was by far the most popular girls' name (about one out of four!), which explains why several women in the Gospels have the name Mary. It is unlikely that Gentile Christians living at the end of the first century in Ephesus or Rome would have known enough about Jewish culture in the first half of the century to come up with such consistently credible names.

The external evidence supporting the historical reliability of Acts is especially impressive. In his gospel, Luke's ability to use the correct title for various officials is renowned: *proconsul* for the Roman officials Sergius Paullus in Cyprus (13:7-8) and Gallio in Corinth (18:12), *politarchs* for the local officials in Thessalonica (17:8), *Asiarchs* for the officials in Ephesus (19:31), and "the chief man" for the leading citizen in Malta (28:7). The narrative in Acts dovetails chronologically and factually with historical events known from sources outside the Bible, such as Herod Agrippa's death in 44 CE after failing to repudiate those who hailed him as a god (12:22-23) and Gallio's brief stint as proconsul in 51-52 CE (18:12-17). Luke's account of Paul's travels, which dominate the second half of the book (Acts 13-28), also dovetails remarkably well with the evidence of Paul's epistles; there are just enough wrinkles in harmonizing the two that we can be reasonably sure Luke was not basing his account on Paul's epistles. Instead, Luke appears

Interview Credibility

Suppose I interviewed you about your grandmother. We spend hours together as you recount her story, her education, her marriage, her children, her community services, and many other details. How do I know what you've told me is true? If I looked up public records, i.e., birth records, marriage certificates, and you got a few of the details wrong, I might have reason to doubt some of the other stories you told me. But if your account of your grandmother agreed with the public records, and I was able to corroborate a few other events with other sources, like newspaper articles or other acquaintances, then I would see you as a reliable witness to your grandmother's life, and give credibility to the rest of the stories.

to be drawing from eyewitness testimony, including his own: he presents himself as part of Paul's entourage in three sections of the book (16:11-40; 20:5-21:26; 27:1-28:16). That he really was there with Paul is especially clear in the last two chapters of Acts, where Luke's account of Paul's voyage and shipwreck displays very specific knowledge of ship routes, sailing practices, and other relevant details.

Cultural context. One of the most important lines of evidence supporting the historical reliability of the Gospels concerns the cultural context of Jesus' sayings as found in the Gospels. On the usual skeptical view, the Gospel authors were Gentile Christians from two or three generations later, natives to parts of the Mediterranean world distant from Galilee and Judea, putting words in Jesus' mouth to address religious and practical issues of their own day. However, greater appreciation of the backgrounds of first-century culture shows this skeptical picture to be off-base. Rather, the Gospels present Jesus addressing Jewish issues of concern to people in Galilee and Judea in his own day, speaking in ways that fit his context as a Galilean teacher.

For example, in the Gospels Jesus most often refers to himself not as Lord or Son of God or even Christ (Messiah), but as "the Son of Man" (82 times, appearing in each Gospel more than a dozen times). This title appears outside the Gospels in the New Testament only four times. The title "the Son of Man" wouldn't even make sense in a Greco-Roman cultural context; one would need to know the Old Testament to have a clue what it meant.

One of the major issues of contention in first-century Christianity was whether men needed to be circumcised to be followers of Christ. Yet Jesus never says a word about circumcision anywhere in the Gospels. This is strange, if the Gospels were composed to address later Christian agendas.

The Gospels report Jesus engaged in controversies with other Jews over the permissible grounds for divorce (Matthew 5:31-32; 19:1-9; Mark 10:2-12; Luke 16:18), a burning issue among the Pharisees in Jesus' day. Furthermore, he addresses the issue in a manner typical of Jewish teachers, citing scripture and contesting misinterpretations of scripture. The Gospels also report conflicts between Jesus and the Pharisees over the Sabbath (Matthew 12:1-12; Mark 2:23-3:6; Luke 6:1-9; 13:10-17; 14:1-6; John 5:9-18; 7:22-23; 9:14-16) and ritual washing rules (Matthew 15:1-11; 23:25-26; Mark 7:1-23; Luke 11:37-41). In these and many other ways, the Gospels' accounts about Jesus' teachings and controversies fit his own time and place—many topics and conversations are nearly incomprehensible if written after the first century, or even after 70 CE.

Objections to the Bible's Historical Reliability

We have only skimmed the surface of the evidence for the historical reliability of the Bible, but it is obvious that the Old and New Testaments are rooted in history. Before turning to our discussion of the authority of the Bible, we should comment briefly on four common objections often raised against its factual accuracy.

Skeptical Scholarship. In modern times, skeptical scholars have used various critical methods to call into question the historical reliability of the Bible. We will comment on these very briefly.

In the Old Testament, many scholars claim that Moses wrote little or none of the Pentateuch (Genesis through Deuteronomy). They theorize that Jews living at the *end* of the Old Testament era compiled the Pentateuch from sources that were first written perhaps in the ninth or eighth century. We have already cited some evidence indicating, at the very least, that the Pentateuch preserves accurate historical information about the patriarchs, Moses, and the exodus of Israel from Egypt. The literary theory about the composition of the Pentateuch, commonly called the Documentary Hypothesis, should not distract us from that evidence of its historicity. We may acknowledge the likelihood that some final editing was done to the Pentateuch centuries after Moses without detracting from its historical credibility.

In the New Testament, many critics have argued that Paul wrote as few as seven of the thirteen epistles that bear his name. They argue that such epistles as 1 and 2 Timothy were composed by students or supporters of Paul years after his death to perpetuate his legacy as they saw it. Other scholars don't agree with this claim, but again it should not be allowed to distract people from the important facts that aren't affected by this issue. From the undisputed epistles of Paul, especially Galatians and 1 Corinthians, we can establish that Paul was an eyewitness of the risen Jesus and that his Gospel message was in agreement with that of the other apostles.

Science. There is a widespread perception that the Bible is incompatible with the findings of modern science. However, it would be more accurate to say that some interpretations of the Bible are incompatible with theories held by some modern scientists.

Problems in reconciling science with the Bible can arise from two directions. On the one hand, such conflicts can be the result of people misunderstanding the Bible. This was the case when people took the Bible to teach that the earth was stationary at the physical center of the universe with all heavenly bodies revolving around the earth. However, the scientists who proved this view to be incorrect also made it clear that they were not impugning the Bible's accuracy. Copernicus was a Catholic priest. Galileo was also a faithful Catholic, and he argued cogently in his writings that the Bible does not teach that the earth is unmoving at the center of the universe. For example, when the Bible talks about sunrise and sunset, it is not teaching a particular view of astronomy, any more than when weather reports today give us the exact times for sunrise and sunset. Such language, called phenomenological language, describes things from the point of the human observer and is accurate within that perspective.

The other source of conflict is when people misunderstand the physical facts of nature. At one point in modern science it was widely believed that the universe was infinitely large and infinitely old. Such a belief seemed validated by the fact that as telescopes got bigger, we saw more and more stars and galaxies. However, in the twentieth century astronomers discovered that the universe, though enormous almost beyond imagination, is finite in size and also finite in age. In other words, it has not always existed. Instead, it had a beginning, and the universe is expanding outward in all directions. Now scientists who do not believe in creation are coming up with naturalistic explanations for the universe's beginning, but these explanations are speculations, not scientific fact. Similarly, the assumption that life must have originated on the earth from non-living chemicals through a purely natural process is not science; it is a philosophical assumption that guides some scientists and limits the kinds of explanations for the origin of life they will even consider.

There are areas of science today where even Bible-believing Christians may hold differing views as to the best way to interpret the statements in the Bible and the facts in the natural world. For example, some conservative Christians believe that Genesis 1 can only be understood to mean that God created the universe in six literal, consecutive, 24-hour days, and therefore that the universe must be less than ten thousand years old. If they are right, most scientists are wrong about the age of the world. Other conservative Christians, who also regard the Bible as the word of God, understand Genesis 1 in a different way, perhaps using the word "days" to refer to long ages, or perhaps viewing the six-day sequence as a thematic, literary arrangement. If they are right, most Christians have until modern times been wrong about the meaning of the days in Genesis 1, just as most were wrong in the past about the Bible teaching that the earth was stationary at the center of the universe. Notice that both of these approaches agree that the Bible and the scientific facts are in agreement; the difference is one thinks the Bible has been misunderstood and the other thinks the facts of nature have been misunderstood.

It is best if we do what we can to make these sorts of controversies less of a distraction from the Gospel. We should help them see that the Bible and evangelical Christianity are not anti-science. We should focus on defending the core claims of the Bible about matters pertaining to science: that the universe is created and that human beings were made in God's image, so that they are distinct in some real ways from the rest of the animal kingdom. We should not address scientific questions (or biblical questions!) beyond our competency. Finally, we should bring the conversation back to the essentials of the Gospel message.

Miracles. The evidence of historical elements in the Bible's narratives is often dismissed by skeptics simply because those narratives include miracles. Such an argument begs the question of whether miracles are possible. If God created the world, then he could do miracles and we should examine the historical information to see if he has done so. If the historical evidence for any of the biblical miracles is strong, then wholesale skepticism about those miracles is not reasonable. And in fact the evidence for the Bible's central miracle, the resurrection of Jesus, is very strong indeed. See the earlier chapter on miracles for a discussion of these issues.

Contradictions. Perhaps the most common objection to the factual reliability of the Bible is that the Bible is supposedly full of contradictions. While apparent contradictions in the Bible can be a serious issue for some people, it can also become an easy way of avoiding dealing with what the Bible does clearly say. Don't feel that it is necessary to disprove every contradiction thrown at you in order for faith in the Bible as God's word to be reasonable. In many conversations the best approach may be to ask for one or two of the most troubling "contradictions" and propose to deal with those as examples of how such issues can be addressed. Then suggest moving on to other matters and maybe coming back to any other apparent contradictions that seem pressing later.

Here are three important qualifications to keep in mind when you are confronted with an apparent contradiction. (1) Unanswered questions are not contradictions. For example, the Bible doesn't tell us when Mary died. That's not a contradiction. (2) Genuine contradictions pertain to meanings, not mere words. This is a crucial principle because words can have different meanings in different contexts. For example, Genesis 22:1 says that God "tested" Abraham, and James 1:13 says that God "tempts" no one. The Greek word used in James 1:13 is the same word used in the Greek translation of Genesis 22:1 (*peirazo*). Is this a contradiction? No, because Genesis is saying that God was putting Abraham through an ordeal that would reveal the maturity of his faith, while James is saying that God never tries to get people to sin. (3) The burden of proof rests on the person charging the contradiction. In other words, merely claiming that something *could be* a contradiction does not mean there is a problem. On the other hand, all you really need to do is to show that it *might not be* a contradiction.

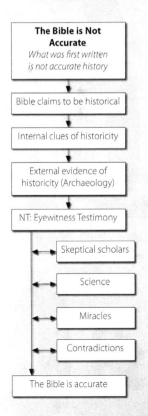

For example, Luke 3:23 says that Jesus was about thirty years old when he began his ministry, while in John 8:57 the Jews say to Jesus, "You are not yet fifty years old." Is it possible these two statements reflect different views of how old Jesus was? It may be *possible*, but it isn't necessary or even a strong argument for a problem.

The best way to be prepared to address alleged contradictions in the Bible is to be thoroughly familiar with the Bible and to be skilled in the application of principles of proper interpretation (what is called *hermeneutics*). Here are some tips to get you started.

First, make sure there is no problem with regard to the correct text or translation of the passages. You can do this easily enough by consulting a couple of good translations, especially those that have study notes. In 2 Kings 23:29, for example, the King James Version says that Pharaoh Neco of Egypt "went up against the king of Assyria." This is a mistake because the Assyrian records say that he went up to *aid* the Assyrians against the Babylonians. The Hebrew expression here, however, can mean "went up to" as well as "went up against," and "went up to" is correct in this context (as modern translations generally show). By the way, this is an example of why using a modern translation is highly recommended: scholars have had hundreds of years to study these things and clear up many such problems.

Second, read the verses in context. Try to understand what each passage means in its own context, without straining to harmonize it with another passage. Often simply reading some of the immediate context will clear up supposed difficulties. For example, Paul's statement that "flesh and blood cannot inherit the kingdom of God" (1 Corinthians 15:50) might seem to contradict other biblical passages that say that Jesus rose from the dead with a physical body (e.g., Luke 24:39, "flesh and bones"). Some people try to force these two texts to harmonize by saying that Jesus' body has flesh and bones but no blood. That's possible (we really do not know), but it is not something either passage is saying. A better approach is to read Paul's statement in context. When we do we find that he amplifies his point by saying "neither can corruption inherit incorruption" (the rest of 1 Corinthians 15:50) and then goes on to explain that our corruptible, mortal bodies must "*put on*" incorruption and immortality (1 Corinthians 15:51-54). In other words, mortals who are mere flesh and blood cannot inherit God's eternal kingdom without having immortality *added* to their physical bodies. Now the contradiction disappears without any forcing.

Third, take into consideration that biblical writings follow certain methods of presentation and may not present things the way we think they should. For example, you might suppose that the Gospels would give us exact transcripts of Jesus' words, but simple comparisons of parallel passages in the Gospels proves this just is not the case. For example, Peter's confession at Caesarea Philippi is worded "You are the Christ, the Son of the living God" (Matthew 16:16), "You are the Christ" (Mark 8:29), and "The Christ of God" (Luke 9:20). These differences would be contradictions or errors *if* the Gospels claimed to be giving us the exact words of Jesus, but that is not a claim they actually make. Bringing false expectations to the Bible is one of the most common ways people come up with apparent contradictions.

THIRD OBJECTION: THE BIBLE IS NOT AUTHORITATIVE

So far we have presented reasons to think that the Bible is authentic and accurate. That is, we have tried to show that the books of the Bible say what they originally said, and that what they say is factually reliable. In a sense, this is enough to serve as the basis for presenting the Gospel of Jesus as the crucified and resurrected Savior. On the other hand, Christians view the Bible as the divinely inspired word of God, not just a collection of historically reliable texts. Outsiders know that the Christian faith involves accepting the Bible as revelation from God, and they have questions about this idea. It is therefore important to be prepared to address some of the most common and basic questions people ask about the *authority* of the Bible. By authority we mean the doctrinal reliability of the Bible. In other words, the issue here is whether the Bible reliably expresses what God wants us to know and do.

We will address this issue of the authority of the Bible in three parts. First, we will look at the claims of authority found in the Bible. Second, we will present evidence for the authority of the Bible. Finally, we will discuss the most important objections against the authority of the Bible.

Was God involved in the writing of the Bible?

The Bible's Claims to Divine Authority

Not every book of the Bible comes with an explicit statement to the effect "This book is inspired by God and carries his authority." However, throughout the Bible we find God's authority expressed in different ways.

The Pentateuch (Genesis through Deuteronomy) claims that God spoke to Moses who made a covenant with Israel based on God's words (e.g., Exodus 19:5-7; 20:1; 24:7-8; Deuteronomy 31:20-26). The historical books from Joshua forward continue the narrative where Deuteronomy leaves off. They continuously interpret events as they unfold in light of the revelations that came through Moses and that prophets like Elijah authoritatively applied to their day. The Psalms perform the same function in song with special focus on God's dealings with David (their main author) and his royal line. The wisdom literature, such as Proverbs and Job, express God's wisdom for his people living in a fallen world. The prophets are most explicit, of course, in claiming that God spoke through them, often introducing their books with "The word of the LORD" (Hoseah 1:1; Joel 1:1; Micah 1:1; Zephaniah 1:1).

These prophets look forward to God fulfilling his promises to the patriarchs, to Israel, and to David in what Jeremiah called a "new covenant" (Jeremiah 31:31).

The New Testament is a collection of books announcing the realization of that new covenant. (*Testament* comes from a Latin word that was used to translate "covenant.") This collection is dominated by the Gospels, which present the words and deeds of Jesus Christ, who inaugurates that new covenant through his death (Luke 22:20). Jesus embodied the authority of God, and the Gospels make him known as he was remembered by Jesus' authoritative spokesmen, the apostles. John recounts Jesus' promise that the Spirit of truth would come and speak to the apostles, testifying with and through them to Jesus (John 14:26; 15:26-27; 16:13). The epistles likewise are written by the apostles or under their authority, expounding the significance of Jesus Christ for the people of God. Paul, for example, asserts that his gospel and doctrine is from Jesus Christ himself and inspired by the Spirit (1 Corinthians 2:13; Galatians 1:11-12), and required his letters to be read in the churches and his instructions obeyed (Colossians 4:16; 1 Thessalonians 5:27; 2 Thessalonians 2:15; 3:14). John opens the Book of Revelation with an exhortation for the book to be read and obeyed (Revelation 1:3). He closes his book with a warning against adding to or taking away from the book (Revelation 22:18-19), implying that it is scripture (cf. Deuteronomy 4:2; 12:32; Proverbs 30:6).

We also find statements in the New Testament affirming the authority of the Old Testament and even some statements referring to some of the other New Testament writings as scripture. Jesus affirmed the same threefold collection of inspired Jewish writings that the Pharisees and many other Jews recognized in the first century: "the Law of Moses and the Prophets and the Psalms must be fulfilled" (Luke 24:44). Jesus regarded the scriptures, which of course at that time included only the Old Testament, as the very word of God, and he asserted without qualification that it would all be fulfilled (see also Matthew 5:17-18; John 10:35). In one of his epistles, Paul quotes as "scripture" a statement that is found in Luke 10:7 (1 Timothy 5:18). The epistle of 2 Peter refers to Paul's writings as scripture (2 Peter 3:16). For the apostles, as for Jesus, scripture was God speaking (2 Timothy 3:16-17; 2 Peter 1:20-21).

Of course, a book is not scripture, the word of God, merely because it says it is. What we find in the Bible, however, is not mere assertions of divine authority. Rather, we find divine authority expressed *in word and deed*. Moses didn't just talk to the Israelites—he parted the Red Sea and led his people out from bondage. Elijah didn't just condemn the prophets of Baal—he defeated them by calling down fire from the Lord God. Jesus didn't just claim to be the resurrection and the life—he sacrificed himself and conquered death by his own resurrection. Paul didn't just claim to speak for Christ—he brought people whom most Jews viewed as dogs into the church and forged a community in which being Jewish or Gentile no longer mattered. This is why appreciating the historical reliability of the Bible is so important. When we understand that the events reported in the Bible really happened, we can see why the Bible has always been viewed by the vast majority of Jesus' followers as the word of God.

Evidence of the Bible's Divine Authority

We have already seen some evidence of the Bible's divine authority. The books of the Bible were produced by people who were involved in the historical unfolding of God's work of revealing himself and bringing redemption to the world. The books have divine authority because they are collectively the permanent means by which we are made aware of what God has done and is doing in the world.

Beyond this foundational understanding of what the Bible is, there are two types of evidence that are particularly important confirmations of the Bible's divine authority: its fulfilled prophecy and its transformational influence.

Fulfilled prophecy in the Bible. No other book in the world contains the kind of specific prophecies found all throughout the pages of the Bible. There is no comparison, for example,

Messianic Prophecies
Hebrew Scriptures that predict the Life & Death of Jesus

Concerning his Birth	Prediction	Fulfillment
Born of a virgin	Isaiah 7:14	Matthew 1:18, 24
Son of God	Psalm 2:7	Matthew 3:17
Seed of Abraham	Genesis 22:18	Matthew 1:1
Tribe of Judah	Genesis 49:10, Micah 5:2	Luke 3:23, 33
House of David	Isaiah 11:1, Jeremiah 23:5	Luke 3:23, 31
Born at Bethlehem*	Micah 5:2	Matthew 2:1
Presented with gifts	Psalm 72:10	Matthew 2:1, 11
Concerning his Nature		
His pre-existence	Micah 5:2	Colossians 1:17
He shall be called Lord	Psalm 110:1	Luke 2:11
Shall be Immanuel (God with Us)	Isaiah 7:14	Matthew 1:23
Shall be a prophet	Deuteronomy 18:18	Matthew 21:11
Special anointing of the Holy Spirit	Isaiah 11:2	Matthew 3:16
Concerning his Ministry		
Preceded by messenger*	Isaiah 40:3	Matthew 3:1
Ministry of miracles	Isaiah 35:5,6	Matthew 9:35
Teacher of parables	Psalm 78:2	Matthew 13:34
Enter Jerusalem on a donkey*	Zechariah 9:9	Luke 19:35
"Stone of stumbling" to Jews	Psalm 118:22	1 Peter 2:7
"Light" to Gentiles	Isaiah 60:3	Acts 13:47, 48
Concerning Events after his Burial		
Resurrection	Psalm 16:10	Acts 2:31
Ascension	Psalm 68:18	Acts 1:9
Seated at the right hand of God	Psalm 110:1	Hebrews 1:3
Prophecies Fulfilled in One Day		
Betrayed by a friend*	Psalm 41:9	Matthew 10:4
Sold for thirty pieces of silver*	Zechariah 11:12	Matthew 26:15
Money to be thrown into God's house*	Zechariah 11:13	Matthew 27:5
Price given for potter's field*	Zechariah 11:13	Matthew 27:7
Forsaken by disciples	Zechariah 13:7	Mark 14:50
Accused by false witnesses	Psalm 35:11	Matthew 26:59,60
Silent before accusers*	Isaiah 53:7	Matthew 27:26
Smitten and spit upon	Isaiah 50:6	Matthew 26:67
Mocked	Psalm 22:7-8	Matthew 27:29
Fell under the cross	Psalm 109:24, 25	Luke 23:26
Hands and feet pierced*	Psalm 22:16	Luke 23:33
Crucified with thieves*	Isaiah 53:12	Matthew 27:38
Made intercession for his persecutors	Isaiah 53:12	Luke 23:34
Rejected by his own people	Isaiah 53:3	John 7:5, 48
Garments parted and lots cast	Psalm 22:18	John 19:23, 24
To suffer thirst	Psalm 69:21	John 19:28
Gall and vinegar offered to him	Psalm 69:21	Matthew 27:34
His forsaken cry	Psalm 22:1	Matthew 27:46
Bones not broken	Psalm 34:20	John 19:33
His side pierced	Zechariah 12:10	John 19:34
Darkness over the land	Amos 8:9	Matthew 27:45
Buried in a rich man's tomb.	Isaiah 53:9	Matthew 27:57-60

Probability of only marked prophecies "accidentally" fulfilled in any one person: 1 in 10^17 (Peter Stoner, Science Speaks)

If the creator of the universe
had a hand in producing a book
like the Bible, how would we
know? What should we expect
if the creator of the universe
wanted to communicate with
us?

Here's one place to start. If the
Bible was influenced by God, it
should stand out from the others
in at least these four areas...

Wide distribution: The Bible
was the most copied handwritten
book in the world, and was the
first book printed by printing
press. It hasn't relinquished the
"best-seller" label since. Well
over 100 million bibles are sold
or distributed every year. Recent
figures estimate somewhere
between 2.5 and 6 billion copies
of the Bible in the world.

Universal Access: According to
the United Bible Society, by the
end of 2007 the whole Bible was
available in 438 languages, the
Old or the New Testament alone
in an additional 1168 languages,
and portions of the Bible in
another 848 languages, for a total
of 2,454 languages. Nothing else
comes remotely close.

Preservation: There have been
numerous attempts to burn, ban,
and systematically eliminate the
Bible, but all have failed. Critics
have often sounded its death
knell, but the corpse never stays
put. The Bible has been subjected
to more abuse, perversion,
destructive criticism, and pure
hate than any other book. Yet it
continues to stand the test of time
while its critics are refuted and
forgotten.

(continued on next page)

between the *Oracles of Nostradamus* and the Old Testament prophecies about Jesus Christ. Other so-called prophecies are so vague and cryptic that they could be "fulfilled" in any number of ways. But the prophecies of the Old Testament are often so detailed that their fulfillments were obvious—so clear, in fact, that many critics have attempted to assign later dates to some of these prophets (e.g., Isaiah 40-66 and Daniel) to make the prophecies come after the events. The Old Testament prophets gave both short- and long-term prophecies, so that the undisputed fulfillment of the short-term predictions would authenticate the validity of the long-term predictions which could not be verified for many years. God intended fulfilled prophecy to demonstrate the divine origin of the scriptures. We will focus first on messianic prophecy—prophecies about the messiah—and then on prophecies about everything else.

It is better to begin with *messianic prophecy* because so much of it is quite specific, and evidence shows that it was all written hundreds of years before the birth of Jesus Christ. The Old Testament was translated into Greek between 250-100 BCE (the Septuagint), so it is obvious that the Hebrew Bible was written before this time. When these messianic prophecies are combined, the prophetic doorway becomes so narrow that only one person can fit through. Jesus and later New Testament figures intended to demonstrate that the whole Hebrew Bible pointed ahead to Jesus as the expected Messiah (Jesus in Luke 24:27, Philip in Acts 8:35, Paul in Acts 17:2-3). Biblical scholars have identified between 100 and 300 Old Testament predictions that were literally fulfilled in the life of Jesus Christ. A messianic impostor might have been able to engineer the fulfillment of a few of these prophecies, but the vast majority would be beyond his reach. The miraculous nature of Jesus's ministry, culminating in his resurrection, could be matched by none other than the promised messiah.

The most explicit and powerful of all messianic prophecies is Isaiah 52:13-53:12, written seven centuries before the birth of Christ. This song of the Suffering Servant reveals that Messiah would suffer sinlessly (53:4-6, 9), silently (53:7), and as a substitute to bear the sins of others (53:5-6, 8, 10-12). Messiah would be subject to "scourging," "pierced through," "cut off out of the land of the living," and placed in the grave of "a rich man in his death." But after his death he will be "lifted up and greatly exalted" (52:13). This is a clear portrait of the rejection, death, burial, and resurrection of Jesus the Messiah. (Jewish scholars since the 12th century have attempted to identify the Servant of this passage with Israel, but the nation is distinguished from the Servant in 53:8, and Israel never suffered sinlessly nor silently as this Servant does.)

General prophecy can also be used to illustrate the supernatural origin of scripture. In many cases these prophecies are so detailed and accurate that skeptical scholars have assigned much later dates to some sections of scripture because they assume that such prophecy is not possible. The accumulating evidence is generally in favor of the earlier dates, but even if we grant the later dates, many powerful examples of fulfilled prophecy remain. Ezekiel's prediction of the destruction of Tyre (Ezekiel 26) claims to have been given in the sixth-century BCE, but higher critics date it after the fifth-century destruction of the city. The ancient city of Tyre was a prominent Phoenician seaport (in modern-day Lebanon) that consisted of two parts, one on the mainland at the coast, and the other on an island about a half mile off the coast. According to this prophecy, Nebuchadnezzar would besiege and destroy the city (26:7-11), many nations would come against it (26:3), the ruins would be scraped from the site and thrown into the sea, leaving a bare rock (26:4, 12, 19), the site would become a place for fishermen to spread their nets (26:5, 14), and the city would never be built again (26:13-14). These specific predictions have been fulfilled in surprising detail. Nebuchadnezzar besieged the mainland city for 13 years (586-573 BCE) and finally destroyed it, but the island city remained intact. This remaining portion continued until Alexander the Great overthrew it in 332 BCE by building a causeway from the coast to the island. To build this causeway, he literally scraped the ruins and debris from the old mainland site (26:4) and threw them "into the water" (26:12). This left the old site "a bare rock" (26:4). "Many nations" (26:3) came against the restored island city, including the Seleucids, the Ptolemies, the Romans, the Muslims, and the Crusaders. But the mainland city was never rebuilt (26:14), and today it remains a bare rock upon which fishermen spread their nets to dry (26:5, 14).

Other remarkable examples of the accuracy of Old Testament prophecies include the details about the overthrow of Nineveh (Nahum 1:3), Babylon (Isaiah 13-14; Jeremiah 51), and the desolation and restoration of Palestine (Leviticus 26; Ezekiel 36), including the name(!) of the Persian ruler who first returned the Jews to their land (Isaiah 45).

The biblical claims for its divine inspiration, combined with the forceful evidence of fulfilled messianic and general prophecy, make a strong case for the inspiration of scripture, especially when these lines of evidence are built upon the case for the historical reliability of the biblical documents developed earlier in this chapter.

The influence of the Bible. Although perhaps not the primary evidence of the Bible's divine authority, its positive influence is certainly a strong confirmation of that authority. For nearly two thousand years the books of the Bible have been transforming both individuals and societies. Of course, the history of Christianity has had its evils, but it has always been the Christian

A Cohesive Unified Message: The Bible was written over 1500 years in 66 books by 40+ authors using 6+ genres in 3 languages on 3 continents and covering topics like God, man, Heaven, marriage, relationships, and yet there it has **one unified message** throughout.

Obviously, these four areas do not prove that the Bible is the inspired word of God. But they may be clues... IF God desired to communicate to the human race through the written word, he ought to be competent at the task. And that means we probably shouldn't first go looking for divine inspiration on the back shelves of a second-hand bookstore, but perhaps we should look first to the most widely printed, translated, distributed book in the history of humanity.

faith informed by scripture that has led to those evils being condemned and eventually abandoned. For example, Christians, not secular humanists, led the way in ridding Europe and America of slavery.

In the biblical view of the world, pagan gods were demoted to inferior spirits and only one God ruled over the whole world. One God meant one set of rules everywhere, allowing for the idea of natural laws on a solid foundation. One God meant that all areas of human knowledge were interrelated. It was therefore this view of the world that led to the formation of the first great universities. It also created the intellectual environment in which modern science originated and flourished. Copernicus, Galileo, Kepler, and Newton were all devout believers in the Bible.

The Bible also taught Jews and Christians to think of human beings neither as gods accountable only to themselves nor as mere animals meant follow their base instincts. Instead, human beings are creatures made in God's image, possessing a unique dignity in the natural world yet one in which they are responsible to the world's maker. This means that might does not make right. Gradually over the centuries, peoples heavily influenced by biblical thought pursued reforms in government and society that ennobled human individuals. As creatures who viewed themselves as beings in the image of the Creator, they valued human creativity in the arts and in technology. Because all human beings share in God's image, Jews and Christians historically have vigorously promoted education for all children.

As Christianity spread throughout the world, missionaries and new believers translated the Bible into more and more languages. In many instances the translators actually began by creating an alphabetic script because the languages had no history of writing at all. In this and other ways, the dissemination of the Bible was the impetus for the rise of literacy throughout the world. No other religious book has had this kind of impact. The Qur'an, for example, has not had the same effect because Muslims believe the Qur'an should be known only in Arabic, and there is a greater emphasis on reciting the Qur'an than actually reading it.

It should be frankly acknowledged that not everyone in the history of Christianity has looked favorably on the translation of the Bible into people's first languages. In the late medieval era the Catholic Church opposed such efforts. They saw them as undermining the unity of the church and of Christian civilization. John Wycliffe in the fourteenth century and William Tyndale in the sixteenth century were declared heretics for translating the Bible into English. One of Martin Luther's most important achievements was his translation of the Bible into German. Despite opposition and even, in the case of Wycliffe, martyrdom, these men revolutionized their society by making the Bible available in the languages of the people. Knowledge of the Bible led to the democratization of the West.

The influence of the Bible for good has continued to this day. Christians informed by their reading of the Bible started most of the non-governmental charitable and relief organizations of the past two or three centuries. The Red Cross, the Salvation Army, and World Vision are just a few of the best known examples.

The blessings that God has bestowed on the world through the Bible are incalculable. Ultimately the reason this is so is that the Bible reliably bears testimony to God's love for all humanity in Jesus Christ. There is no greater transforming power in the world.

Objections to the Bible's Divine Authority

We close with consideration of three of the most common objections to the divine authority of the Bible. These objections concern the canon of scripture, alleged ethical problems in the Bible, and the question of diverse interpretations of the Bible.

Challenges to the canon of scripture. How do we know that the right books are in the Bible? The collection of books that belong in scripture is known as the *canon* (from a Greek word meaning rule or standard). This question about the canon is often posed as an objection to trusting what the Bible says. Let's think about this point of the question before addressing it with specifics.

There are only two possible problems with the canon. It might not contain books that should be there, or it might contain books that should not be there. Of course, one could imagine the canon having both of these problems. Consider each concern one at a time. Suppose the Bible is "missing" some books that should be there. If that's the problem, it doesn't affect the doctrinal reliability of the books that are there. For example, suppose Jacob, Abraham's grandson, had written a book that at one time was considered scripture but somehow got lost and has been missing for over two thousand years. That would be a shame, and perhaps we would be somewhat poorer for it, but what we do have in the Bible would still be good. So this concern really doesn't constitute a problem for the reliability of the Bible as it now stands.

On the other hand, if the Bible included books it should not have, that could be a problem. How much of a problem would depend on how much the inclusion of those books might have altered the teachings of Christianity as a whole.

With regard to the Old Testament, the books that historically people have most often questioned have not played a large role in Christian theology. The books of Ecclesiastes, Song of Solomon, and Esther are three books in the Old Testament that have been seriously questioned. None of these short books has played a major role in Christian doctrine (or in Jewish doctrine, although Esther is the basis for the Jewish holiday of Purim). Each makes its contribution, which would be missed if taken out, but Christianity would remain intact without them.

There are also a number of other books that some Christians include in the Old Testament but others do not. These books are called the *Deuterocanonical* books by those who include them (notably Catholics and Eastern Orthodox), meaning that they belong on a kind of second tier within the canon. In other words, they recognize that those books are not of the same authority as, say, Genesis or Psalms or Jeremiah. Those who reject these books as scripture (Protestants) call them the *Apocrypha* ("hidden away"), meaning that they should be excluded from the canon. These books include 1 and 2 Maccabees, Tobit, Judith, Baruch, two books of Wisdom, and some later additions to Esther and Daniel. Except for a passing reference or two that Catholics have cited in support of praying for the dead, little hangs doctrinally on whether one accepts these books or not. One reason that Protestants think these books do not belong in the Old Testament is that they were not part of the Hebrew Bible, and even to this day are not part of the Jewish Bible.

In the New Testament, there was some dispute in the early church about Hebrews, James, 2 Peter, 2 and 3 John, Jude, and Revelation. Here the situation is different from that of the Old Testament, because these books, especially Hebrews, James, and Revelation, have had significant influence in Christian thought. It should be noted, though, that the main concern with these books was that there was uncertainty as to who wrote them (especially Hebrews). Except for Revelation, there really was no concern about the doctrine of these books. Frankly, those who questioned Revelation did so because they didn't understand it. Debates over Revelation and the other books dissipated quickly and it became clear to practically everyone which books belonged in the New Testament. Since the late fourth century, essentially all Christians have accepted all 27 books of the traditional New Testament.

Since about the early 1980s, a growing number of people have criticized the whole idea of a canon of Scripture, especially with regard to the New Testament. Their complaint has not been that some books don't belong there, but that having a canon at all excludes some viewpoints from early Christianity. In effect, then, this is a complaint about what books were not included in the traditional canon of the New Testament. Sparking this complaint was the discovery and translation of a number of early writings by people who had a radically different way of understanding Christianity than what one finds in the four Gospels or the epistles of Paul. Most of these "excluded" writings reflect beliefs that scholars loosely call Gnostic. The *Gnostics* believed in a secret, hidden knowledge (Greek, *gnosis*) imparted by Jesus that would enable those initiated into the secrets to escape the limitations of the material world.

Chief among the "Gnostic" or Gnostic-like writings are the so-called Gospel of Thomas, the Gospel of Mary (i.e., Mary Magdalene), and the Gospel of Peter. To call them "Gospels" is rather misleading, as they are nothing like the Gospels in the New Testament. Our knowledge of the texts of these books depends primarily on one tattered manuscript for each. There is one fourth-century manuscript of a Coptic translation (from a Greek original) for *Thomas* and one fourth- or fifth-century Coptic manuscript, that is missing much of the book, for *Mary*. There is a Greek manuscript for Peter, but it is also incomplete, and it dates from the eighth century. Imagine if that was all the manuscript evidence we had for the Gospels of Matthew, Luke, and John!

Nearly all scholars agree that *Mary*, *Thomas*, and *Peter* were written in the second century. In other words, pretty much everyone agrees these books were written fifty to a hundred years later than the four Gospels in the New Testament. No one argues that Mary, Thomas, or Peter wrote these books. None of these books provides enough in the way of historical anchoring in places, times, or events to warrant thinking of these books as historical in content. Instead they contain esoteric, speculative statements like "The nature of matter is resolved into the roots of its own nature alone" (*Mary* 23) and "Split a piece of wood, and I am there; lift up the stone, and I am there" (*Thomas* 77).

Sober historians and other scholars acknowledge that these Gnostic Gospels do not provide authentic information about the historical person of Jesus. Those who promote these Gospels do so not to add accurate information about Jesus but to deny that there is any authoritative information about Jesus. Their claim is that the biblical Gospels are just some of the many different books written about Jesus from many different points of view. That is why it is important to recognize that in fact the biblical Gospels are by far our most reliable source of historical facts about Jesus—a point that even some agnostic and skeptical scholars acknowledge.

Alleged ethical problems in the Bible. Critics of the Bible may argue that the Bible contains contradictions or historical errors, but usually that is not what bothers them most. Generally speaking, the strongest criticisms of the Bible are ethical. In particular, the Old Testament comes under especially harsh criticism.

Perhaps the most often cited ethical criticism of the Bible is that it claims that God ordered Joshua to kill every man, woman, and child in Canaan. The notion of God commanding genocide is perceived by both believers and non-believers alike as ethically troubling. What shall we say about this question?

In Deuteronomy, here is what God commands the Israelites:

> When the LORD your God brings you into the land that you are entering to take possession of it, and clears away many nations before you, the Hittites, the Girgashites, the Amorites, the Canaanites, the Perizzites, the Hivites, and the Jebusites, seven nations more numerous and mightier than you, 2 and when the LORD your God gives them over to you, and you defeat them, then you must devote them to complete destruction. You shall make no covenant with them and show no mercy to them. 3 You shall not intermarry with them, giving your daughters to their sons or taking their daughters for your sons, 4 for they would turn away your sons from following me, to serve other gods. Then the anger of the LORD would be kindled against you, and he would destroy you quickly. 5 But thus shall you deal with them: you shall break down their altars and dash in pieces their pillars and chop down their Asherim and burn their carved images with fire. (Deuteronomy 7:1-5 ESV)

The usual understanding of verses 1-3 is that God was telling the Israelites to kill literally every individual in the seven nations listed. However, verses 4-5 do not fit easily with that reading of verses 1-3. If God had just told the Israelites to leave literally not one person alive from those nations, what is the point of forbidding intermarriage with them? There would be no one to marry if they carried out the command literally (see also Deuteronomy 20:16-17).

If we take the early chapters of Joshua literally, it would seem that his army did kill every last person among the Canaanites. Ten times in Joshua 10:28-11:14 we read that Joshua "struck" each city "with the edge of the sword," often adding that he "left none remaining" or something to the same effect. Then we read, "So Joshua took the whole land, according to all that the LORD had spoken to Moses, and Joshua gave it for an inheritance to Israel according to their divisions by their tribes. Thus the land had rest from war" (Joshua 11:23). If we stop right there, we would have to conclude that all the Canaanites were literally wiped out, dead, and the land was now occupied by Israelites alone.

Turn the page, however, and we find God telling Joshua, "You are old and advanced in years, and very much of the land remains to be possessed" (Joshua 13:1). The book refers in later chapters to Canaanites who were still living in various places in the land (Joshua 16:10; 17:12-18). Evidently the Israelites had gained enough of a foothold in the land that Joshua had assigned territory to each of the tribes, but they had not killed everyone and in general struggled to take control in those territories (e.g., Joshua 19:47). This situation is confirmed in the Book of Judges which follows immediately after Joshua and opens with a military offensive in which the Israelites defeat a Canaanite army of ten thousand men (Judges 2:1-4)!

We therefore see evidence both in Deuteronomy, which introduces God's command to wipe out the Canaanites, and in Joshua, which repeatedly says that this command was carried out, that it did not mean that the Israelites were to kill literally every man, woman, and child. Judges confirms this point conclusively. Evidently the language about killing every last person, leaving no one remaining, destroying them completely, is hyperbole. Most people have no trouble recognizing hyperbole when it's part of their own culture, but find it shocking or absurd when it's part of someone else's culture. A man who triumphantly announces that he made "a ton of money" will not be taken literally in our culture, but someone unfamiliar with this exaggerated idiom might mistakenly take it literally. Likewise, a man who asserts that his favorite football team "killed" the opposing team is not speaking literally. It appears that a similar stylized use of exaggerated language is being used in Deuteronomy and Joshua.

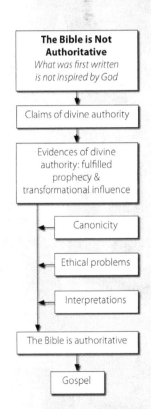

What about slavery? This issue may be addressed more briefly. We need to understand first what "slavery" in the context of the Old Testament was—and more importantly, what it was not. Slavery in the Old Testament was more like indentured servitude than what in modern times is called slavery. Kidnapping people in order to own them or to sell them as slaves was forbidden (Exodus 21:16). This one statute alone would have outlawed the entire slave trade of centuries ago that made human chattel out of millions of people from Africa.

The usual way a person became a "slave" in ancient Israel was that a poor Israelite would indenture himself to another Israelite. In those cases, the slave would be freed after a certain number of years (usually seven) unless the slave chose to remain in his master's employ for life (Exodus 21:1-6; Leviticus 25:35-42). Slaves were not to be treated with severity (Leviticus 25:43). People from the surrounding pagan nations could be indentured for life—again, though, not by kidnapping or forcing them into such servitude (Leviticus 25:44-46).

The point is that "slavery" in the Old Testament was a humane institution that gave poor people a way to survive and to provide for their families. It was part of a very different culture from the one in which we live today. It was also not at all the same as the slavery practiced in the American

South.

The problem of different interpretations of the Bible. The last objection to the divine authority of the Bible we will consider is very different from the ones already discussed. This objection argues that the Bible cannot function as a divine authority because it has no objective meaning. The Bible is like a wax nose, so we are told, that can be twisted any way a person wants. Look at the problem of slavery in the Bible just considered. People used to quote the Bible to justify owning slaves. Other people argued that the Bible condemned slavery. How can the Bible be an authoritative revelation from God if it isn't clear what the Bible means?

This objection, though it may be voiced with all sincerity, rests on three faulty assumptions. The first is *an exaggerated view of the extent to which Bible-believing Christians disagree in their understanding of the Bible.* It is true that they disagree on a number of topics, such as the age of the universe, whether Christians can or should speak in tongues today, or how to interpret the Millennium in Revelation 20. Yet they also agree on the more important issues, such as that God is the sole creator of the universe, that speaking in tongues is not essential for salvation, and that the hope of the church is the return of Jesus Christ.

We should also point out that many religious groups today that quote the Bible actually place their faith in something else. That is, they quote the Bible because other people respect it, but the real source of their beliefs is some other book or some supposed prophet or something else. If we restrict our attention to Christian groups that affirm the Bible to be the only reliable revelation from God on which our beliefs should be based, we will find a high degree of unity on essential doctrines. These include the Trinity, Jesus Christ as God incarnate, the physical resurrection of Christ, and salvation by grace alone through faith in Christ alone.

The second faulty assumption is *an underestimation of the extent to which people are capable of misunderstanding the truth.* Whether by making innocent mistakes, being ignorant and careless, or deliberately lying, people all too often misunderstand objective facts. Look at how economists and politicians manage to come up with diametrically opposed interpretations of the same hard numerical data. The fault is not in the numbers, but in those who are using the numbers to support their agendas. Scientists often disagree on which hypothesis best explains the data from their experiments. Lawyers can present persuasive-sounding arguments for a man's innocence or guilt using the same evidence. Differences of belief are a pervasive, unavoidable part of life. The fact that people come up with different interpretations of the Bible is not a poor reflection on the Bible. It is simply what happens when different people look at the same text.

The third faulty assumption is *an overly pessimistic view of the possibility of resolving differences of interpretation.* Yes, people understand the Bible differently, as they do practically everything else in life. This does not mean that there is no way for an individual to reach a sound conclusion as to which understanding is correct. In most cases of conflicting interpretations of the Bible, it is possible to learn enough to reach an informed, solidly based view of the matter. Again, this is the way things are in every area of thought. Take the issue of slavery again. While it is true that conflicting interpretations of the Bible were debated when slavery was practiced, it is not true that there is no way to resolve the dispute reasonably. A careful study of all that the Bible says on the subject was and is sufficient to reach some definite conclusions on the issue. For example, as noted previously, the Bible states explicitly that kidnapping people for the purpose of selling them is forbidden (Exodus 21:16). When we apply proper methods of interpretation to passages in the Bible (see our earlier discussion of interpretive method in this chapter), we will grow in our understanding of its meaning. Granted, we will not reach perfect knowledge. The Bible is absolutely reliable; our understanding of it is not. That fact does not make the Bible any less authoritative.

SUPPLEMENTAL READING

Apologetics Study Bible. Nashville: Holman Bible Publishers, 2007. Study Bible with detailed footnotes and articles addressing the whole range of issues pertaining to the reliability of the Bible.

Archaeological Study Bible, Zondervan, 2005. Another study Bible, with abundant articles highlighting significant archaeological finds that help explain and understand the world of the Bible.

Archer, Gleason L. *New International Encyclopedia of Bible Difficulties*. Grand Rapids: Zondervan, 1982, 2001. Archer's introductory essay on how to approach alleged discrepancies and errors in the Bible is a classic. It is followed by hundreds of answers to such problems.

Bauckham, Richard A. *Jesus and the Eyewitnesses: The Gospels as Eyewitness Testimony*. Grand Rapids: Eerdmans, 2006. Respected conservative scholar defends the view that the Gospels are based on eyewitness testimony.

Blomberg, Craig L. *Making Sense of the New Testament: Three Crucial Questions*. Grand Rapids: Baker Academic, 2004. The first and longest of the three chapters is on "Is the New Testament historically Reliable?" A good popular-level introduction.

_____. *The historical Reliability of the Gospels*. 2nd ed. Downers Grove, IL: InterVarsity Press, 2007. The heart of this excellent book is a study of alleged contradictions and historical problems in the Gospels that makes responsible use of scholarly methods.

Boa, Kenneth D., and Robert M. Bowman Jr. *20 Compelling Evidences that God Exists: Discover Why Believing in God Makes So Much Sense*. Colorado Springs: Cook, 2005. See chapters 9-12 for a popular-level survey of the reliability of the Bible.

Brisco, Thomas V. *Holman Bible Atlas. Broadman & Holman Reference*. Nashville: Broadman & Holman, 1997. Color maps and photographs bring biblical locations to life and gives a sense of the reality "on the ground" of the Bible's narratives. This is just one of several excellent Bible atlases currently available.

Bruce, F. F. *The New Testament Documents: Are They Reliable?* 5th ed. Downers Grove, IL: InterVarsity Press, 1960. Short, older book, but a classic that is still one of the best introductions to the subject.

Burridge, Richard A. *What Are the Gospels? A Comparison with Graeco-Roman Biography*. 2nd ed. Grand Rapids: Eerdmans; Dearborn, MI: Dove Booksellers, 2004. Academic study (by a non-evangelical) demonstrating that the Gospels fit the genre of Greco-Roman biography.

Copan, Paul. *Is God a Moral Monster? Understanding the Old Testament God*. Grand Rapids: Baker, 2011. Addresses such common concerns as harsh penalties in the Law, treatment of women, slavery, and genocide.

Copan, Paul, and William Lane Craig, eds. *Come Let Us Reason: New Essays in Christian Apologetics*. Nashville: B&H, 2012. Includes several excellent essays on the historical reliability of the New Testament, as well as the issues of genocide and slavery in the Old Testament.

Fant, Clyde E., and Mitchell G. Reddish. *Lost Treasures of the Bible: Understanding the Bible through Archaeological Artifacts in World Museums*. Grand Rapids: Eerdmans, 2008. Fascinating review of many important archaeological discoveries of importance to placing the Bible in historical context.

Howard, David M. Jr., and Michael A. Grisanti, eds. *Giving the Sense: Understanding and Using Old Testament historical Texts*. Grand Rapids: Kregel Academic, 2003. Includes several articles by leading evangelical scholars on the historical reliability of the Old Testament.

Kaiser, Walter C. Jr. *The Old Testament Documents: Are They Reliable & Relevant?* Downers Grove, IL: InterVarsity Press, 2001. Excellent overview of the reliability of the Old Testament text, history, and message, and of its relevance for us today.

Kitchen, Kenneth A. *On the Reliability of the Old Testament*. Grand Rapids: Eerdmans, 2003. This culminating major work by an influential conservative Christian scholar takes an unusual approach: it begins at the end of Old Testament history and works backwards.

Komoszewski, J. Ed, M. James Sawyer, and Daniel B. Wallace. *Reinventing Jesus: How Contemporary Skeptics Miss the Real Jesus and Mislead Popular Culture*. Grand Rapids: Kregel, 2006. Popular-level book that includes excellent sections on the text and canon of the New Testament.

Mangalwadi, Vishal. *The Book that Made Your World: How the Bible Created the Soul of Western Civilization*. Nashville: Thomas Nelson, 2011. An evangelical Christian scholar and humanitarian who is a native of India, Mangalwadi presents a superb account of the transforming influence of the Bible in Western civilization–and a warning of what the West is in danger of losing.

Matthew, Victor H. *Studying the Ancient Israelites: A Guide to Sources and Methods*. Grand Rapids: Baker Academic, 2007. Excellent introductory textbook for putting the Old Testament historical narratives into their physical and historical context. Its lengthy chapter on archaeology actually explains how archaeologists do their work and what its limitations are.

Rydelnik, Michael. *The Messianic Hope: Is the Hebrew Bible Really Messianic?* NAC Studies in Bible & Theology. Nashville: B&H, 2010. Important defense of the traditional Christian belief that the Old Testament does contain predictive prophecies of the coming of Christ.

Tov, Emanuel. *Textual Criticism of the Hebrew Bible, 3rd ed., rev. and expanded*. Minneapolis: Fortress Press, 2012. The most up-to-date and comprehensive textbook on the subject, suitable for scholars and advanced students.

Wenham, John. *Christ and the Bible. 3rd ed.* Eugene, OR: Wipf & Stock, 2009. Classic book accessible to most readers, basing Christian acceptance of the canon of scripture on the authority of Christ.

Study Guide for Is the Bible Reliable?

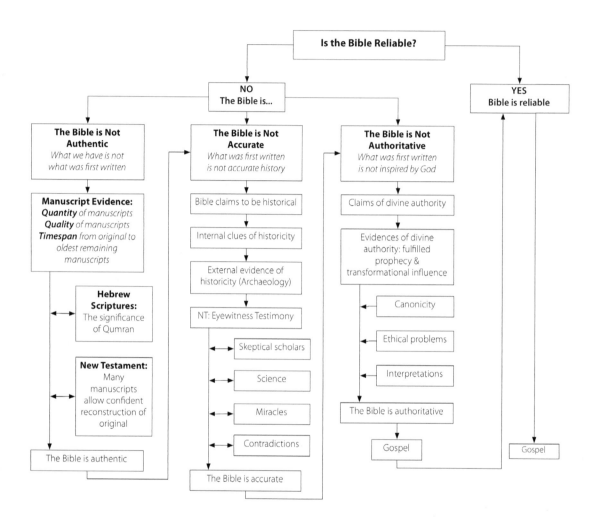

Is the Bible Reliable?

NO
The Bible is...

YES
Bible is reliable

The Bible is Not Authentic
What we have is not what was first written

The Bible is Not Accurate
What was first written is not accurate history

The Bible is Not Authoritative
What was first written is not inspired by God

Manuscript Evidence:
Quantity *of manuscripts*
Quality *of manuscripts*
Timespan *from original to oldest remaining manuscripts*

Bible claims to be historical

Claims of divine authority

Internal clues of historicity

Evidences of divine authority: fulfilled prophecy & transformational influence

External evidence of historicity (Archaeology)

Hebrew Scriptures:
The significance of Qumran

NT: Eyewitness Testimony

Canonicity

Skeptical scholars

Ethical problems

New Testament:
Many manuscripts allow confident reconstruction of original

Science

Interpretations

Miracles

The Bible is authoritative

Contradictions

The Bible is authentic

Gospel

Gospel

The Bible is accurate

Key Illustrations

Telephone Game

Everyone remembers the telephone game from childhood. One boy whispers a phrase to the girl sitting next to him, and the message is whispered around the circle. The last person says aloud what he thinks the message is, often with hilarious results. Through many transmissions, the message has become grossly distorted. The process of copying the Bible has been compared to this game. But in order to make the comparison fair, we would have to make this adjustment. The first person would say the message out loud to the person sitting next to him and the message would be repeated out loud around the entire circle. If someone deliberately changed the message or got it wrong by accident, anyone who caught the mistake would be able to correct them. The Bible was not copied in secret or through hushed voices, but was conducted openly.

JFK Witnesses

Suppose a man wrote a book today claiming that after he was shot in Dallas, John F. Kennedy came back to life, appeared to groups of people around the country for a couple of weeks and then disappeared. How many copies would he sell? Probably quite a few. But could this new view gather a large following? Probably not. There are simply too many eye witnesses to the events of 1963 still alive today to contradict this fiction. The book might garner a few headlines, but it would only be months before its believers could be found only in the fringes of society. And yet the stories of Christ's death and resurrection were circulated immediately in the very place where he died and the first Gospels were written down within 30-40 years. There was simply not enough time for myths to be created and propagate–too many eyewitnesses remained.

Interview Credibility

Suppose I interviewed you about your grandmother. We spend hours together as you recount her story, her education, her marriage, her children, her community services, and many other details. How do I know what you've told me is true? If I looked up public records, i.e., birth records, marriage certificates, and you got a few of the details wrong, I might have reason to doubt some of the other stories you told me. But if your account of your grandmother agreed with the public records, and I was able to corroborate a few other events with other sources, like newspaper articles or other acquaintances, then I would see you as a reliable witness to your grandmother's life, and give credibility to the rest of the stories.

Key Verses

Eyewitness Claims:

John 19:35 (NLT) This report is from an eyewitness giving an accurate account; it is presented so that you also can believe.

1 John 1:1 That which was from the beginning, which we have heard, which we have seen with our eyes, which we have looked at and our hands have touched–this we proclaim concerning the Word of life.

2 Peter 1: 16 For we did not follow cleverly devised tales when we made known to you the power and coming of our Lord Jesus Christ, but we were eyewitnesses of his majesty.

Claims of historicity:

Luke 1:1-4 Many have undertaken to draw up an account of the things that have been fulfilled among us, ²just as they were handed down to us by those who from the first were eyewitnesses and servants of the word. ³Therefore, since I myself have carefully investigated everything from the beginning, it seemed good also to me to write an orderly account for you, most excellent Theophilus, ⁴so that you may know the certainty of the things you have been taught.

Acts 2:22 "Men of Israel, listen to this: Jesus of Nazareth was a man accredited by God to you by miracles, wonders and signs, which God did among you through him, as you yourselves know.

Claims to be the Word of God:

2 Timothy 3:16 All scripture is inspired by God and profitable for teaching, for reproof, for correction, for training in righteousness

2 Peter 1:20-21 Above all, you must understand that no prophecy of scripture came about by the prophet's own interpretation. ²¹For prophecy never had its origin in the will of man, but men spoke from God as they were carried along by the Holy Spirit.

1 Corinthians 2:13 This is what we speak, not in words taught us by human wisdom but in words taught by the Spirit, expressing spiritual truths in spiritual words.

Were Paul's letters really scripture? Peter thought so...

2 Peter 3:15-16 And regard the patience of our Lord to be salvation; just as also our beloved brother Paul, according to the wisdom given him, wrote to you, ¹⁶as also in all his letters, speaking in them of these things, in which are some things hard to understand, which the untaught and unstable distort, as they do also the rest of the scriptures, to their own destruction.

Study Questions

1. What is the difference between the Authenticity, Accuracy, Authority, and Accumulation of the Bible? Why is it important to clearly identify which of these issues is most troubling a friend before launching into a defense of the Bible?

2. Define the three lines of manuscript evidence used to demonstrate the authenticity of all ancient documents, including the Bible. How does the Bible compare to other ancient documents?

3. Respond to this statement: "What about the many, many times the Bible was copied? Couldn't errors have crept into and significantly distorted the text?"

4. List a few verses that give the Bible's claim to historical accuracy. What would you say to the charge that this is just circular reasoning?

5. How do other historical and archaeological sources support the accuracy of the biblical record? Give examples from both the Old and New Testaments.

6. Even if the Bible is an authentic and historically accurate document, does that necessarily mean that it is inspired by God and bears his authority? How would you support inspiration?

7. Listed below are some of the problems that cause people to question the Bible. Give a brief response to each:

   • Multiple Interpretations

   • Science

   • Ethical Issues

   • Apparent Errors

   • Canonicity

<u>Notes</u> _____

QUESTION 5: DOES GOD MAKE SENSE IN A WORLD FULL OF SUFFERING?

Often-Asked Questions:

- If God is all-good and all-powerful, why did he make a world with so much suffering? Why do innocent people suffer from things like disease and natural disaster?

- If God is so good, loving, and powerful, why doesn't he put an end to suffering now?

- How could a loving God send people to hell?

- Did God create evil? If God knew man would sin and bring evil into this world, why did he bother to create him in the first place?

We must be extremely sensitive to someone going through a time of suffering, or someone on the sidelines of a loved one's pain. No *intellectual* answer is *emotionally* satisfying in the midst of personal pain. Don't try to give reasons for why God allowed a specific act of evil or suffering to occur. Just because we can see good come from a bad situation doesn't mean that that is why it happened. We don't have access to that information, we won't on this side of eternity, and it comes across as arrogant and insulting when we do. For someone in the midst of a difficult situation, the best approaches are pastoral, not philosophical.

When a person is ready and willing to explore a thoughtful response to the dilemma with you, we recommend looking at the way every worldview answers (or fails to answer) the question.

Three Options

We must be clear that the problem of evil is not just a Christian problem, but perhaps the toughest subject with which all philosophies and religions must wrestle. How to reconcile the concept of evil and God has baffled man for centuries. The problem has often been described in a manner similar to this argument:

1. An all-powerful God *could* prevent or stop evil and human suffering.
2. An all-good God *would want to* prevent or stop evil and human suffering.
3. But our experience shows that evil and human suffering still exist.
4. Therefore…

An examination of this problem reveals three major approaches to this quandary: evil exists and God doesn't (atheism); God exists and evil doesn't (pantheism); or somehow they both exist (theism) but there is an explanation. These explanations for how God and evil can both exist either shrink or excuse God: God exists, but is not all-powerful (finitism or dualism); God exists, but is not all-good (evil God or fatalism); or God is all-powerful and all-good, and has a justifiable reason for allowing evil (Christian theism among others).

First Option: Evil Exists And God Doesn't

The atheist solves the problem by eliminating God. Evil and suffering are taken as givens, but the existence of God is not. Prominent thinkers throughout the centuries such as Epicurius, David Hume, H.G. Wells, Bertrand Russell, and Daniel Dennett have concluded, on the basis of their observations of suffering and evil, that an all-good and all-powerful God probably does not exist. Because of the prevalence of evil in the world, they resolved the classic argument like this: **(4) Therefore, an all-good, all-**

"Natural" evil often refers to suffering inflicted on innocent parties by natural phenomena, such as hurricanes, tsunamis, earthquakes, plagues, and other diseases and disasters. "Moral" evil usually refers to the harmful actions and consequences of people. The innocent suffer because of man's hatred (e.g., war), because of his overindulgence (e.g., the drunk driver who kills an innocent family), and because of his greed (e.g., many starving to death while others hoard surpluses).

It may be helpful to make two observations in this discussion.

- The lines between natural and moral evil are blurring - many diseases and natural disasters can be traced to human activity.

- Most people have experienced far greater pain as a result of moral evil than natural evil. How do we account for the presence of both classes of evil, and is there a reasonable response to the plight they present?

"There is, unfortunately, no guarantee that a plausible response to the theoretical problem of evil will prove practically helpful. Indeed, when in the throes of sorrow, silence is often far more appropriate or fitting than words. But while silence sometimes suits us better than words, many if not most of us are all too aware that the theoretical problem will abide silence for only so long before it once again raises its voice and demands our attention. Hence, it must be dealt with in its own time and place."

–Stewart Goetz, "The Argument from Evil," *Natural Theology*, 2009.

"If a good God made the world why has it gone wrong? And for many years I simply refused to listen to the Christian answers to this question because I kept on feeling whatever you say, and however clever your arguments are, isn't it much simpler and easier to say that the world was not made by any intelligent power? Aren't all your arguments simply a complicated attempt to avoid the obvious?' But then that threw me back into another difficulty. My argument against God was that the universe seemed so cruel and unjust. But how had I got this idea of just and unjust? A man does not call a line crooked unless he has some idea of a straight line. What was I comparing this universe with when I called it unjust? If the whole show was bad and senseless from A to Z, so to speak, why did I, who was supposed to be part of the show, find myself in such violent reaction against it? A man feels wet when he falls into water, because man is not a water animal: a fish would not feel wet. Of course I could have given up my idea of justice by saying it was nothing but a private idea of my own. But if I did that, then my argument against God collapsed too–for the argument depended on saying that the world was really unjust, not simply that it did not happen to please my fancies. Thus in the very act of trying to prove that God did not exist–in other words, that the whole of reality was senseless–I found I was forced to assume that one part of reality–namely my idea of justice–was full of sense. Consequently atheism turns out to be too simple."

–Lewis, *Mere Christianity*, 1952.

powerful God is impossible or at least unlikely.

The false assumption made is that the existence of an all-good, all-powerful God is incompatible with the current level of suffering in the world. On the contrary, if there is an all-good, all-powerful God, then the resolution could be stated another way: **(4) Therefore, there was a purpose for allowing evil and evil will be destroyed one day.** Read the last three chapters of Revelation for a description of how God plans to do just that. For a further exploration on the Bible's position on the causation and cessation of evil, see the Biblical Theism section later in this chapter.

The key observation to make in this section is to notice what happens when God is eliminated. At first, it seems as if the emotional tension has been resolved. "Where was God when _____ happened?" Or, "How could God have allowed _____?" These are followed by "Well, I guess he isn't there. Problem solved." But it has been replaced by a new problem. If there is no God, then there is no objective "right & wrong" and there is no basis for complaint. If there is no God, then the universal sense of "that's not the way it is supposed to be" is meaningless.

Given these observations, it becomes clear that the atheistic position on the problem of evil offers neither comfort for the present nor hope for the future. There is no meaning or justification for suffering, there will be no justice for those who cause it, and there is no meaningful hope that the situation will ever improve. While our world has made breathtaking advancements in science and technology, our track record on morality provides little evidence for optimism.

Although we are specifically dealing with the problem of evil, it is critical that we re-examine the evidence for God as a whole. A current tactic used against theism is to graphically highlight examples of apparently gratuitous suffering, considering that argument sufficient for dismissing the existence of God. But it isn't proper to isolate this issue as the only relevant argument for or against the evidence of God.

The discussion about evil must be weighed in context with evidence from the universe, the origin of life, and the source of morality (See Question 1).

Second Option: God Exists And Evil Doesn't

The pantheist argues that evil cannot be real if his view of God (God is all and all is God) is correct. They resolve the argument with **(4) Therefore our experience of evil is an illusion.** The teachings of Vedanta Hinduism express evil as only a passing appearance, an illusion. There is only one reality, and that reality is good, regardless of how we perceive it. The illusion of evil is like thinking a coiled rope is a snake until one is close enough to see that it's only a rope. In America, the best known proponent of evil as an illusion is Christian Science.

There are two major objections to this alternative:

To accept it, we must deny our own senses and consistent personal experiences. All around us we see suffering resulting from evil. Man's inhumanity to man is apparent as we observe hatred, murders, robbery, famines, wars, etc. If we deny these, on what grounds can we verify the pantheist's position? If we can't trust our senses and experience about evil, how can we know that our senses and experience are not deceiving us when we accept pantheism as a whole? Furthermore, if all true reality is God, then from where do these deceitful sensory experiences originate?

For the majority of pantheists, the difficulties compound with reincarnation. According to the principles of karma, any suffering incurred is payback for wrongs committed in this life or a prior one. So on one level, suffering is an illusion we must see beyond, but at the same time, my suffering is my fault. Worse, the suffering of "the innocent child" is her fault. For a fuller response to the issue of reincarnation, see the appendix to Question 9.

Finally, we should be clear that pantheism directly contradicts the statements of Christ and the Bible (Judges 2:11-15; Psalms 5:4-5; 51:2-5; Micah 3:1-3; Matthew 23:13-36; Galatians 5:19-26). For a closer look at the trustworthiness of Christ and the Bible, see Questions 2, 4, and 6.

The second option is invalid because it violates our own personal experiences and reason, and it goes contrary to the testimony of Christ and the Bible. When pantheism is no longer seen as a viable or desirable option, we can move on the theistic options.

Third Option: God And Evil Both Exist

We have four choices here. The first choice is finitism—evil is greater than God. The second choice is dualism—God and evil are co-eternal opposites. The third choice is an evil God—God himself is the source of evil and suffering. The fourth choice is Biblical theism—God is greater than

---

The **atheist's** line of reasoning:

(1) If God were all-powerful, he would destroy evil.

(2) Evil is not destroyed.

(3) Therefore, an all-good, all-powerful God is impossible or at least unlikely.

The **pantheist's** line of reasoning:

(1) God is everything.

(2) God is good.

(3) Evil still seems to exist.

(4) Therefore, our experience of evil is an illusion.

evil and will one day defeat it.

Non-biblical Theisms

Finitism. Philosophers such as Edgar S. Brightman and Peter Bertocci attempt to deal with the dilemma of God and evil by proposing a God who is finite in his powers and is thus unable to control or stop evil. God wants to aid us in our suffering, but he is not all-powerful and therefore he is helpless. When we look closely at this approach, we discover several pitfalls.

First, the finitist makes the same false assumption that the atheist makes. Both conjecture that God is incapable of defeating evil because he has not done it yet. Finitism fails to consider that God's timing is not human timing. The fact that God has not defeated evil today does not eliminate his ability to do it later.

Second, there could never be any hope of a solution. The finitist assumes that if man will join the conflict against evil and come to God's aid, man and God will ultimately win in the cause of good. But this assumption has no basis, for if a finite God cannot overcome evil, there is certainly no assurance that man's participation on the side of good will be the crowning blow that defeats evil.

Finitism directly contradicts the Bible's description of both the character of God and how he intends to deal with evil. Fifty-six times the bible declares that God is almighty (e.g., Revelation 19:6, a reference to his omnipotence). The Bible also predicts that God will ultimately defeat evil (Revelation 21-22). Refer back to Question 4 for a discussion on the trustworthiness of the Bible.

Dualism. Dualism assumes that God and evil are co-eternal opposites. This view is similar to finitism because it rescues the goodness of God at the expense of his omnipotence. But dualism holds God to be equal with evil rather than less than evil. Although there are variations of this position from ancient Greek and Zoroastrian theology to the process theology of the last century, all who hold this view build it on the following premises.

The first premise for co-eternality states that nothing can be the source of its opposite; light cannot be the source of darkness, or vice versa. The second premise states that evil is a thing, and if God were the only eternal source of all things, then he would be the cause of evil. Therefore, God and evil must exist together for all eternity or else God would be responsible for evil.

Both of these presuppositions are false. There are three problems with the first premise. First, it is possible for evil to occur out of good. This would not occur intrinsically but incidentally. A man may kill a dog while backing out of his driveway. There is nothing intrinsically evil about backing an

---

The **finitist's** line of reasoning:

(1) God exists.

(2) If God were all-powerful, he would destroy evil.

(3) Evil is not destroyed.

(4) Therefore God is not all-powerful.

The **dualist's** line of reasoning:

(1) God exists.

(2) Nothing can be the source of its opposite

(3) Evil exists, and if God were the only eternal source of all things, then he would be the cause of evil.

(4) Therefore God and evil are co-eternal opposites.

automobile out of a driveway, but accidentally the animal is slain. Second, just because we have opposites, this does not mean that we have a first-cause opposite for each. For instance, take the concepts of fat and thin. They are opposites, but this doesn't necessitate an eternal fat as opposed to an eternal thin. Third, the concept of two ultimate forces that are in eternal opposition, each having the same amount of power, is not logical. Philosophers have presented this dilemma in terms of an absolute irresistible force coming in conflict with an absolute immovable object. If the force cannot move the object, it is no longer irresistible. If the object can be moved, it is no longer immovable. Either evil is greater than God, or God is greater than evil. It is logically absurd to have them as absolute coequals in eternal opposition.

We can prove the second premise false by demonstrating that evil is not a thing. Evil does not have an existence of its own; it is a corruption of that which already exists. We generally think of evil in negative terms—e.g., *un*sanitary, *un*healthy, *un*reliable, *un*civilized, *in*curable, etc. All these terms present evil as a negation of good.

St. Augustine and St. Thomas Aquinas both struggled with the identity of evil. They concluded that evil is real but not a substance in and of itself, because everything created by God is good. Evil, then, is an absence or privation of something good. Blindness was used as an example of the privation of sight. Aquinas noted that a thing is called evil for lacking a perfection it ought to have; the lack of sight is evil in a man but not in a stone.

There is no such thing as a perfect state of rottenness.

Evil does not exist by itself, because it does not exist apart from good. For example, rot can exist in a tree only as long as the tree exists. There is no such thing as a perfect state of rottenness. A rusting car and a decaying carcass illustrate the same point. Evil exists as a corruption of some good thing; it is a privation and does not have essence by itself.

 **Key Illustration:** Rot, Rust

Dualism directly contradicts the Bible's affirmation of God's omnipotence and sovereignty, and its authors never recognize co-eternal opposites in the universe. Moses describes the one sovereign God in Deuteronomy 4:35, and the Prophet Isaiah echoes this (Isaiah 45:5). Christ himself discusses the defeat of Satan in Luke 10:17-19. Scripture not only accounts for one sovereign, almighty God, but also validates the statement that evil is a privation and not a thing in and of itself. Paul tells us in Colossians 1:16 that God created all things, and 1 Timothy 4:4 says that all things created were good.

Evil God. This position says that God is all-powerful, but he is sadistic and, therefore, not all-good. There are no serious proponents of this view, for carried to its logical conclusion, it leads to atheism. Both the cruel-God view and the atheistic view reject the notion of a good God and hold to the reality of evil. The former attributes the evil to God whereas the atheist

In this chapter we describe the classic biblical approach to the origin of both personal and natural evil, that is, Adam & Eve's sin brought disastrous consequences upon themselves and to all of creation.

Over the past century or so, as many in the church have adopted a view of creation where the earth and countless living creatures existed long before Adam arrived and sinned, theologians have wrestled with whether or how to attribute natural disasters to these actions. While no broad consensus has been reached, here are four of the leading candidates:

1. Direct Attribution: For many pastors and theologians, the theological dependency of natural evil on Adam's sin trumps all other considerations. This can be a major reason to remain committed to a young-earth model of origins.

2. Satan: Many theologians and thinkers have tied the origin of natural evil to the sin of Satan. The Bible isn't clear on the timing of Satan's fall, sometime before Adam shows up, providing a possible way to link natural evil to a personal choice. C. S. Lewis pursued this idea in *The Problem of Pain*, and Greg Boyd has recently explored it in *Satan and the Problem of Evil*.

3. Retroactive effect: In his 2009 book, *The End of Christianity*, William Dembski recognizes that an omnipotent God is not bound by time and could have retroactively applied the consequences of the fall to creation, or rather, he could have responded *in advance* to Adam's sin.

4. Natural consequence of creative process: Some theologians and thinkers have theorized that much of what we label "natural evil" is simply a by-product of the world necessary for the development and sustainability of life. Plate tectonics are responsible for earthquakes, tsunamis, and the existence of continents. The same forces that killed many thousands created a habitable world for billions of people. Great storms bring destruction and replenish the land with water and nitrogen. For some, the same mechanism responsible for horrible birth defects, DNA mutation, is the natural process that God used to bring all creatures into existence. Most of these writers would argue that the declarations in Genesis 1 of the "goodness" of creation do not imply that the earth was free of decay, disorder, destructive forces, or non-human death. Rather, God used these patterns to bring into existence this world where we live and can choose to worship him.

** Proponents of 2 & 3, and those of 4 who retain a literal Adam & Eve, can make the observation that God's initial interaction with them took place in a garden, perhaps segregated from the rest of the world which had been affected by chaos. Only after they sin and get expelled from the garden do they personally encounter the effects of a fallen world.

simply admits the existence of evil. The cruel-God position usually has been espoused by atheists writing satirically about theism.

Biblical Theism.

The Bible stipulates that there is an all-good (Habakkuk 1:13), all-powerful (Revelation 4:8) God, who recognizes the reality of evil (Romans 1:18-32), and will one day end evil and restore peace (Revelation 21:3-4). When the critic examines biblical theism, he poses two difficult questions: (1) Why did an all-good, all-powerful God allow evil? (2) Why hasn't God put an end to evil?

Causation. The first question is one of causation. Why did God allow evil to occur in the first place? In answering this question, it is important to determine the point in time when evil entered history. This requires a summary of the biblical account of the origin of evil:

God created the universe without evil and suffering. He also created man perfect, with the ability to freely love or reject the God who created him (Genesis 1). Scripture says throughout that God desires to have loving fellowship with man (2 Chronicles 16:9; Jeremiah 29:11; John 4:23; 1 Peter 3:18). But the ability to reject as well as accept is essential to any relationship. God did not force his love on man but gave him the privilege of a choice.

The magnitude of any choice is determined by the size of the consequences. Choosing between Coke and Pepsi is not a major choice in life, but choosing between apples and arsenic is. The consequences of accepting or rejecting God make this the choice of supreme importance. God told man that if he chose to embrace him, their fellowship and blessings could continue. To spurn God and his commandments, however, would bring separation from him (spiritual death) and physical death as well (Genesis 2). Genesis 3 tells us that man chose to go his own way rather than follow God's. Man thus suffered the consequences of spiritual and physical death. It was at this point that evil and suffering entered the world. Theologians call this choice and its attendant consequences "the Fall," when humankind fell away from God.

So we see that God did not create nor is he responsible for evil and sin. God's plan had the potential for evil when he gave man freedom of choice, but the actual origin of evil came as a result of man who directed his will away from God and toward his own selfish desires. Evil, remember, is not a thing, but a corruption of a good thing already created by God. God told man what to do, but man corrupted himself by choosing to disobey God. God's way is the perfect way and anything less than complete obedience to his instructions will bring problems into the process. God is not to blame for man's disobedience; man is the moral agent who is responsible.

Suppose, for example, a man purchases a lawn tractor. The dealer delivers the tractor and provides ample instructions as well as an extensive operations manual. As soon as the dealer leaves, the new owner throws away the manual and ignores the instructions. He drives out into his backyard and begins to randomly press buttons and pull levers until the lawn mower begins smoking and the engine shuts down. The potential for misuse of the equipment was always there, but the manufacturer had given specific instructions on how to use it properly and had warned of the consequences of misuse. Whose fault is it that the machine broke down? Man ignored the instructions for the tractor. God's creation had the potential for evil, but God did not promote it in any way. It only came about when man chose to ignore God's instructions and warning.

Key Illustration: Operations Manual

Because of the Fall, mankind became imperfect. This state of imperfection yielded temporal and eternal consequences.

The temporal consequences encompass both moral and natural evil. Moral evil is caused by man's inhumanity to man. Man in his fallen nature often seeks to promote himself at the expense of others. The suffering of innocent people is part of the insidiousness of evil. If only the wicked suffered, we would call that justice; but because there are innocent victims, there is a problem of injustice.

It is easy to associate moral evil with the fall of man, but how does the theist relate natural evil to the Fall? This occurs when the innocent are afflicted by natural phenomena such as typhoons and tornadoes. The Bible tells us that man's fall included not only a curse on him but also a curse on the creation around him (see Genesis 3:14-19; Romans 8:18-23; Revelation 22:3). We live today in a disease-death environment. God did not originally design it this way; it has changed as a result of man's sin. This is an abnormal state which God will rectify when sin is removed (see Revelation 21:3-4; 22:3). Eden saw no natural disasters or death until after the sin of man, and there will be no natural disasters or death in the new heavens and earth when

God puts an end to evil.

The temporal consequences are harsh, but the eternal consequences are even more grave, for they involve our relationship with God. When man ceased to follow the perfect way of God, he was no longer a perfect being (Romans 3:23; Isaiah 53:6; 59:2). The justice of God demanded that a penalty be paid for man's disobedience. The judgment for sin is eternal separation from the holy God (Romans 6:23). This separation is defined by God as a confinement in hell forever (Matthew 25:46; Revelation 20:14-15). See the appendix at the end of this chapter for a discussion of three other issues that relate to this question (the fall of angels and men, the justice of hell, and the alternatives available to God when he created man).

Thus, human choice caused evil to enter our world and wrought temporal and eternal consequences upon mankind and his environment. Now we must turn to God's solution to man's problem of sin.

Two attributes of God's character must be kept in balance to understand how God resolves the dilemma. God's justice demands death as the penalty for the rejection of his command, and God's love seeks a solution to man's terminal condition. God cannot change the penalty because it is just, and it is in keeping with his character. But, out of his great love for his creation, he paid the penalty for man. God substituted himself and made possible man's redemption from sin.

Key Illustration: Tibetan Ruler ▷

A story is told of a Tibetan ruler who once declared that anyone caught stealing would lose his hand to the ax. Throughout the kingdom, as violators were discovered, each was brought to the king and summarily lost his hand. One day guards brought an old woman before him, and when he asked her whether or not she had stolen the item, she responded affirmatively. He turned to her and said, "You have been found guilty as charged, and the penalty is the loss of a hand. I cannot change the verdict even though you are my mother, but my love for you is great, *and* I am willing to pay the price for you." And with that, he laid his hand on the chopping block and had it severed from his arm. His only choice was to substitute himself for one he *loved*. The woman was guilty and the penalty had to be paid. Had he excused her without payment he would have no longer been a just king.

Through substitution, God can satisfy both demands of his character. God is a righteous judge, and he cannot change his verdict on man's rebellion. What he did do, though, was offer to pay the penalty for us. Now the choice is up to us; we can pay the penalty ourselves, or accept the payment of our heavenly Father. The penalty *will* be paid. The only question is, who will pay it?

God has still left us with the ability to accept or reject him and his payment. As before, each choice has a consequence. If we accept God's

It can be helpful to consider what God would have to do in our present environment to eliminate the painful consequences of human choices. Every time an act of violence is attempted, God would have to make the weapons harmless. Bullets would turn to mush, clubs and knives would become soft, and so forth. If someone driving on a mountain road loses control on a turn, God would have to intervene, perhaps by lifting the car on a gust of wind and gently putting it back on the road. In effect, our lives would have to be cushioned by hundreds of miracles to protect us from the consequences of our actions.

payment, we enter into a personal relationship with Christ, we are restored to fellowship, and we are guaranteed eternal life. If we reject God's offer, we will spend eternity in separation from God.

Make sure you take the opportunity to make the Gospel clear at this point. For further help, refer to Question 11.

We have established the cause of evil to be the disobedient choice of man, but there is still an unattended problem. Even if God didn't cause evil, why hasn't he stopped it?

Cessation. The first question was one of *causation*, and the second question is one of *cessation*. "Why hasn't God stopped evil if he can?" Most people want God to wipe out all evil that affects them, but they want to set the conditions for God's eradication process. They would like to see God eliminate the cruel world leaders, murderers, and thieves, along with the natural disasters and diseases that afflict the world. But God is not interested in a partial containment of evil. He promised that he will someday permanently put an end to evil. To do this, he must not only move against actual evil but also potential evil.

Let's imagine that God stopped all evil at 12 o'clock. How many people would be left at 12:01? God showed us with Noah and the Flood that if he removes actual evil and leaves potential evil behind, actual evil eventually returns. Even though God hasn't done it yet, we have God's promise that he will put an end to evil and suffering in the future (2 Peter 3:7-12; Revelation 19:1-2, 11-21; 20:7-15; 21:4-8).

Key Illustration: 12 o'clock Deadline

The Bible tells us that the world today is in an abnormal state. God did not begin creation with evil and suffering, and he will one day eliminate evil and suffering from his creation. The question should not be, "Will God stop evil?" but, "When will he stop evil?"

Peter gives us a glimpse of why God is so patient. The early church suffered many persecutions and the Christians clung to the promise of Christ's return. They knew that suffering and pain would then end. Knowing this, they questioned Peter as to why it was taking Christ so long to come.

Peter answered, "The Lord is not slow about his promise, as some count slowness, but is patient toward you, not wishing for any to perish but for all to come to repentance" (2 Peter 3:9). By delaying his return, Christ is extending the opportunity for people to turn to him and thus escape eternal punishment. When Christ comes, there will be no more chances, for time will have run out. If a person has not accepted God's substitute before then, it will be too late.

It is imperative that we view temporal suffering in light of God's perspective. Believers are not in the land of the living going to the land of the dying. They are in the land of the dying going to the land of the living. One reason why God delays the return of Christ and allows temporal suffering to continue is to allow more people to hear about and accept Christ, and thereby escape eternal suffering. God could send Christ today and stop temporal suffering, but when he does all opportunity to know Christ as Savior goes with it. Pose this question to a friend who is concerned with why God allows suffering to continue: If God had sent Christ and eliminated all suffering the day before you had a chance to understand and accept Christ as Savior, where would you be now? God delays putting an end to evil in order to allow us more opportunities to share the Gospel of Christ with others.

Key Illustration: Minister & Barber

The following story illustrates how man refuses to see God's solution to evil:

A minister and a barber who boasted of being an atheist walked one day through a disreputable part of the city. As they looked around, the barber said, "This is why I can't believe in a God of love. If he is as kind as they say, why does he permit all this poverty, disease, and squalor? How can he allow all this drug-dealing and vandalism?"

The minister said nothing until they came across an unkempt and filthy man with hair down his back and a half inch of stubble on his face. Then he said to the atheist, "You can't be a very good barber or you wouldn't let people like this live around here without a haircut and a shave."

Indignantly, the barber answered, "Why blame me for that man's condition? I can't help it if he's like that. He's never given me a chance! If he would only come to my shop, I could fix him up and make him look like a gentleman!"

With a penetrating look, the minister said, "Then don't blame God for allowing people to continue in their selfish ways. He constantly invites them to come to him and be changed. The reason they are slaves to sin and evil habits is because they refuse to accept the One who died to save and deliver them."

God is greater than evil, and he will indeed put an end to evil and suffering. Christ defeated evil through his work on the cross (1 Corinthians 15:54-57) and will finalize that defeat by confining evil in hell forever.

Was God the cause of evil? No! Man in his rebellion against God caused evil to enter this world. Why doesn't God stop evil now? He allows temporal evil to continue so that more may come to know him. God did not create this world as the best of all possible worlds, but as *the best possible way to attain the best possible world*. At great personal sacrifice to himself, God has counted and underwritten the cost of redeeming his creation. The story of the boy and his sailboat gives a clear picture of the sacrifice made by God for his creation:

The young boy used to play for hours by the lake with the sailboat he had carefully made. One day, a strong wind blew his boat away and he was heartbroken. Several weeks later when he passed a hobby shop, he noticed his sailboat in the window. He rushed inside and told the store-keeper that the sailboat in the window was his. The store-keeper replied, "That boat belongs to me now, and if you want it, you will have to buy it."

For six weeks the boy worked every job he could find and finally saved enough for the boat. Finally when he bought it, he walked out of the shop and said to his little boat, "I made you and I have bought you; you are now twice mine."

Summary

We have three possible solutions to the dilemma of the coexistence of God and evil. The first affirms the existence of evil but denies the existence of God. The major objection to this first option is that it denies God's existence, thereby rendering both suffering and the moral wrong-doing that it inflicted as ultimately meaningless. The position provides meaningless hope for improvement or justice, and proves emotionally and intellectually unsatisfying. We referred to Question 1 for a more detailed analysis of why atheism is untenable.

The second solution says that God exists but evil doesn't. If we think of evil as an illusion, we have to reject our own personal experience. This position also requires a rejection of Christ and the Bible. Since overwhelming evidence demonstrates the existence of evil, the second option is untenable.

The third possible solution allows for the existence of both God and evil. This leads to three more choices:

Evil is more powerful than God. This rests on the assumption that God is unable to end evil because he has failed to do so thus far. This is a false assumption, and the position as a whole is contradictory to scripture.

God and evil are co-eternal and coequal. Perceiving evil as a privation rather than a thing helps dispel this viewpoint. Not only is this choice erected on faulty logic but it also contradicts scripture. The reliability of scripture has been substantiated in Question 4.

God is greater than evil. We must ask two major questions here. First, "Why did God allow evil to begin with?" Second, "Why does God allow evil to continue?" Evil and suffering entered the world as a result of man's disobedience to God. God desired a loving relationship with man. Though created perfect, man could accept or reject God. He chose to reject God, and the consequences of this sin were both temporal and eternal. The temporal consequences included both moral and natural evil. The eternal consequences demanded that he be eternally separated from God. God's solution to man's problem was to substitute himself for man on the cross,

If there is no God, then there is ultimately nothing wrong with the world.

but each person must still make the choice of accepting or rejecting God's free offer of salvation.

Even though man's rebellion against God brought about evil, we still have to find out why God, who has the power, has not yet stopped evil. God allows temporal suffering to continue so that more can accept Christ and escape eternal suffering. The promise we have from God is that he will ultimately defeat evil and confine it in hell. This third choice not only explains evil, but provides hope for the future.

Appendix On The Fall, Hell, And God's Alternatives

In this question, there are three side issues that may need to be considered when exploring God's solution to man's problem. The three issues are: the fall of Satan, the justice of hell, and the alternatives available to God when he created man. We survey these topics in case they should ever come up in a discussion, but we should never raise more questions than a person asks.

The fall of angels and men. The original appearance of evil in the creation of God came through the choice of Satan. Satan and the other angels were spirit-beings whom God had created before the story in Genesis 3, but beyond that, the Bible doesn't say. They were created with the capacity of choosing whether or not to serve and love God. After a period of time, Satan and a group of other angels acted in willful disobedience. They chose to serve and love themselves rather than God. The angels who went with Satan are known today as fallen angels or demons. Many of the angels did not follow Satan but chose to continue following God; these angels still love and serve God today. Our conclusions about man's ability to choose also apply to the angels' choice. God allowed the potential for evil, but this did not make him the producer of evil. The introduction of evil came as a result of a willful choice to disobey God. Most of what we know of this interaction is taken from Isaiah 14 and Ezekiel 28.

Some time after the fall of Satan, God created man as a responsible moral agent. The tempter manifested himself in the Garden of Eden, and it was not long before the parents of the human race succumbed by pursuing their own course instead of God's. Man's fellowship with God was broken and thus evil and suffering entered our world. The major distinction between the fall of man and the fall of the angels is that all the angels ever in existence were alive when Satan disobeyed. But when man fell, there were only two humans in existence. Their imperfection was passed down as a result of their sin, and the whole human race was in need of salvation.

Someone once illustrated this problem by starting to button his shirt with the first button in the second hole. After that, all of the other buttons went into wrong holes as well. The story of Adam's fall became our story as well; sin is highly contagious. There is not only a social heredity but also a spiritual heredity of sin.

The justice of hell. Many people question the love of God because of the biblical concept of hell. Some would rather have God solve man's problem of separation by either allowing everyone into heaven (universalism) or by annihilating the wicked. Both alternatives stand in contrast to the testimony of Christ and the Bible. In his Sermon on the Mount, Christ described some attitudes that could send people to hell (Matthew 5:22). Later he explained that hell is a place of weeping and gnashing of teeth (Matthew 8:12; 25:30) as well as a place of eternal fire (Matthew 25:41) and punishment (Matthew 25:46). The Apostle Paul declared that the penalty for sin is eternal separation from God (Romans 6:23). The concept of universalism is a violation of man's free choice. Hell is the consequence of man's rebellion against God. As we have said before, if you remove the consequences of a choice you no longer have a choice. If God brought everyone to heaven, he would do so against the wishes of many. C.S. Lewis once observed that there is a real sense in which the doors of hell are locked from the inside. While no one wants to be there, they will be there by their own choice. By rebelling against the will of God and rejecting his costly provision of salvation, they will continue forever in their rebellion and separation from God. If all people end up in heaven, there is no real consequence to sin and we don't really have free choice.

Which is the greater evidence of love: to let evil and suffering continue its ravages or to ultimately confine it? Evil must be contained, and hell is the place where God contains it. Suppose a group of terrorists walked into your home and killed your family. If they were apprehended by the police, would you consider it appropriate for the police to let them go or would you want the terrorists confined so they could kill no more? Obviously the more loving and just thing to do would be to contain the evil. Hell is required if justice and peace are to be restored in the kingdom of God.

To maintain a good garden, a gardener must periodically hoe out the weeds and carry them away. If he fails to preserve the garden in this way, it will soon be overrun by the weeds, and the garden will no longer exist. In the same way, if God does not remove the unrighteous, there will be no godly creation.

This separation from God is the just consequence of man's rebellion against God. Hell not only displays the justice of God, but it also displays his love. God's love is expressed best in his solution to the problem of hell, the giving of himself as a substitute for man's penalty. But God did not force his love on man—he gave us a choice. No real exchange of love could take place between God and man without choice, for man would just be a robot. When the unbeliever chooses not to accept God's payment for his sin, God says, "My love for you recognizes your choice to be separated from Me, and thus I give you a place to exist in rebellion for all eternity." To the believer God says, "I love you so much that I will contain evil in hell forever so that peace and harmony can be restored to creation."

God does not send man to hell. Man sends himself by rejecting God's offer of salvation and restoration. Christ claimed he came not to send us but to save us from hell, if we would only believe (John 3:17).

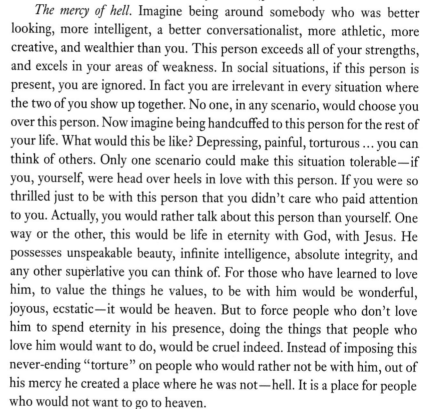

Key Illustration: Another Look at Hell

The mercy of hell. Imagine being around somebody who was better looking, more intelligent, a better conversationalist, more athletic, more creative, and wealthier than you. This person exceeds all of your strengths, and excels in your areas of weakness. In social situations, if this person is present, you are ignored. In fact you are irrelevant in every situation where the two of you show up together. No one, in any scenario, would choose you over this person. Now imagine being handcuffed to this person for the rest of your life. What would this be like? Depressing, painful, torturous … you can think of others. Only one scenario could make this situation tolerable—if you, yourself, were head over heels in love with this person. If you were so thrilled just to be with this person that you didn't care who paid attention to you. Actually, you would rather talk about this person than yourself. One way or the other, this would be life in eternity with God, with Jesus. He possesses unspeakable beauty, infinite intelligence, absolute integrity, and any other superlative you can think of. For those who have learned to love him, to value the things he values, to be with him would be wonderful, joyous, ecstatic—it would be heaven. But to force people who don't love him to spend eternity in his presence, doing the things that people who love him would want to do, would be cruel indeed. Instead of imposing this never-ending "torture" on people who would rather not be with him, out of his mercy he created a place where he was not—hell. It is a place for people who would not want to go to heaven.

Other options available to God. Since God knows everything, he knew that man would turn from him. So why didn't he design his creation differently? Did God have any other options?

God could have chosen not to create man at all. But God is worthy of all blessing, honor, glory, and dominion (Revelation 5:13), and it seems natural that his plan would allow for him to display and receive glory. He is a loving God who desires to be loved back. In his omniscience, God knew that the best way to reveal his glory was to redeem a corrupt and wicked creation and make all things new.

God could have created man perfect and without choice. But without responsible choice there is no capacity for love. Man would be a robot.

Imagine getting up in the morning and finding yourself married to a robot. It could only respond in the way it was programmed. When you switch it on, it marches around saying, "I love you, I love you, I love you." No one would desire that kind of atmosphere for long. There would be no real communication, love, or response. The beauty of a loving relationship is that people love one another because of their own desire, and not because they are forced into it.

In analyzing God's options, we must remember that only God is omniscient, omnipotent, and all-good. Understanding this, we know that the option he chose was the best of all options for attaining his goals. But this does not mean that we are now in the best of all possible worlds. The best of all possible worlds is yet to come. There, man will have freedom, including a freedom not to sin. God says that the world in which we live is the best possible way for us to obtain the best of all possible worlds. God's plan will bring the greatest good but not without costing God a great deal. Not only does he suffer as a result of his creatures' disobedience, but he also paid an unfathomable price, the cross, so that he could redeem sinful men and women.

Supplemental Reading

C.S. Lewis, *The Problem of Pain*. HarperOne, 2009 Lewis offers rich insights on this subject and this book is worth several readings.

John W. Wenham, *The Goodness of God*. InterVarsity Press, 1974. An extensive treatment that draws principles from God's actions in the Old Testament. Wenham attacks the problem head-on and does not settle for simplistic answers.

Dembski, William. *The End of Christianity: Finding a Good God in an Evil World*. B&H Academic, 2009.

Alcorn, Randy. *If God Is Good: Faith in the Midst of Suffering and Evil*. Multnomah Books, 2009.

Study Guide for Q5: Does God Make Sense in a World Full of Suffering?

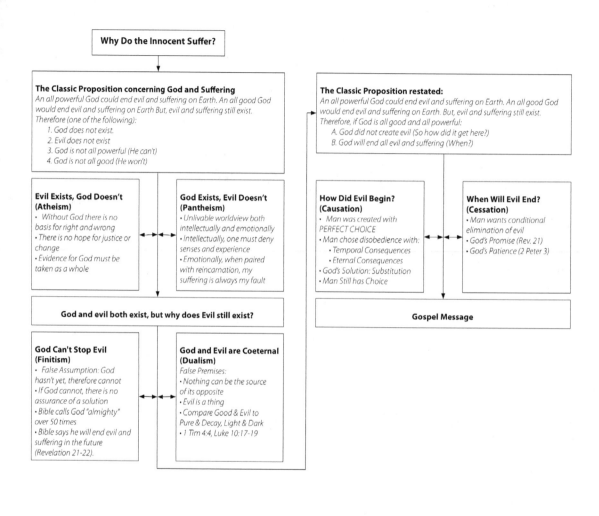

Why Do the Innocent Suffer?

The Classic Proposition concerning God and Suffering
An all powerful God could end evil and suffering on Earth. An all good God would end evil and suffering on Earth But, evil and suffering still exist. Therefore (one of the following):
1. God does not exist.
2. Evil does not exist
3. God is not all powerful (He can't)
4. God is not all good (He won't)

Evil Exists, God Doesn't (Atheism)
• *Without God there is no basis for right and wrong*
• *There is no hope for justice or change*
• *Evidence for God must be taken as a whole*

God Exists, Evil Doesn't (Pantheism)
• *Unlivable worldview both intellectually and emotionally*
• *Intellectually, one must deny senses and experience*
• *Emotionally, when paired with reincarnation, my suffering is always my fault*

God and evil both exist, but why does Evil still exist?

God Can't Stop Evil (Finitism)
• *False Assumption: God hasn't yet, therefore cannot*
• *If God cannot, there is no assurance of a solution*
• *Bible calls God "almighty" over 50 times*
• *Bible says he will end evil and suffering in the future (Revelation 21-22).*

God and Evil are Coeternal (Dualism)
False Premises:
• *Nothing can be the source of its opposite*
• *Evil is a thing*
• *Compare Good & Evil to Pure & Decay, Light & Dark*
• *1 Tim 4:4, Luke 10:17-19*

The Classic Proposition restated:
An all powerful God could end evil and suffering on Earth. An all good God would end evil and suffering on Earth. But, evil and suffering still exist. Therefore, if God is all good and all powerful:
A. God did not create evil (So how did it get here?)
B. God will end all evil and suffering (When?)

How Did Evil Begin? (Causation)
• *Man was created with PERFECT CHOICE*
• *Man chose disobedience with:*
  • *Temporal Consequences*
  • *Eternal Consequences*
• *God's Solution: Substitution*
• *Man Still has Choice*

When Will Evil End? (Cessation)
• *Man wants conditional elimination of evil*
• *God's Promise (Rev. 21)*
• *God's Patience (2 Peter 3)*

Gospel Message

Key Illustrations

Rot, Rust

Evil does not exist by itself, because it does not exist apart from good. For example, rot can exist in a tree only as long as the tree exists. There is no such thing as a perfect state of rottenness. A rusting car and a decaying carcass illustrate the same point. Evil exists as a corruption of some good thing; it is a privation and does not have essence by itself.

Operations Manual

Suppose, for example, a man purchases a lawn tractor. The dealer delivers the tractor and provides ample instructions as well as an extensive operations manual. As soon as the dealer leaves, the new owner throws away the manual and ignores the instructions. He drives out into his backyard and begins to randomly press buttons and pull levers until the lawn mower begins smoking and the engine shuts down. The potential for misuse of the equipment was always there, but the manufacturer had given specific instructions on how to use it properly and had warned of the consequences of misuse. Whose fault is it that the machine broke down? Man ignored the instructions for the tractor. God's creation had the potential for evil, but God did not promote it in any way. It only came about when man chose to ignore God's instructions and warning.

12 O'clock Deadline

Let's imagine that God stopped all evil at 12 o'clock. How many people would be left at 12:01? God showed us with Noah and the Flood that if he removes actual evil and leaves potential evil behind, actual evil eventually returns.

Minister & Barber

A minister and a barber who boasted of being an atheist walked one day through a disreputable part of the city. As they looked around, the barber said, "This is why I can't believe in a God of love. If he is as kind as they say, why does he permit all this poverty, disease, and squalor? How can he allow all this drug-dealing and vandalism?"

The minister said nothing until they came across an unkempt and filthy man with hair down his back and a half inch of stubble on his face. Then he said to the atheist, "You can't be a very good barber or you wouldn't let people like this live around here without a haircut and a shave."

Indignantly, the barber answered, "Why blame me for that man's condition? I can't help it if he's like that. He's never given me a chance! If he would only come to my shop, I could fix him up and make him look like a gentleman!"

With a penetrating look, the minister said, "Then don't blame God for allowing people to continue in their selfish ways. He constantly invites them to come to him and be changed. The reason they are slaves to sin and evil habits is because they refuse to accept the One who died to save and deliver them."

Key Verses

John 9:1-3 As Jesus was walking along, he saw a man who had been blind from birth. [2]"Teacher," his disciples asked him, "why was this man born blind? Was it a result of his own sins or those of his parents?" [3]"It was not because of his sins or his parents' sins," Jesus answered.

2 Peter 3:9 The Lord isn't really being slow about his promise to return, as some people think. No, he is being patient for your sake. He does not want anyone to perish, so he is giving more time for everyone to repent.

Revelation 21:1-8 Then I saw a new heaven and a new earth, for the old heaven and the old earth had disappeared. And the sea was also gone. [2]And I saw the holy city, the new Jerusalem, coming down from God out of heaven like a beautiful bride prepared for her husband.

[3]I heard a loud shout from the throne, saying, "Look, the home of God is now among his people! He will live with them, and they will be his people. God himself will be with them. [4]He will remove all of their sorrows, and there will be no more death or sorrow or crying or pain. For the old world and its evils are gone forever."

[5]And the one sitting on the throne said, "Look, I am making all things new!" And then he said to me, "Write this down, for what I tell you is trustworthy and true." [6]And he also said, "It is finished! I am the Alpha and the Omega–the Beginning and the End. To all who are thirsty I will give the springs of the water of life without charge! [7]All who are victorious will inherit all these blessings, and I will be their God, and they will be my children. [8]But cowards who turn away from me, and unbelievers, and the corrupt, and murderers, and the immoral, and those who practice witchcraft, and idol worshipers, and all liars–their doom is in the lake that burns with fire and sulfur. This is the second death."

Study Questions

1. Please state this question, "Why do the innocent suffer?" in its classical form to show that you understand the problem.

2. Give two responses to the statement, "God exists, evil doesn't."

3. What is the problem with defining evil as a "thing"?

4. Respond to this charge: "Since evil exists and God created this world, then God must be the cause of evil and suffering." (This question is one of causation.)

5. If God has the power and desire to stop evil and suffering, why hasn't he done so yet? (This question is one of cessation.)

6. What has God done to solve the problem of evil and suffering?

7. How does this affect life now? How will it affect the next life?

Notes

QUESTION 6: IS CHRIST THE ONLY WAY TO GOD?

Often-Asked Questions:

- Isn't Christianity too narrow?

- Since all religions are basically the same, does it matter what you believe?

- Isn't the choice of which religion you take just a matter of personal preference?

- An estimated 75 percent of the world population is not Christian—can they all be wrong?

- Christ can be the only way to God for you, but how can you claim that he is the only way for everybody?

Three Options

Tension mounts whenever there is a discussion regarding the exclusive claims of Jesus Christ. Since its beginning, orthodox Christianity has held that the only access to God is through Christ. At first glance this seems arrogant and intolerant. When we address the problem, we find three possible responses.

The first option *denies* that Christianity claims to be exclusive. Christianity is viewed as just one part of a grand mosaic that links God and man, and that any claims to exclusivity are misguided. The second option acknowledges Christianity's claim to exclusivity, but states that it is *wrong* to hold such a position. If Christ is the only way to God, a lot of sincere people will be excluded. The third option is that Christianity is exclusive and may be correct.

First Option: Christianity Is Not Exclusive

The first option portrays Christianity as a very broad and accepting religion that would eliminate no one who sincerely seeks God. Christianity, according to some people, is just one of an assortment of religions. They believe that within the matrix of religions there are some technical distinctions, but all the religions are, in essence, the same. It doesn't matter how you get to God as long as you get there.

This concept has been portrayed in a number of ways. Some people see the journey to God as one of a series of caravans (different religions) seeking the same destination (God) from different directions. Others have represented God as the hub of a wheel with the spokes of the wheel representing the major world religions. Man can get to God regardless of which spoke he chooses. Still others see God sitting on top of a mountain, and the paths that lead to the peak are the different religions available to man. Such a broad and accepting view of Christianity may sound appealing *but it is not based on the claims of Christ and his disciples.*

According to the Bible, the concept that everyone is lost without Christ originates with Christ himself. Consider these verses:

> "For God so loved the world, that he gave his only Son, that whoever believes in him should not perish but have eternal life. For God did not send his Son into the world to condemn the world, but in order that the world might be saved through him. ***Whoever believes in him is not condemned, but whoever does not believe is condemned already, because he has not believed in the name of the only Son of God*** (John 3:16-18).

I said therefore to you, that you shall die in your sins; for unless you believe that I am he, you shall die in your sins (John 8:24).

Jesus said to him, "I am the way, and the truth, and the life; no one comes to the Father, but through Me" (John 14:6).

Christ was unique among the founders of world religions. Some promoted their *teachings* as the only way to God, but Christ promoted *himself* as the only way to God. This claim was based on two premises: that Jesus was God's equal in a way that no other human in history could claim, and therefore, he was positioned to reconcile God and mankind as no other person or system could.

Christ claimed not only exclusivity but also deity. As the God-man, he boldly stated, "If you knew Me, you would know My Father also" (John 8:19). To know him was to know God. Later, Christ mentioned that all who had seen him had seen God: "He who has seen Me has seen the Father" (John 14:9).

Another means Christ used to claim that he was God was the important phrase, "I AM." For example, Jesus said, "Truly, truly, I say to you, before Abraham was born, I AM." (John 8:58). This was equivalent to claiming that he himself was YHWH (Yahweh). Exodus 3:14 reads, "God replied to Moses, 'I AM WHO I AM. This is what you are to say to the Israelites: I AM has sent me to you.'" By calling himself the I AM, Christ was at the same time claiming to be Jehovah God.

Christ supported his case for deity by ascribing to himself various attributes of God. He claimed eternality (John 17:5) and omnipresence (28:20). He also spoke of his sinlessness (John 8:46). His indirect claims included (1) his acceptance of worship by men (Matthew 14:33; John 9:35-39; 20:27-29); (2) his ability to forgive sins (Mark 2:5-11; and Luke 7:48-50); and (3) his claim that all men would face him in judgment (John 5:24-28).

Christ clearly claimed to be the only way and his apostles affirmed this in their writings. Here are three examples:

And there is salvation in no one else, for there is no other name under heaven that has been given among men, by which we must be saved (Acts 4:12).

For the wages of sin is death, but the free gift of God is eternal life in Christ Jesus our Lord (Romans 6:23).

But even though we, or an angel from heaven, should preach to you a Gospel contrary to that which we have preached to you, let him be accursed (Galatians 1:8).

The apostles recognized that Christ was God as well as the only way

---

"At the heart of every major religion is a leading exponent. As the exposition is studied, something very significant emerges. There comes a bifurcation, or a distinction, between the person and the teaching. Mohammed, to the Qur'an. Buddha, to the Noble Path. Krishna, to his philosophizing. Zoroaster, to his ethics.

Whatever we make of their claims, one reality is inescapable. They are all teachers who point to their teaching or show some particular way. In all of these, there emerges an instruction, a way of living. It is not Zoroaster to whom you turn. It is Zoroaster to whom you listen. It is not Buddha who delivers you; it is his Noble Truths which instruct you. It is not Mohammed who transforms you, it is the beauty of the Qur'an that woos you.

By contrast, Jesus did not only teach or expound his message. He was identical with his message... He did not just proclaim the truth. He said, 'I am the truth.' He did not just show a way. He said, 'I am the way.' He did not just open up vistas. He said, 'I am the door. I am the Good Shepherd. I am the resurrection and the life.'"

–Ravi Zacharias, *Jesus Among Other Gods*, 2002.

Who Was Jesus?

Did Jesus really claim to be the only way?
· John 3:18 - He who believes in him is not judged; he who does not believe has been judged already, because he has not believed in the name of the only begotten Son of God.
· John 8:24 - I said therefore to you, that you shall die in your sins; for unless you believe that I am he, you shall die in your sins.
· John 14:6 - Jesus said to him,"I am the way, and the truth, and the life; no one comes to the Father but through me."

Did Jesus really claim to be God?
· John 8:19 - "If you knew me, you would know My Father also."
· John 14:9 - "He who has seen me has seen the Father."
· John 10:30 - "I and the Father are one."
· Matthew 26:63-64 But Jesus remained silent. The high priest said to him,"I charge you under oath by the living God: Tell us if you are the Christ, the Son of God." 64"Yes, it is as you say," Jesus replied."But I say to all of you: In the future you will see the Son of Man sitting at the right hand of the Mighty One and coming on the clouds of heaven."

I AM statements
· Exodus 3:14 - And God said to Moses,"I AM WHO I AM"; and he said,"Thus you shall say to the sons of Israel,'I AM has sent me to you.'"
· John 8:58 - "Truly Truly, I say to you, before Abraham was born, I AM."
· John 8:24, 28; 18:5

His disciples knew that he claimed to be God and the only way to him:
· Thomas – John 20:28 - "Thomas said to him,'My Lord and my God!'"
· Peter – Acts 4:12 - And there is salvation in no one else, for there is no other name under heaven that has been given among men, by which we must be saved.
· John – John 1:13-14 - In the beginning was the Word, and the Word was with God, and the Word was God. 14The Word became flesh and made his dwelling among us. We have seen his glory, the glory of the One and Only, who came from the Father, full of grace and truth.
· Paul – Colossians 1:16-17 - For by him all things were created: things in heaven and on earth, visible and invisible, whether thrones or powers or rulers or authorities; all things were created by him and for him. 17He is before all things, and in him all things hold together.
· Paul – Titus 2:13-14 - While we wait for the blessed hope–the glorious appearing of our great God and Savior, Jesus Christ, 14who gave himself for us to redeem us from all wickedness and to purify for himself a people that are his very own, eager to do what is good.
· (Author of Hebrews) – Hebrews 1:8 - "But about the Son he says,"Your throne, O God, will last for ever and ever, and righteousness will be the scepter of your kingdom."
·John – 1 John 5:20 - "We know also that the Son of God has come and has given us understanding, so that we may know him who is true. And we are in him who is true–even in his Son Jesus Christ. He is the true God and eternal life."

Even his enemies knew that he claimed to be God!
· Matthew 26:65-66 - Then the high priest tore his clothes and said,"He has spoken blasphemy! Why do we need any more witnesses? Look, now you have heard the blasphemy. 66What do you think?" They answered, "He is worthy of death!"
· Mark 2:6-7 - Now some teachers of the law were sitting there, thinking to themselves, 7"Why does this fellow talk like that? He's blaspheming! Who can forgive sins but God alone?"
· John 5:18 - For this reason the Jews tried all the harder to kill him; not only was he breaking the Sabbath, but he was even calling God his own Father, making himself equal with God.
· John 10:30-33 - I and the Father are one." 31Again the Jews picked up stones to stone him, 32but Jesus said to them,"I have shown you many great miracles from the Father. For which of these do you stone me?" 33"We are not stoning you for any of these," replied the Jews,"but for blasphemy, because you, a mere man, claim to be God."

Did he mean the things he said? Or was "the greatest teacher in history" misunderstood by everyone?

to God. John made this clear by describing him as "the Word" (John 1:1, 14). Paul spoke of Christ as the one who created all things and who holds all things together through his divine power (Colossians 1:16-17). He also addressed Jesus as "our great God and Savior, Christ Jesus" (Titus 2:13).

Skeptics speculate that Christ could not have meant what the apostles understood him to say. It is important that we understand that not only did his disciples hear him proclaim his exclusivity and deity, but so did the critics of his day. Frequently when he made these dramatic claims, the Jews accused him of blasphemy. They correctly understood the implications of what he was saying, realizing that he was making himself to be an equal with God. This, of course, would indeed have been blasphemous if Christ's claims were not true (Mark 2:6-7; 14:61-64; John 5:18; 10:30-33). Many people today have tried to redefine the person and work of Christ in more general and broad terms. It is significant, however, that both his friends and his enemies recognized that he was claiming to be God and the sole means to God.

It is not enough to understand that Christ claimed to be the only way to God, we also need to understand *why*.

All religious (and non-religious) systems acknowledge that there is a difference between our ideal behavior and our actual behavior, a difference between the *best* life choices and the choices we have made. The Bible calls this gap "sin." All religious systems offer plans to close that gap, to minimize the amount of sin we commit. ***But Jesus taught that our sin has separated us from a holy God.*** There is no amount of good that we can do that will "undo" this situation. The only way for man to bridge the gap between himself and God was through his acceptance of Christ's payment for his sin. All of the alternatives available to us apart from the sacrifice of Christ are based on systems of human effort and merit. If we seek to bridge the gap through our own good deeds we will fall woefully short.

The death of Christ would have been a supreme blunder and a tragic waste if people could get into heaven by any other means: "for if righteousness comes through the Law, then Christ died needlessly," (Galatians 2:21). Why would God make such a radical sacrifice if there was any other way? Read Question 9 for a more detailed study on why our own good works cannot be sufficient to gain salvation.

If the Bible makes it so clear that Christ claimed to be God, and the only way to God, and his disciples affirmed his claims, how do people deny this? They do so because (1) they are unaware of the teachings of the Bible, so we must expose them to the relevant passages in scripture. Or (2) they assume the Bible is in error, then we need to address the problem of the trustworthiness of the Bible (see Question 4).

Christianity is Not Narrow

Christ made exclusive claims

The Disciples affirmed Christ's exclusive claims

What about good deeds

See Question 9 on good works

The Biblical record is wrong

See Question 4 on accuracy of the Bible

Why did Christ make such claims?

Christianity is narrow

It is essential that we understand Christianity's position through the ages. Christ insisted that he was man's only solution for the problem of sin. That is a very narrow and restrictive assertion. The question is no longer whether or not Christianity is narrow, but whether it is right.

Second Option: Christianity Is Exclusive And Wrong

The second option recognizes that Christianity claims to be the only way to God but denies the validity of such a claim. This rejection is often a result of two false assumptions. The first assumption, common in our tolerant society, is that **exclusiveness**, by its very nature, makes something suspect if not entirely wrong. Therefore Christianity's intolerance for other paths to God means it cannot be right. Second, there are millions of sincere worshipers whose religions lay outside the confines given by Christianity. Even if Christ were right for us, it doesn't mean he is right for everyone. The assumption is that we have no right to declare the **sincere beliefs** of others wrong. These assumptions must be dealt with if we hope to show that Christianity is both narrow and right.

The best way to address these false assumptions is to discuss and illustrate them outside of the context of religion. In this issue, perhaps more than any other, the use of secular illustrations can help avoid the culturally-indoctrinated sense of revulsion that many feel when Christians claim to have a monopoly on God.

False Assumption #1: Exclusiveness = Wrong.

The assumption here is that anything this narrow-minded has to be wrong. Most of us were brought up to believe that tolerance is a virtue, and that discrimination and exclusion is morally unacceptable. We have finally cast most of our racist and misogynistic language out of acceptable conversation. We've vilified the whites-only clubs out of existence, and we've nearly done the same with "men-only" establishments.

But despite the examples that show why we object to exclusivity, the assumption behind this objection is not valid. A position can be narrow and wrong, or it can be narrow, and right. Just being exclusive doesn't make something either right or wrong. Someone once said, "Tolerance in personal relationships is a virtue, but tolerance in truth is a travesty." We've found John Stott's delineation of three types of tolerance to be very helpful. Truth is always intolerant of error. The fact that one plus one will always equal two is very narrow, but it is also right.

Life is full of examples of things that are narrow and true. For instance, when we fly in an airplane we want a narrow-minded pilot, one who will land on the runway, not the highway; land right side up and not upside down; and land when he is told, not before or after. Suppose someone feels that

"Tolerance is one of today's most coveted virtues. But there are at least three different kinds of tolerance.

"First, there is *legal* tolerance: fighting for the equal rights before the law of all ethnic and religious minorities. Christians should be in the forefront of this campaign. Second, there is *social* tolerance, going out of our way to make friends with adherents of other faiths, since they are God's creation who bear his image. Third, there is *intellectual* tolerance. This is to cultivate a mind so broad and open as to accommodate all views and reject none. This is to forget G. K. Chesterton's witty remark that "the purpose of opening the mind, as of opening the mouth, is to shut it again on something solid." To open the mind so wide as to keep nothing in it or out of it is not a virtue; it is the vice of the feeble-minded."

–John Stott to *Christianity Today*, 2003 ("Why Don't They Listen?")

Key Illustration: Airplane & Unleaded Fuel

the automakers are being unnecessarily exclusive by specifying "unleaded fuel only" for his automobile. If he resisted this narrow confine by using diesel fuel or, cheaper but worse yet, water, his car would fail to operate. The specifications may be narrow, but nevertheless they are valid. ***Exclusivity doesn't make something false, nor does it make something true.***

False Assumption #2: Sincerity = Right

The second major objection to Christianity's exclusiveness is that it eliminates many sincere people who are seeking God through other means. The assumption is that because these people have **sincere beliefs,** they can't be wrong. Sincerity, or the lack of it, however, has nothing to do with determining truth. We can be sincere and right or we can be sincere and wrong. We can cite numerous examples to show that sincerity by itself does not make something true. In 1978 over 900 people who had followed their spiritual leader Jim Jones to Guyana were conned into drinking poisoned Kool-Aid. In 1997, 39 people following Marshall Applewhite in San Diego committed suicide hoping to join a spaceship coming with a nearby comet. They were sincere in their faith in their leader, but it was a misplaced faith. It led them to pain and death, not peace and prosperity.

Key Illustration: Nurse & Oxygen Tank

A nurse in a large metropolitan hospital changed an oxygen tank in an oxygen tent for one of her patients. She went about her duties with the utmost sincerity, but on the next set of rounds another nurse found the patient dead. The tank she had affixed to the tent was filled with nitrogen, not oxygen. It had been improperly labeled at the warehouse. The nurse sincerely believed what she was attaching to the tent was oxygen, but it was not, and the consequences were deadly.

One of the most famous football plays from the 1960's resulted from a wrong but sincere belief. In the 1964 game against San Francisco, defensive end Jim Marshall of the Minnesota Vikings picked up a fumble and fought off tacklers repeatedly for 66 yards until he crossed the goal line. Thinking he had scored a touchdown, he threw the ball away out of the endzone. Marshall, however, crossed the wrong goal line and his errant throw scored a safety for the 49ers.

Key Illustration: Flat Earth Theory

All these people were extremely sincere in their beliefs, but they were sincerely wrong. Sincerity does not make something right or wrong. Truth must be determined apart from sincerity. For centuries, popular opinion stated that the earth was flat. Today, the scientific consensus is that the earth is roughly spherical. Our understanding of the shape of the earth was arrived at by objective criteria, not by popular opinion. It is round, and our belief or lack of belief in that fact will not change it one bit. Similarly, the truth of Christianity cannot be determined on the basis of belief or lack of belief, but on the basis of objective criteria. For further study on this, see Question 3.

But what about those other sincere faiths?

We know about the claims of Christianity, but it would be helpful to compare them with those of the other major world religions. Whenever we hear someone say "all religions are basically the same," we immediately know two things: (1) that the person has little *in-depth* knowledge of the various religions; and (2) we know that the person is probably not intimately involved in *any* one religion, otherwise he would at least know the distinctions of *his own*.

The major religions differ in their perception of who God is, in their view of ultimate human destiny, and in their means of attaining salvation. To see this, consider five great world religions: Hinduism, Buddhism, Judaism, Islam, and Christianity.

Let's look first at the different views of God. The Christian is a trinitarian. He believes in only one true God, but in the unity of the Godhead there are three eternal and coequal Persons. The Jew and the Muslim are strong unitarians. They believe in only one true God, there is no separate Son or Spirit. The philosophical Hindu is a monist (all is one) or pantheist whose god is an eternal, non-personal, abstract being without knowable attributes. God is an It rather than a Person. The popular sects of Hinduism are polytheistic, worshipers of many gods. Various sects of Buddhism hold a variety of views on God. These sects are either polytheistic, pantheistic, or often atheistic. As we can see, there is a great divergence in views just on the identity of God.

Next, we can draw our attention to the issue of man's destiny. Where is man headed when life is finally over? For the Christian, believers will spend eternity in heaven, though this is often described in the Bible as a new earth. There, they will experience a personal existence, meaningful responsibilities, and have fellowship with God forever. Among Jews today we find a broad spectrum of views on man's destiny. Many say that nothing exists after this life is over. Others believe they will go to life hereafter that will be enjoyed in the company of their Messiah. Muslims believe they will join Allah in heaven for an eternity of sensual pleasure and gratification. Hindus believe they eventually will end up becoming one with the impersonal supreme being (Brahman) in a state of nirvana. The individual ceases to have his own personal identity of existence. Buddhists aspire to nirvana as a state of total nothingness, a final annihilation of individual consciousness. On the surface, each of these religions speaks of an ultimate destiny for man, but that destiny is vastly different.

How does man achieve his destiny in each of the major religions?

Helpful clarification of narrow: Christianity is only narrow in the how–not the who. That is to say, it is narrow about the path to God (faith in Jesus), but it's very open about who is able to get to God. From its inception, Christianity crossed all social boundaries. Young and old, rich and poor, men and women, merchants and slaves and aristocrats across the empire and well beyond embraced the Christian faith and were accepted. Even today it doesn't matter how much money you have, what ethnicity you are, what job you work, what your background is, what family you're from, or what caste system you were born into. It's a level playing field wide open to all who come and believe. Galatians 3:28 says, "There is neither Jew nor Greek, there is neither slave nor free man, there is neither male nor female; for you are all one in Christ Jesus."

According to Christianity, he enters heaven by his acceptance of Christ's payment on the cross for his sin. Christianity's solution is based on faith in Jesus Christ, not on man's good works.

The Jew who believes in heaven qualifies for it by turning back to God and living a moral life. There is no assurance of salvation since it will be determined by man's own efforts. The Muslim tries to be worthy of salvation by believing in the five doctrines of Islam and by performing the duties of the Five Pillars of Islam. But it all depends on his behavior and the final decision of Allah, so he cannot be sure.

The Hindu believes he achieves his desired state of oneness with Brahman through a series of reincarnations. The law of karma says a Hindu reaps in the next life the rewards or punishments of the present life. The Buddhist believes he earns his own release from the endless chain of reincarnations by following the Four Noble Truths and the Eightfold Path.

Four of these five religions seek salvation from this world and in the next through human effort, but the effort is different for each. Christianity recognizes the frustration and futility of man's own efforts and declares that man's salvation must rest solely in the provision and grace of God. Study Questions 9-12 for a deeper look at the nature of salvation as described by the Bible.

The major religions differ in their perspectives of God, man's destiny, and the means of salvation. While these ideas are not widely understood, the big surprise to most people is that *they all claim to be exclusively right*. Christianity is not the only religion with exclusive claims. Jews, Muslims, and Buddhists also all believe they have found the only true way to God. Hindus are the only ones who might equivocate on an exclusivity clause. Ramakrishna stated that "many faiths are but different paths leading to one reality, God." On the surface, it appears that Hindus allow for different ways to get to nirvana.

A closer look at Hinduism reveals that the Hindu allows for an openness to other faiths but stresses the superiority of his own. If all faiths are but different paths, we might wonder if the Hindu would allow his children to be brought up as Christians. There is really only one path by which an outsider can enter the fold. He must live a pious life and then, after many transmigrations, his soul may be at last reborn into a Hindu family.

Many people today assume that all religions are different paths on a mountain, heading upward in the same direction, all worshiping the same God. If we have learned anything in our quick survey of these five major religions, we have learned that they aren't even on the same mountain.

Each of these religions seeks to answer man's questions regarding his origin, destiny, and current role in the universe. Their answers, though

A Basic Comparison of the "Big 5" World Religions as They Describe Themselves

	Who or What is God?	Life or lives?	Eternal Destiny?	To achieve eternal destiny?	Any other ways?	Who was Jesus? (According to modern religious leaders)	Did Jesus die on the cross, and was he physically resurrected?
Judaism	Monotheistic - One God, infinite and personal	One life of obedience to the Law, then ?	Some believe Paradise with Messiah, others do not believe in any kind of afterlife.	Turn back to God and live a moral life under the Law	No	A wise teacher, perhaps a prophet, but not the Messiah of Israel, nor divine in any way.	He died, but was not resurrected.
Christianity	Monotheistic - Trinity, one God existing as Father, Son, and Holy Spirit	One life, then judgment	Eternity in Heaven	Accept Christ's payment on the cross for sin	No	Jesus Christ is both fully God and fully man. God in human form.	Yes.
Islam	Monotheistic - Allah, the one eternal, omnipotent God, unable to be reduced to a name.	One life, then judgment of works on a scale	Eternity in Paradise	Believe in the 5 doctrines of Islam and perform the 5 pillars of faith.	No	A prophet of God, sinless, miracle working prophet of God, but not divine, and superseded by Mohammed.	No. A prophet of God would not be killed like that. Jesus was taken to heaven without being crucified.
Hinduism (Views differ greatly across sects)	Monistic, Pantheistic, Polytheistic	Many reincarnations following rules of karma	Nirvana, a oneness with Brahman, end of individual	Live a pious life, and after a series of reincarnations, live a pious life in a Hindu family	No	A great son of God like Ramakrishna, partly divine, perhaps enlightened.	No official teaching, but some teach that an enlightened being would have passed peacefully into the next phase of existence.
Buddhism (Views differ greatly across sects)	Polytheistic, Pantheistic, Atheistic	Many reincarnations following rules of karma	Nirvana, a state of nothingness, peace	Follow the 4 Noble Truths and the Eightfold Path to be released from chain of reincarnations	No	An enlightened being like the Buddha.	No official teaching, but some teach that Jesus "coming alive" in his followers' hearts is far more significant than whatever might or might not have happened in history.

similar at first glance, are dramatically different when scrutinized closely. How can all of these religions be right at the same time? They disagree with each other in the three major issues of who God is, where man is going, and how he is going to get there. How can we square Hinduism's teaching that God is impersonal with Christianity's teaching that God is personal? Islam, Christianity, and Judaism all have a God to whom they pray. Philosophical Hinduism, Buddhism, and modern New Age religions believe all is one, and that God is not "out there" but rather "everywhere" including "in me." These questions are only the tip of the iceberg of contradictions among the major religions.

One of the most basic laws of logic, on which all rational conversation depends, is the **law of non-contradiction**. Simply stated, the law of non-contradiction says that if two statements about one particular issue contradict each other, or make mutually exclusive claims, then (1) only one of them is true, or (2) they are both false. They cannot both be true in the same sense and at the same time. If statement A contradicts statement B: Either A is true and B is false, or A is false and B is true, or A is false and B is false.

If someone says, "All dogs shed hair," and another person says, "Poodles don't shed hair," then either both are wrong or one is right. They can't both be right. If Christ claims to be the only way to God and Mohammed says there is another way to God, then either Christ is right and Mohammed is wrong, or Christ is wrong and Mohammed is right, or they are both wrong. They cannot both be right.

Since the major religions make mutually exclusive claims, the law of non-contradiction applies. Either one of them is right and the rest are wrong, or they all are wrong; they cannot all be right.

Here again it is vitally important that we remember not just that Jesus claimed to be the only way to God, but *why* he claimed to be the only way. The AIDS illustration may help:

Imagine three men dying of AIDS. One contracted the HIV virus through promiscuous sexual activity with prostitutes, another—a lifelong heroin addict—got it though a dirty needle. The third man, a hemophiliac, was infected by a transfusion with contaminated blood. Two of the individuals were involved in illicit or illegal activities, but all three face the same prognosis—an untimely demise to an incurable disease. They are all taking AZT to treat the symptoms. Although not a cure, AZT slows the effects of the virus, prolonging and enhancing the life of an AIDS victim.

Now imagine that today the cure for AIDS is announced, "TZA", a completely different compound than the one in wide usage. While this new compound appears to cure AIDS, it has disastrous effects if combined with AZT - patients must choose one or the other.

Christianity is Narrow and Wrong

↓

False Assumptions:
· *Sincere belief is enough*
· *Exclusiveness is wrong*

↓

All religions are different

↓

All religions are narrow

↓

Law of non-contradiction

↓

Question:
Not is it narrow, but is it true?

Key Illustration: AIDS Cure

The drug addict resolved to clean up his life. In addition to the AZT treatments, he kicked his habit, got a job, and started taking care of himself. Life is good, better than it has been in years, why mess with what is working? The hemophiliac has also attained a pretty normal life with AZT, so he continues his normal treatments. Only the sex-addict accepts the offer to take TZA. He is cured! The other two men, in spite of their good lives and best efforts, will still die from the complications of AIDS someday.

All systems of good works operate like spiritual AZT—every religion and almost any system of good works prolongs and enhances this life. They can help a person "sin less" thereby making life better and usually longer. Where do these good works fit into a person's eternal destiny? Well, they don't. Just like AZT, they make possible a better life, but fail to change the eventual outcome. We all have an incurable disease called sin. <u>No amount of "sinning less" will let us reach a state of "sinless."</u> No amount of future good can undo the damage already done. We don't need a spiritual crutch, we need a cure. Jesus offers a cure, a solution to the sin problem that no one else can provide.

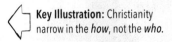
Key Illustration: Christianity narrow in the *how*, not the *who*.

Jesus's offer of salvation is narrow in the *how*, not the *who*. Many religions over the centuries have been very narrow in their selection criteria. Hindus were trapped in their caste, Jewishness is determined by bloodline, and in several religions the only path to salvation for women was to be married to a practicing man. Jesus offers salvation for free to any man, woman of any tribe, or color. Paul rejoices that there is no longer any Jew nor Gentile, slave nor free, man nor woman, for Christians are one in Christ Jesus (Galatians 3:28).

We stated earlier that the hard question facing Christianity was not whether it is narrow, but whether it is true. The exclusiveness of Christ's claims is no reason to declare him wrong. We must proceed to our third option where we will analyze whether or not Christianity is true.

Third Option: Christianity is Exclusive and True

We know from Christ's own claims that Christianity is narrow. What we must determine now is whether or not Christianity is true. If Christ was not who he claimed to be, then we are left with some very uncomfortable alternatives. If Christ was not the only way to God, he was either a liar or a lunatic. Neither of these choices is very palatable, but they are our only options if Christ was not Lord of all. Christ was not merely a good man or a great teacher.

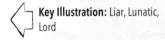
Key Illustration: Liar, Lunatic, Lord

The very character of Christ argues persuasively against his being a liar. He spoke of truth and virtue on every occasion. His life exemplified the very message he proclaimed. In fact, very few people will make this claim. The evidence is weighted heavily in favor of Christ being a paragon of truth and virtue rather than a liar.

The consistent life and testimony of Christ make it clear as well that he was not a lunatic. A lunatic displays abnormalities and imbalance as a part of his lifestyle. When we analyze the life of Christ we do not find inconsistencies and imbalance. To the contrary, we discover a man who is mentally sound and balanced.

If Christ is not a liar nor a lunatic, then he is who he claimed to be—Lord of all, the only way by which man can be saved. The objective data for the truth of Christianity comes from two sources—the Bible and the legal historical evidence for the Resurrection—and we have already supported the truth of both these sources. See Question 4 for information regarding the reliability of the Bible, and see Question 2 for a detailed explanation of the evidence for the Resurrection.

Incidentally, it is often helpful to use a diagram to present the claims and credentials of Christ. In the following chart the left column lists some of the unique claims he made, and the right lists some of his credentials that back up his claims.

UNIQUE CLAIMS OF CHRIST	CREDENTIALS OF CHRIST
• Claimed to have power to forgive sins. • Claimed to be sinless. • Claimed to fulfill Old Testament messianic prophecies. • Claimed that he would rise from the dead and raise all men. • Claimed that he would come again and judge the world. • Claimed to be the exclusive way to salvation.	• His sinless life (even his enemies acknowledged this). • His miracles (power over nature, disease, demons, death). • His unique character and teaching. • His fulfillment of hundreds of messianic prophecies. • His power to change lives. • His resurrection from the dead.

His works (credentials) authenticate his words (claims), and the nature of his claims leads us to the liar, lunatic, Lord trilemma, because these are the only real options about Jesus. (A fourth option that he was a legend was addressed in Questions 2 & 4.)

Even though there is ample evidence in favor of the truth of Christianity, there are still a couple of questions that may need to be addressed. The first concerns the Jews. Many people assume that Christianity is a Gentile religion or that to become a Christian, a Jew must stop being a Jew. Others have raised this issue because Jews worship the one true God of Abraham. So why aren't they going to heaven?

A little history is needed to put this question into context. In the early church, the problem facing believers was not how a *Jew* could become a

Christian but how a *Gentile* could become a Christian. Early Christianity was predominantly Jewish. Almost the entire cast of the Gospels is Jewish, as are almost all the characters in Acts up through the first ten chapters of the book. When a Gentile named Cornelius became a Christian in Acts 10, the Jewish Christians had difficulty believing it was possible. Jesus was a Jew, as were all of the apostles. Paul tells us in Philippians 3:4-11 how he needed Christ for salvation even though he was the epitome of a good Jew. Every one of the New Testament writers, with the exception of Luke, was a Jew. The New Testament revealed that in Christ, Jews and Gentiles could come together into one body without distinction.

> For I am not ashamed of the Gospel, for it is the power of God for salvation to everyone who believes, to the Jew first and also to the Greek (Romans 1:16).

> There is neither Jew nor Greek, there is neither slave nor free man, there is neither male nor female; for you are all one in Christ Jesus (Galatians 3:28).

> For he himself is our peace, who made both groups into one, and broke down the barrier of the dividing wall (Ephesians 2:14).

> For there is one God, and one Mediator also between God and men, the man Christ Jesus (1 Timothy 2:5).

It is important for Jewish people to know that to become Christians, they do not have to forsake their Jewishness any more than Irishmen would have to forsake being Irish. There are Gentile Christians and Hebrew Christians. A Jew does not have to abandon his heritage to become a Christian.

The Jew, just like any other man, must deal with his sin and the separation it has caused between him and God. The standard set by God is perfection, and the Jew doesn't measure up to that standard any better than the Gentile does (Isaiah 53:6). Paul, "a Hebrew of Hebrews," speaks of the common dilemma in Romans 3:9-10: "What then? Are we better than they? Not at all; for we have already charged that both Jews and Greeks are all under sin; as it is written, 'There is none righteous, not even one.'" The penalty for this imperfection is death and separation from God.

What is the solution to man's problem of sin? Man can pay the penalty himself or accept a substitute in his place. (The futility of seeking to pay the debt with our own efforts is examined in Question 9.) In the Old Testament, man escaped the penalty of his sin by presenting an unblemished animal as a sacrifice in his stead. But the debt was only covered, not canceled, and the next year on the Day of Atonement it had to be covered again. Christ said

Key Illustration: One Million
Dollars

his sacrifice of himself ended for all time the need for another sacrifice. He canceled the debt for all who would come to him.

Imagine that you have just borrowed $1 million and the bank discovers you cannot pay it back. Perhaps you can pay the interest, but you have no means of reducing the principal. Then someone comes along and not only pays the current interest payment but pays the principal as well. At that point, your debt is canceled and you are again financially solvent. Christ paid not only the interest but also the principal on our debt of sin. All we have to do is accept that payment.

This is all the Jew must do as well. He must come to a personal relationship with Jesus if he wants to be reconciled to God. Romans 3:29-30 says, "Or is God the God of Jews only? Is he not the God of Gentiles also? Yes, of Gentiles also, since indeed God who will justify the circumcised by faith and the uncircumcised through faith is one." The God of all creation makes salvation available for all people through his Son Jesus.

Many believe that Christianity's exclusion of Judaism as a way to God is just nitpicking. Their problem can be stated in this way:

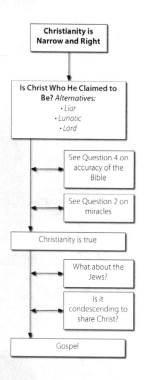

(1) Judaism worships the one true God in the Old Testament.
Christianity proclaims Christ and the God of the Old Testament as one.
Therefore, Judaism in reality believes in the same God.

But what is not understood here is that the Jew rejects Christ as the Son of God, so the proposition should be stated in this way:

(2) Judaism rejects Christ as the Son of God.
Christ is the Son of God and the only way to the Father.
Therefore, Judaism in reality has rejected the only way to the Father.

Either Christ is right or wrong. If he is right, and we have tried to show that he is, then the Jew must come through him to get to God. Paul agonized over this situation. In Romans 9:2-4 he wrote, "I have great sorrow and unceasing anguish in my heart. For I could wish that I myself were cursed and cut off from Christ for the sake of my people, those of my own race, the people of Israel." There has been no revelation from God since that time that provides an alternative.

A second question we sometimes hear concerns the proclamation of Christianity to others. Because of the great missionary mindset of Christianity, the question is posed, "Isn't it unloving, intolerant, condescending, even arrogant, to preach that Christ is the only way to God?"

To some people Christianity appears harsh and unloving. We must balance this negative reaction with two crucial points: It was the same Christ who said he was the only way (John 14:6), and who gave the Great Commission to take this message to everyone (Matthew 28:19-20).

Since Christianity is true, even though it is narrow, it would be unloving if we didn't share Christ's solution with others.

We can illustrate this by imagining a scientist who has just discovered a complete cure for cancer. He now faces the dilemma of whether he should share his discovery.

If he shares it, he risks offending some who are seeking other techniques to cure the problem. The scientist will challenge the theories of other researchers when he shares his discovery and thus risk their scorn. But since his only alternative is to let people die in their ignorance, the loving thing would be to share the cure, even though some might misunderstand the offer. Likewise, the world has need of Christ and we must lovingly share him with people.

In all this, we must remember to expose Christianity to others—not impose it. Christ never called us to force him on anyone. Our task is to present Christ in a loving way and allow men and women the choice of accepting or rejecting him.

If these two supplementary questions are not raised by your non-Christian friend, you can move right into a presentation of the Gospel. It is not enough for a person to recognize intellectually that Christ is the only payment available for sins. He must personally accept Christ as his own Savior from sin. For a detailed presentation of what is essential for salvation, refer to Question 11.

Summary

The first option we considered is that Christianity is not narrow, but then we faced the problem that Christ claimed not only to be the exclusive way to God but also to be God himself. The disciples also affirmed what Christ taught. When the question arose, "Where do good deeds fit in if salvation comes through Christ alone?" we referred to Question 9.

If, after being exposed to Christ's claims in scripture, a person persists in denying the truth of such testimony, then his problem is not with this question but with the question addressed in Question 4, "Is the Bible reliable?"

The testimony is clear that Christ claimed to be the only way. A person must decide if he believes this claim is true or false.

The second option we looked at is that Christianity is narrow and wrong. We found the assumption behind this option to be false. Truth is not determined on the basis of sincerity or beliefs. Nor can a faith be discredited simply because it is narrow.

After a brief examination of five major religions, we concluded that, contrary to popular belief, they are all different and not basically the same. We also noted that Christianity is not the only religion that claims to be the only right one. Then with help of the law of non-contradiction, we saw that either one and only one of the religions of the world is right, or they are all wrong; no two of them can be right. This left us with the task of determining if Christianity is true.

The third option claimed that Christianity is both narrow and true. The unique claims of Christ lead to only three alternatives: he was a liar, a lunatic, or the Lord. The evidence from the Bible and the Resurrection give sufficient objective data to warrant a positive response to the question of the truthfulness of Christ.

Two other questions might have to be worked through before the Gospel is presented: "What about the Jews—do they need Christ?" and "Is it condescending to share Christ with others in the world?"

We concluded finally that Christianity is narrow and right because it is true. Without Christ there is no solution to man's problem of sin and separation from God.

Supplemental Reading

In this chapter we cover both the identity of Jesus and the comparison to the other major world religions.

Olasky, Marvin. *The Religions Next Door*. Broadman & Holman Books, 2004.

Corduan, Winfried. *Neighboring Faiths: A Christian Introduction to World Religions*. IVP Academic, 2012.

Tennet, Timothy C. *Christianity at the Religious Roundtable: Evangelicalism in Conversation with Hinduism, Buddhism, and Islam*. Baker Academic, 2002.

Zacharias, Ravi. *Jesus Among Other Gods*. W Publishing Group, 2002.

Grindheim, Sigurd. *God's Equal*. Bloomsbury T&T Clark, 2013.

Bowman, Robert and J. Ed Komoszewski. *Putting Jesus in His Place*. Kregel Publications, 2007.

Bock, Darrell L. and Daniel B. Wallace. *Dethroning Jesus: Exposing Popular Culture's Quest to Unseat the Biblical Christ*. Thomas Nelson, 2010.

Study Guide for Is Christ the Only Way to God?

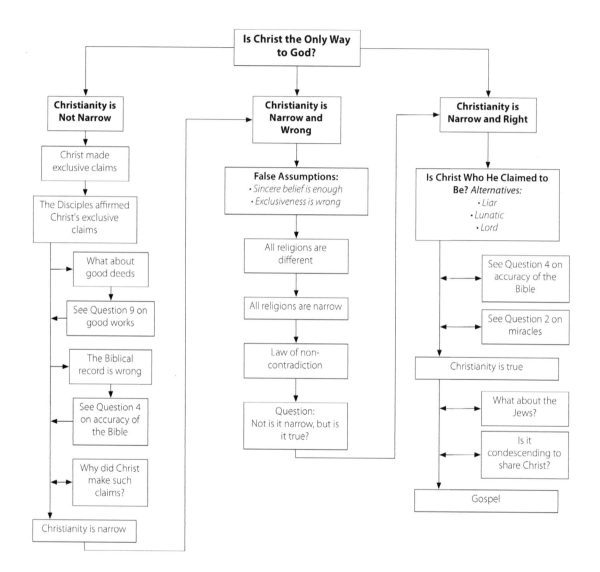

Key Illustrations

Nurse & Oxygen Tank

A nurse in a large metropolitan hospital changed an oxygen tank in an oxygen tent for one of her patients. She went about her duties with the utmost sincerity, but on the next set of rounds another nurse found the patient dead. The tank she had affixed to the tent was filled with nitrogen, not oxygen. It had been improperly labeled at the warehouse. The nurse sincerely believed what she was attaching to the tent was oxygen, but it was not, and the consequences were deadly.

Flat Earth Theory

Sincerity does not make something right or wrong. Truth must be determined apart from sincerity. For centuries, popular opinion stated that the earth was flat. Today, the scientific consensus is that the earth is roughly spherical. Our understanding of the shape of the earth was arrived at by objective criteria, not by popular opinion. It is round, and our belief or lack of belief in that fact will not change it one bit.

Unleaded Fuel

Suppose someone feels that the automakers are being unnecessarily exclusive by specifying "unleaded fuel only" for his automobile. If he resisted this narrow confine by using diesel fuel or, cheaper but worse yet, water, his car would fail to operate. The specifications may be narrow, but nevertheless they are valid.

Liar, Lunatic, Lord

Jesus Christ claimed to be God. If he was wrong, and wasn't God, then we have a dilemma. If he knew he wasn't God then he was a Liar, a deceiver, and hardly a good moral teacher. If he really believed he was God (but wasn't) then he would be insane, not unlike a man who believed he was Napoleon, and hardly the wisest teacher ever to walk the planet. Jesus was either a Liar, a Lunatic, or just who he claimed to be–Lord.

Three Types of Tolerance

"Tolerance is one of today's most coveted virtues. But there are at least three different kinds of tolerance.

"First, there is *legal* tolerance: fighting for the equal rights before the law of all ethnic and religious minorities. Christians should be in the forefront of this campaign. Second, there is *social* tolerance, going out of our way to make friends with adherents of other faiths, since they are God's creation who bear his image. Third, there is *intellectual* tolerance. This is to cultivate a mind so broad and open as to accommodate all views and reject none. This is to forget G. K. Chesterton's witty remark that "the purpose of opening the mind, as of opening the mouth, is to shut it again on something solid." To open the mind so wide as to keep nothing in it or out of it is not a virtue; it is the vice of the feeble-minded."

–John Stott to *Christianity Today*, 2003 ("Why Don't They Listen?")

Key Verses

John 14:6 Jesus said to him,"I am the way, and the truth, and the life; no one comes to the Father but through me."

John 8:24 I said therefore to you, that you shall die in your sins; for unless you believe that I am he, you shall die in your sins.

John 3:16-18 he who believes in him is not judged; he who does not believe has been judged already, because he has not believed in the name of the only begotten Son of God.

John 10:30 "I and the Father are one."

Matthew 26:63-64 But Jesus remained silent. The high priest said to him,"I charge you under oath by the living God: Tell us if you are the Christ, the Son of God." 64 "Yes, it is as you say," Jesus replied."But I say to all of you: In the future you will see the Son of Man sitting at the right hand of the Mighty One and coming on the clouds of heaven."

Acts 4:12 And there is salvation in no one else, for there is no other name under heaven that has been given among men, by which we must be saved.

Galatians 1:8 Let God's curse fall on anyone, including myself, who preaches any other message than the one we told you about. Even if an angel comes from heaven and preaches any other message, let him be forever cursed.

Aids Cure Illustration

Imagine three men dying of AIDS. One contracted the HIV virus through promiscuous sexual activity with prostitutes, another–a lifelong heroin addict–got it though a dirty needle. The third man, a hemophiliac, was infected by a transfusion with contaminated blood. Two of the individuals were involved in illicit or illegal activities, but all three face the same prognosis–an untimely demise to an incurable disease. They are all taking AZT to treat the symptoms. Although not a cure, AZT slows the effects of the virus, prolonging and enhancing the life of an AIDS victim.

Now imagine that today the cure for AIDS is announced, "TZA", a completely different compound than the one in wide usage. While this new compound appears to cure AIDS, it has disastrous effects if combined with AZT - patients must choose one or the other.

The drug addict resolved to clean up his life. In addition to the AZT treatments, he kicked his habit, got a job, and started taking care of himself. Life is good, better than it has been in years, why mess with what is working? The hemophiliac has also attained a pretty normal life with AZT, so he continues his normal treatments. Only the sex-addict accepts the offer to take TZA. He is cured! The other two men, in spite of their good lives and best efforts, will still die from the complications of AIDS someday.

Study Questions

1. Respond to this statement, "God is the hub of the wheel with the spokes representing the major world religions. Man can get to God regardless of which spoke he chooses."

2. How would you respond to the person who says, "Jesus never really claimed to be the only way to God"? What passages would you use to show his claim?

3. Respond to these objections to the exclusive claims of Christ:

   • Sincere belief is enough.

   • Exclusiveness is wrong.

4. What is the essential difference between Christianity and the other world religions?

5. Summarize the "Law of Non-contradiction" and explain how it supports the belief that Christianity can be both narrow and true.

6. Give a summary of the liar, lunatic, Lord argument and describe its implications.

Notes

QUESTION 7: WILL GOD JUDGE THOSE WHO NEVER HEARD ABOUT CHRIST?

Often-Asked Questions:

- Would God condemn an innocent heathen simply because he never heard about Christ?

- What about religious people who don't know about Christ and call their god by a different name?

- What happened to people before the coming of Christ?

- What about infants and people who are mentally incapable of understanding the Gospel?

When a person begins to grasp the exclusiveness of the Gospel (Question 6), it is almost inevitable that some version of this question surfaces in their mind. In some cases this objection may be raised as an evasive maneuver when the implications of the Gospel are beginning to get too close to home. More often, however, it comes up because they wonder, *Is God fair? Does God even care?* Something would be desperately wrong if humans showed more compassion than God for those who are lost.

Some try to minimize this problem by arguing that (1) those who have not heard about Christ are innocent because of their ignorance and will not be judged. If, on the other hand, these people are subject to divine judgment, there are only two remaining possibilities—God's judgment is either (2) unfair or (3) fair. Many question the justice of God at this point because they falsely assume that God will hold people accountable for that which they have no way of knowing. But the scriptures are clear that God's judgment is perfectly just and that no one who stands before God will accuse Him of being unfair. How can this be?

First Option: God Will Not Judge Those Who Have Not Heard

These concerns have led some people to the conclusion that those who have never heard about Christ will escape the judgment of God. From this perspective, passages such as the Great Commission make no sense at all. Christian missionaries would not only be wasting their lives but may be doing great harm. By preaching the Gospel to those who were unaware of Christ, they have brought people from a state of innocence to a state of moral culpability. The death and resurrection of Jesus Christ should have been kept a secret! But scripture disagrees strongly. One of the primary mandates given to followers of Christ is to tell others about him. These are the last words of Jesus recorded by Matthew and Luke, the marching orders to his disciples before he left the earth:

> "Go therefore and make disciples of all nations, baptizing them in the name of the Father and of the Son and of the Holy Spirit, teaching them to observe all that I have commanded you. And behold, I am with you always, to the end of the age." (Matthew 28:19–20, ESV)

> "But you will receive power when the Holy Spirit has come upon you, and you will be my witnesses in Jerusalem and in all Judea and Samaria, and to the end of the earth." (Acts 1:8, ESV)

The Bible is clear on the reality of divine judgment. The idea that all people will be saved regardless of their actions or beliefs may be more appealing, but reality is not determined by what we would like to be true.

The following section summarizes the scriptural teaching on the love and holiness of God. Judgment is necessary because of his character.

God is love[1] and this love was manifested when he "sent his Son to be the propitiation [satisfaction] for our sins"[2] "We know love by this, that he laid down his life for us"[3]. God wants no one to spend an eternity apart from him but "desires all men to be saved and to come to the knowledge of the truth"[4]. The Lord is "compassionate and gracious, slow to anger, and abounding in loving-kindness and truth."[5] It is not his desire that any should perish, but that all should come to repentance[6]. God is not only loving and merciful, but he is also holy and just and, therefore, he cannot overlook sin.[7] Sin is a universal human condition,[8] and it causes a breach between man and God[9]. Sin leads to death,[10] and the wrath of God abides on all who are separate from Christ.[11] All have sinned, and those who have not been "justified as a gift by his grace through the redemption which is in Christ Jesus"[12] are under divine condemnation[13] and must stand before God in judgment.[14] Human works, sincerity, and religion are not enough to avert this judgment, because apart from Christ we are enemies of God.[15] But those in Christ are at peace with God and for them there is no condemnation.[16]

[1] 1 John 4:8

[2] 1 John 4:10.

[3] 1 John 3:16; Romans 5:5-8

[4] 1 Timothy 2:4

[5] Exodus 34:6

[6] 2 Peter 3:9; cf. Deuteronomy 30:19; Ezekiel 18:23, 32

[7] Habakkuk 1:12-13

[8] 1 Kings 8:46; Psalms 51:5; Romans 3:9, 23; 1 John 1:8

[9] Isaiah 59:2

[10] Romans 6:23

[11] John 3:18, 36

[12] Romans 3:24

[13] Romans 3:10-20; 5:16-19

[14] John 5:27-29; Revelation 20:11-15

[15] Romans 5:10

[16] Romans 5:1; 8:1.

The supreme authority for truth on these matters is divine revelation, not human opinion. We must be clear, there is no single passage in scripture that neatly addresses the eternal plight of all the categories of people who didn't hear a meaningful explanation of Jesus during their lifetime. However, the scriptures offer enough principles to enable us to gain a reasonably accurate perspective on this question. (The authority of scripture to speak of and for God is pretty essential to this question. If significant doubts remain, revisit these issues in Question 4.)

The sidebar summarizes the scriptural teaching on the love and holiness of God. Judgment is necessary because of his character.

People are not lost because they have not heard. They are lost because they have sinned and thus are separated from God. We die because of disease, not because of ignorance of the proper cure. Tuberculosis was a leading cause of death in urban environments for thousands of years, until the past century and the advent of antibiotics to cure it. "Cause of death" in every one of those cases is "bacterial infection of the lungs," not "lack of antibiotic."

Second Option: God's Judgment of Those Who Have Not Heard Is Unfair

When a person realizes that God *will* judge the unevangelized, he might object that this is unfair, raising questions about the justness of God. How can God judge people for things they don't know?

How will God judge? Unlike a human judge, God knows the complete truth including the thoughts and intentions of the heart. He judges impartially, as in, not on a curve. He judges according to what we have done, not according to what we know or don't know. *"I the Lord search the heart and test the mind, to give every man according to his ways, according to the fruit of his deeds." Jeremiah 17:10*

It is our natural tendency to assume that people who didn't have the training or upbringing as we did simply don't know the things we know. But the Bible and our experience shows that no one is completely in the dark. **The key principle in answering this question is that God's judgment is based on the knowledge that people already have.** He will not hold them accountable to a message about Christ that they never received. People will be judged according to the revelation they have been given and the moral standard they acknowledged. Responsibility is proportionate to revelation, and God knows exactly how much revelation a person received and exactly how he or she responded to it. Just as there are different degrees of responsibility, so there are evidently different degrees of punishment for those who chose to reject the revelation they had been given. *"And from everyone who has been given much shall much be required" (Luke 12:48, see also Matthew 11:21-24; Hebrews 2:2-3).*

How much knowledge do people who do not know about Christ really have about spiritual things? According to the scriptures, they are not in total darkness about God, sin, or even salvation.

Everyone knows enough about God to seek Him. Underlying the objection about the unevangelized is the assumption that they are completely ignorant of God and therefore innocent or unaccountable. This is unfounded because their ignorance is only relative, not absolute. Paul's description of man's rebellion against the one true God in Romans 1:18-25 is the central biblical text on this issue. Verse 20 describes the ***external revelation*** of God to all mankind: "For since the creation of the world His invisible attributes, His eternal power and divine nature, have been clearly seen, being understood through what has been made, so that they are without excuse." The creation points beyond itself to the One who made it, and no one can plead ignorance of the Creator, because all people have access to this general revelation of God. *General revelation* is the spiritual knowledge available to all people, while *special revelation* refers to God's more direct means of communication to some people through dreams, visions, angels, and especially the Bible.

The universe manifests God's "invisible attributes," including His "eternal power and divine nature." God's eternality, omnipotence, omniscience, and wisdom are "clearly seen" in creation, but because of their unrighteousness, men have suppressed these evident truths about God (Romans 1:18). This revelation of God in nature is also affirmed by Psalm 19: "The heavens are telling of the glory of God; and their expanse is declaring the work of His hands. Day to day pours forth speech, and night to night reveals knowledge" (Psalm 19:1-2). Paul told the residents of Lystra that in His creation God "did not leave himself without witness" (Acts 14:15-17). Those of us who spend much of our lives with the night sky shrouded by the light pollution of cities and suburbia may be tempted to take lightly these passages. We need to remember that for most of history the majority

Two Types of External Revelation

1. General - The spiritual knowledge available to all people.

2. Special - Direct communication to people through dreams, visions, angels and especially the Bible.

of men and women lived much closer to nature. Under the constant witness of the stars, thousands of years of mankind looked up at night and knew that something bigger than us was at work. This may explain why every people group in history embraced some form of religious or spiritual tradition.

God has revealed himself to all people not only externally in nature but also through **internal revelation**: *"That which is known about God is evident within them; for God made it evident to them" (Romans 1:19)*. Though fallen, humans are still *"made in the likeness of God" (James 3:9)* with a spiritual dimension and inner awareness of the existence of God. God *"has also set eternity in their heart" (Ecclesiastes 3:11)*, and it is "the fool" who suppresses this knowledge by saying in his heart, "There is no God" (Psalms 14:1). *"For the wrath of God is revealed from heaven against all ungodliness and unrighteousness of men, who suppress the truth in unrighteousness" (Romans 1:18)*.

There is a general revelation, therefore, of the existence and power of the eternal God to which people must respond. Those who reject or suppress the light they have been given are "without excuse" and under the wrath of the Living God. They may never have heard about God the Son, but they have already rejected the truth that they know about God the Father.

At this point someone may respond, "What about the dedicated followers of other religions? Surely they are not rejecting the light they have about God." Once again, Romans 1 gives us an answer:

> For even though they knew God, they did not honor Him as God, or give thanks; but they became futile in their speculations, and their foolish heart was darkened. Professing to be wise, they became fools, and exchanged the glory of the incorruptible God for an image in the form of corruptible man, and birds and four-footed animals and crawling creatures. Therefore God gave them over in the lusts of their hearts to impurity, that their bodies might be dishonored among them. For they exchanged the truth of God for a lie, and worshiped and served the creature rather than the Creator, who is blessed forever. Amen.

According to Paul, the religions of man were spawned not out of a search for truth, but as a perversion of the truth that mankind originally had. Contrary to popular opinion, many religions did not evolve but devolved from a primal monotheism to a debased polytheism and animism. Because of unrighteousness, people quickly turned from knowledge of God to their own futile speculations, "and their foolish heart was darkened." They substituted the creation for the Creator and developed their own ways of salvation.

*Not all faith traditions retain a meaningful concept of "salvation," and we need to be sensitive about applying the Christian usage of the term indiscriminately. However, they all differentiate between better and worse states for this life and/or the next, and "doing good not bad" is the central mechanism for earning for yourself the better state.

It is significant that all non-Christian religions teach that salvation is achieved by human effort, ritual, sacrifice, and devotional service.* These systems of salvation by works minimize two essential truths: the wretchedness of sin and the holiness of God. To be saved, a person must recognize his inability to atone for his own sins and cast himself on the mercy of the one true God. Jesus made it clear that human works will never bridge the moral gap between man and God; the only acceptable work is faith in Christ (John 6:28-29, 40).

There are truths in non-Christian religions because of general revelation, but there are also serious falsehoods in the critical areas of God, man, sin, and salvation due to a suppression of general revelation. Because of distortions like idolatry, those who participate in pagan religions actually compound their guilt by rejecting the external and internal revelation that they already have about the Creator. Sin always has consequences. Thousands of years of some cultures rejecting Christ have led to the tragic situation we have today, with billions of people stranded in societies marked by spiritual deception.

Everyone knows there is a standard that they don't meet. Romans 1 proclaims that people cannot plead ignorance of God the Father, though they may not have heard about God the Son. Romans 2 adds that all people also have an awareness of sin. They may not share the same set of moral principles, but everyone has *moral standards*, including the relativist. These standards emerge clearly whenever someone criticizes another. "Therefore you are without excuse, every man of you who passes judgment, for in that you judge another, you condemn yourself; for you who judge practice the same things" (Romans 2:1). Even the cannibal shows that he knows cannibalism is wrong when you try to kill and eat *him* for dinner tonight.

Not only do we have moral standards, we are all guilty of violating them. For instance, most people believe that consideration for the interests of others is preferable to selfishness, but how many consistently live up to this standard? Most people agree that they should treat their spouses with kindness and respect, but who is perfect in their conformity to this principle?

Thus, when someone says, "If a person who does not know about Christ lives up to his own standard, he should not be judged," we can respond, "That sounds reasonable—if he flawlessly obeys his moral code, he should be considered innocent. But are there any people who do so?" Now and then someone may say, "Well, I have a friend who is a wonderful human being. He doesn't believe in God, and yet he is a caring, compassionate, and consistently helpful person." This will always be a third party, because others we know can sometimes maintain the appearance of living in conformity to their moral beliefs. But it is an exceedingly rare person who can say, "To the best of my knowledge, I have always kept my moral standards and never

The perfect justice of God. If God is loving and fair, can he really condemn people who haven't had a chance to make a decision about Jesus Christ? If he does judge them, how can we commit ourselves to such a God?

While the Bible does not develop the theme of those who have not heard as deeply as we would like, it does provide several principles we can use in responding to this important objection. One of these is that God is holy and just in all his ways: "Surely, God will not act wickedly, and the Almighty will not pervert justice" (Job 34:12). God has "fixed a day in which he will judge the world in righteousness" (Acts 17:31; also see Genesis 18:25–"Shall not the Judge of all the earth deal justly?"–and Romans 3:3-5). On that day, no one will defiantly accuse God of injustice.

Romans 2:2-16 reveals three important aspects of the judgment of God: (1) God judges according to truth (Romans 2:2-5). Unlike a human judge, God knows the complete truth (including the thoughts and intentions of the heart; Hebrews 4:12), and his justice is not clouded by error. (2) God judges according to works (Romans 2:6-10). His judgment is contingent on whether a person obeys the truth or obeys unrighteousness. (3) God judges according to impartiality (Romans 2:11-16). "There is no partiality with God" (Romans 2:11; see 1 Peter 1:17).

violated them." (See Question 9 about good works.)

People may try to minimize or rationalize sin, but they are not ignorant of it. They have a law inscribed in their hearts, and their *conscience* is aware of it:

> For when Gentiles who do not have the Law do instinctively the things of the Law, these, not having the Law, are a law to themselves, in that they show the work of the Law written in their hearts, their conscience bearing witness, and their thoughts alternately accusing or else defending them, on the day when, according to my Gospel, God will judge the secrets of men through Christ Jesus (Romans 2:14-16).

One can sear his conscience (1 Timothy 4:2), but he cannot eliminate it. The conscience is a divinely given internal testimony to all people of their moral inadequacy. The first-century Roman philosopher Seneca wrote, "We are all wicked; what we blame in another each will find in his own bosom." The Roman poet Ovid confessed, "I see and approve the better course—I follow the worse." And the 18th-century English critic Samuel Johnson wisely observed, "Every man knows that of himself which he dare not tell his dearest friend."

The unevangelized person then is not as ignorant as we might have thought. In his heart he is aware of the eternal and omnipotent Creator, and he knows about his own moral guilt. If he responds to these two truths rather than suppressing them, he will be moving in the direction of God's solution.

God promises that those who seek him will find him. Each person has some knowledge about God and sin for which he is accountable. This revelation requires a response and, in this sense, everyone has a chance. God is aware of the light that each one has, and he knows the response of each human heart. We saw earlier that because he is fair, God will not hold anyone accountable for any knowledge he did not receive. But God is also holy and must judge those who do not respond to the truth they have. Salvation is a gift of God's grace—completely free; no one can earn or deserve it. God is therefore under no obligation to justify anyone, let alone those who fail to respond to the revelation they have received.

Every individual must shoulder his own burden of responsibility for making a decision about salvation. No one else can do this for him. There is a twofold revelation about God and sin, and every person's response should also be twofold: acknowledge need (forgiveness of sin) and abandon themselves to the mercy of the Creator (God). Both elements are found in Hebrews 11:6: *And without faith it is impossible to please him, for whoever would draw near to God must believe that he exists and that he rewards those who seek him.*

As the philosopher Blaise Pascal noted three and half centuries ago, there is a God-shaped vacuum, and "infinite abyss" in the heart of every person. When they recognize this need for God and respond to the knowledge they have, God himself will respond and reward that person. The Bible often affirms that those who seek God will find him: "And you will seek me and find me, when you search for me with all your heart" (Jeremiah 29:13). "You, O Lord, have not forsaken those who seek you" (Psalms 9:10). "The Lord is near to all who call upon him" (Psalms 145:18). "The Lord is good to those who wait for him, to the person who seeks him" (Lamentations 3:25). David exhorted his son Solomon, "The Lord searches all hearts, and understands every intent of the thoughts. If you seek him, he will let you find him; but if you forsake him, he will reject you forever" (1 Chronicles 28:9; cf. 2 Chronicles 15:2). "Wisdom" offered her treasures to those who would seek her: "I love those who love me; and those who diligently seek me will find me" (Proverbs 8:17; also see Matthew 7:7-8).

Other verses tell us that God is actively involved on the other end of this process: "For the eyes of the Lord move to and fro throughout the earth that he may strongly support those whose heart is completely his" (2 Chronicles 16:9). "For thus says the Lord God, 'Behold, I myself will search for my sheep and seek them out'" (Ezekiel 34:11), Jesus proclaimed, "For the Son of Man has come to seek and to save that which was lost" (Luke 19:10).

Seeking God is more than an intellectual process; it also involves a moral willingness:

> And this is the judgment, that the light is come into the world, and men loved the darkness rather than the light; for their deeds were evil. For everyone who does evil hates the light, and does not come to the light, lest his deeds should be exposed. But he who practices the truth comes to the light, that his deeds may be manifested as having been wrought in God (John 3:19-21).

John 7:17 also relates the moral dimension to the reception of spiritual truth: Jesus said, "If any man is willing to *do* God's will, he shall *know* of the teaching, whether it is of God, or whether I speak from myself." After his vision of the sheet, Peter came to understand that "God is not one to show partiality, but in every nation the man who fears him and does what is right, is welcome to him" (Acts 10:34-35; cf. 17:26-27).

On the other hand, David wrote that no one seeks after God or does good (Psalms 14:2-3) and Paul agreed (Romans 3:10-12). Evidently, this means that no one pursues God with a whole heart or merits salvation by his works; apart from God's grace no one would seek him. Yet we are still responsible.

Unfortunately, these passages are often used as an excuse for lazy evangelism. "No one seeks after God, so I don't need to be looking out for them. And people that ask questions or raise objections are just throwing up a smokescreen." We must acknowledge that in these places the Bible affirms our innate brokenness and inability to seek after God on our own, but elsewhere the Bible speaks of the Holy Spirit "drawing" or "convicting" us (John 6:44, 16:8). **When the Holy Spirit is internally drawing a person to faith, the outward appearance looks like someone *seeking* after God.**

Those who respond positively to the light they have received will gain the knowledge that leads to salvation, and those who suppress it remain under the wrath of God. There is therefore no biblical warrant or need for a second chance.

God has seen fit to use his children as his primary means of providing additional light to those who want more. The New Testament strongly emphasizes the need for missions, so that all may be exposed to the Good News about Jesus.

> For there is no distinction between Jew and Greek; for the same Lord is Lord of all, abounding in riches for all who call upon Him; for "Whoever will call upon the name of the Lord will be saved." How then shall they call upon Him whom they have not heard? And how shall they hear without a preacher? And how shall they preach unless they are sent? Just as it is written, "How beautiful are the feet of those who bring glad tidings of good things!" (Romans 10:12-15)

Missionaries must be sent so that people who have not heard may hear and believe. This was the point of Christ's Great Commission: "Go therefore and make disciples of all the nations, baptizing them in the name of the Father and the Son and the Holy Spirit, teaching them to observe all that I commanded you" (Matthew 28:19-20). Our Lord's last words prior to His ascension anticipated the spread of the Gospel throughout the whole world: "But you shall receive power when the Holy Spirit has come upon you; and you shall be My witnesses both in Jerusalem, and in all Judea and Samaria, and even to the remotest part of the earth" (Acts 1:8). After the Good News spread throughout Judea (Acts 1-7), it reached the Samaritans in Acts 8 through the ministry of Philip.

The incident with the Ethiopian eunuch (Acts 8:26-40) is a good illustration of God's provision of further light to a person who responds to the light he has received. The Ethiopian wanted to know more about the Suffering Servant of Isaiah 53, and God sent Philip to preach Jesus to him. A similar illustration appears in Acts 10 with the conversion of the Gentile centurion Cornelius and his household. Beginning in Acts 13, the missionary journeys of Paul and others carried the message of Jesus throughout the Roman Empire to Jews and Gentiles who needed to hear it.

There have been setbacks, but today this message has expanded in an unprecedented way all over the globe. Massive revivals have taken place in Africa, Indonesia, and other countries; millions have attended Christian rallies in South Korea; Gospel radio broadcasts reach all over the world through powerful transmitters; Christian organizations with global vision are reaching millions of people each week through newspapers, literature, films, and distribution of food and supplies. Our myopic impression is that Christianity is big in the United States, but irrelevant in much of the world. On the contrary, less than 10% of all Christian adherents, less than 15% of Protestants, and less than 25% of evangelical traditions make their home in the USA.

In fact, over the past 20 centuries since Jesus walked the earth, there are very few people groups and population centers where his Gospel has never been proclaimed. A few modern thinkers about this topic like to turn the question back on the questioner, "Are you sure there are so many who have never heard or had the opportunity to hear about Jesus at any point in their lives?"

Too often we think of God in Lilliputian terms. He is not an elderly gentleman looking down on earth from a celestial perch, biting His fingernails and saying, "I hope that missionary makes it. I hope he gets there in time!" If He really is the omniscient and omnipotent creator and sustainer of the universe, the Lord can get the message through, no matter where a person is (cf. Psalms 139:7-12). We cannot put Him in a box and limit the ways He might use to do this. Use the *time and distance* illustration in the sidebar to help clarify this point.

The Bible repeatedly tells us that God can speak directly to the human heart. Consider, for example, the call of Abraham in Genesis 12, Nebuchadnezzar's dream in Daniel 2, God's warning to the magi in Matthew 2, Christ's appearance to the Pharisee Saul in Acts 9, Cornelius's vision of an angel in Acts 10. Missionaries sometimes report stories of similar divine encounters today as well as unusual circumstances, obviously engineered by God to lead people into a knowledge of Christ.

Mary Teegardin, a missionary to South Thailand, remembered a Muslim village leader who was directed in a dream to come to a missionary hospital to learn about Jesus and believe in him. During that very week a missionary doctor who had worked in the Middle East for years made an unannounced visit to the same hospital. Because this doctor spoke fluent Arabic, he was able to share Christ with this Muslim.

Illustration: Is God bound by time and distance?

Is it possible that there is someone here in this city who has never heard a meaningful explanation of the love and sacrificial death of Jesus Christ and his offer of forgiveness and eternal life? Of course. It's not only possible, but it's probable.

Could a person here, who has never heard about Jesus Christ, reach out to God and ask for information or help? Perhaps they are experiencing emptiness in the midst of material success, or existential despair in the midst of difficulty. Could they cry out, "God, if you're really there and if it's possible to have some personal real connection with you, I'd like to know how." Of course. If you are having this conversation with a friend who hasn't embraced faith, then they may be having this very experience.

If this person who had never heard about Jesus Christ asked for more information, do you think God could somehow connect him with someone who DID know about Jesus Christ so he could pass on the message? And is that possible? Of course. If God's God, if he created the world and everything in it, and if he can get the message to this person here in our city, why couldn't the God who made the whole world get the message to somebody on the other side of it from us? It's a big problem for you and me, but not a big problem for an all-knowing and all-powerful God. Couldn't God get the job done if he wanted to?

In recent decades there seems to have been an explosion of reports of Muslims having dreams that directed them to ultimate faith in Jesus. Several of these testimonies are posted online at answering-islam.org.

An incident that took place in 19th-century India illustrates the effective power of even a tiny fragment of God's Word. A caravan was crossing from one part of India to another and a missionary was traveling with it. As it passed along, a Hindu was so overcome by heat and weariness that he sank down, and was left to perish on the road. The missionary saw him and kneeling by his side when the other travelers had passed on, whispered into his ear, "Brother, what is your hope?" The dying man raised himself a little, and with his last effort gasped out, "The blood of Jesus Christ His Son cleanseth from all sin." The astonished missionary wondered how this man, to all appearance a heathen, came to know Christ. Then he noticed a piece of paper grasped tightly in the dead man's hand. To his delight he saw it was a single leaf from the Bible containing the first chapter of John's first epistle in which these words appear. On that single page, this Hindu had found eternal life. (Story collected by John Richardson Phillips, who included it in his 1876 book, *Remarkable Providences and Proofs of a Divine Revelation*)

The Spirit of God uses the Word of God through men and women of God to make the message about the Son of God available to all who want to know the truth. There is no limit to the creative ways God can use to bring about this process.

What about those who lived before Christ? How could any of them have come to a knowledge of the true God? The *basis* of salvation has always been the sacrificial death, burial, and resurrection of Christ Jesus. Though the saving work of Christ was future, God saw it from before the foundation of the earth. Not bound by time, the Lord applied the benefits of the death of Christ to all who called upon God for salvation. The *means* of salvation has always been faith, not works. The Old Testament clearly teaches that man is sinful and in need of God's grace (Isaiah 59:2; 64:6; Psalms 6:1-2; 51:1-13). Thus, an Israelite needed to acknowledge his sin and turn to God in repentance and faith, and this was demonstrated through the offering of animal sacrifices at the temple. These sacrifices could never atone for all sin, they had to be offered again and again. The prophets looked forward to the time when God would provide ultimate atonement (Isaiah 53). We can look back and see clearly that these ritual sacrifices all pointed ahead to the sacrifice of God's Son. In Old Testament times, people did not clearly understand this; like Abraham (Genesis 15:6), they were justified by grace through faith, and the object of that faith was God. But with the progressive revelation of the New Testament, the content of faith now includes the finished work of Christ.

The Old Testament also offers a few examples of Gentiles who came to know the one true God. These include Rahab the prostitute (Joshua 2), Ruth the Moabite (Ruth 1), Naaman the Syrian (2 Kings 5), and even the Assyrians in Nineveh, who repented at the preaching of Jonah (Jonah 3). Though it's not quite as clearly described, a case can be made that Babylonian king Nebuchadnezzar and Darius the Mede made professions of faith in Israel's God. Rahab and Ruth married Jewish men and became part of Israel, while the other examples remained in their own lands.

What about infants and those mentally incapable of understanding the Gospel? Although the Bible is not explicit on this issue, it does provide certain principles and examples which suggest that God does not hold accountable those who do not have the capacity to make a decision about Him. When the recently emancipated Israelites rebelled against God and Moses and wanted to return to Egypt, God declared that they would all die in the wilderness. But Numbers 14:29 says that those who were under 20 would be spared this judgment. The younger generation was not held accountable for the sins of their fathers. Instead, they were allowed to take possession of Canaan; "Moreover, your little ones who you said would become a prey, and your sons, who this day have no knowledge of good or evil, shall enter there, and I will give it to them, and they shall possess it" (Deuteronomy 1:39).

The issue here is the same one that runs throughout this chapter—the fairness of God. Based on this example, God will be fair to those who are incapable of making an intellectual and moral response to Him.

The doctrine of infant salvation cannot be proved from the Bible, but there are some passages that imply that infants are in some special way kept by the power of God. Christ's teaching in Matthew 18:3-14 and 19:14 points in this direction:

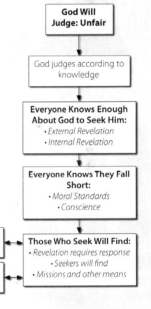

> See that you do not despise one of these little ones, for I say to you, that their angels in heaven continually behold the face of my Father who is in heaven.... Thus it is not the will of your Father who is in heaven that one of these little ones perish.... Let the children alone, and do not hinder them from coming to me; for the kingdom of heaven belongs to such as these (Matthew 18:10, 14; 19:14).

King David, after the loss of the infant born out of his adultery with Bathsheba, said, *"But now he has died; why should I fast? Can I bring him back again? I shall go to him, but he will not return to me"* (2 Samuel 12:23). Though David sinned, he knew the child would be with God, and he anticipated seeing him again.

Some people also look at Revelation 5:9, *"for you were slain, and by your blood you ransomed people for God from every tribe and language and people and nation"* as a partial reference to infant salvation. The argument is that this could account for the salvation of people in every tribe and nation that existed. If infants are covered by the atoning work of Christ, it is likely that these people will constitute a large percentage of the redeemed in heaven. (It is possible that this verse offers a partial solution to the problem of the American Indians before Columbus and other large groups unreached by missionaries.)

God Will Judge: Fair

↓

Knowledge of God

↓

Knowledge of Sin

↓

Knowledge of Solution

Third Option: God's Judgment Of Those Who Have Not Heard Is Fair

When a person realizes that God's judgment is fair, it is time to personalize this question to show how it applies to him or her. We said that God judges according to the knowledge each individual has received and does not hold people accountable for what they could not know. But the other side of the coin is that God *does* hold us accountable for the knowledge we have received, and the person who asked this question is already aware of the message of the Gospel. Therefore, the real issue for him is no longer the unevangelized but himself. So we must ask, "What are *you* going to do with Jesus Christ?"

This question cannot be used as a dodge to avoid a decision about Christ. Those who have heard the Gospel and rejected it are doubly guilty—they have rejected not only the Father but also the Son. And the scriptures are clear about the judgment that awaits those who have refused God's offer of salvation. The wrath of God abides on them (John 3:36; cf. Hebrews 2:3; 10:26-31).

Even those who have not heard about Christ have some knowledge about God, sin, and the solution of casting oneself upon the mercy of the one true God. This knowledge from general revelation is not contradicted but completed by special revelation.

Knowledge of God. The scriptures reveal His character most clearly in the person of Jesus Christ (cf. John 1:14, 18).

Knowledge of sin. God's standard is perfection (Matthew 5:20, 48), and all of us fall short of that standard (Romans 3:23). Apart from Christ, we are under the condemnation of God (Romans 3:9; 6:23).

Knowledge of solution. God has provided a solution for sin through the work of His Son. We must acknowledge our need for His gift of righteousness and receive that gift by a choice of faith (Luke 19:10; John 1:12; 3:16; 14:6; 2 Corinthians 5:21; 1 Peter 3:18).

Summary

When a person comes to understand Christ's claim to be the only way to the Father, he will probably wonder what happens to those who never heard about Jesus Christ. Some avoid the problem by claiming that these people will not be judged. That would solve the problem (and eliminate the need for missions), but it is not a viable option. The Bible repeatedly teaches the universality of sin and the judgment that sin produces. We must all stand before the holy God in final judgment because of sin.

This may seem unfair until we understand certain biblical principles about the justice of God and the knowledge of the unevangelized. God's justice is perfect, and it is based on the amount of light that each person has received. No one is entirely ignorant about the Creator, because, even apart from the special revelation of his Word, he has made himself known to all through general revelation. This includes his external revelation through the creation and his internal revelation in the human heart.

Nor is anyone completely ignorant about the problem of sin. We all have moral standards that we cannot consistently maintain, and our conscience tells us of our moral inadequacy. This revelation about God and sin requires a response, and those who acknowledge their need and appeal to God for the answer will receive further light. God uses His children to carry the Good News about Christ to all parts of the world where people are seeking the one true God.

The basis of salvation in all ages has been the same—the redemptive work of Christ. The means of salvation has always been grace through faith. The content of this faith in the case of those who lived before Christ was not as specific as it is now because of progressive revelation. It is evident that infants and the mentally impaired are not held accountable to make a response they are incapable of making.

Those who ask this question must realize that, when they stand before God, the question will not be, "What about those who haven't heard?" but, "You heard the truth about Jesus Christ. How did you respond to Him?"

Supplemental Reading

Don Richardson, *Eternity in Their Hearts* (Regal Books). This absorbing book explores the almost universal concept of a supreme God in "primitive" and advanced cultures.

R.C. Sproul, *Objections Answered* (Regal Books). See chapter 3 for a fine presentation of the answers to this question.

Nash, Ronald H. *Is Jesus the Only Savior?* Zondervan, 1994.

Morgan, Christopher W., Robert A. Peterson, eds. *Faith Comes by Hearing: A Response to Inclusivism*.

Study Guide for Will God Judge Those Who Have Never Heard About Christ?

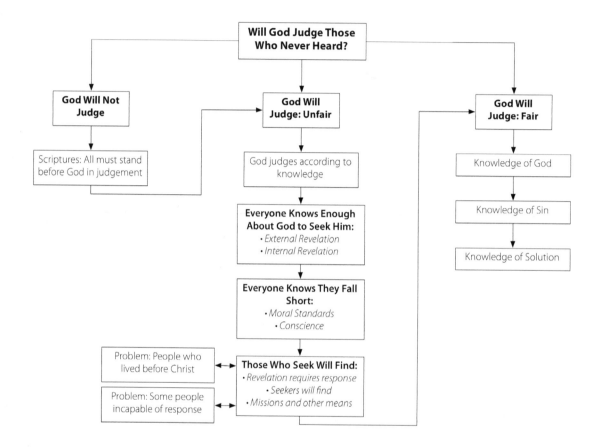

Key Illustrations

Tuberculosis

We die because of disease, not because of ignorance of the proper cure. Tuberculosis was a leading cause of death in urban environments for thousands of years, until the past century and the advent of antibiotics to cure it. "Cause of death" in every one of those cases is "bacterial infection of the lungs," not "lack of antibiotic."

Illustration: Is God bound by time and distance?

Is it possible that there is someone here in this city who has never heard a meaningful explanation of the love and sacrificial death of Jesus Christ and his offer of forgiveness and eternal life? Of course. It's not only possible, but it's probable.

Could a person here, who has never heard about Jesus Christ, reach out to God and ask for information or help? Perhaps they are experiencing emptiness in the midst of material success, or existential despair in the midst of difficulty. Could they cry out, "God, if you're really there and if it's possible to have some personal real connection with you, I'd like to know how." Of course. If you are having this conversation with an friend who hasn't embraced faith, then they may be having this very experience.

If this person who had never heard about Jesus Christ asked for more information, do you think God could somehow connect him with someone who DID know about Jesus Christ so he could pass on the message? And is that possible? Of course. If God's God, if he created the world and everything in it, and if he can get the message to this person here in our city, why couldn't the God who made the whole world get the message to somebody on the other side of it from us? It's a big problem for you and me, but not a big problem for an all-knowing and all-powerful God. Couldn't God get the job done if he wanted to?

Acts 14:15-17 "Friends, Why are you doing this? We are merely human beings like yourselves! We have come to bring you the Good News that you should turn from these worthless things to the living God, who made heaven and earth, the sea, and everything in them. [16]In earlier days he permitted all the nations to go their own ways, [17]but he never left himself without a witness. There were always his reminders, such as sending you rain and good crops and giving you food and joyful hearts."

Key Verses

Job 34:12 Surely, God will not act wickedly, and the Almighty will not pervert justice.

Genesis 18:25 Shall not the Judge of all the earth deal justly?

Luke 12:48 (NLT) "But people who are not aware that they are doing wrong will be punished only lightly. Much is required from those to whom much is given, and much more is required from those to whom much more is given.

1 Timothy 2:4 for he wants everyone to be saved and to understand the truth.

2 Peter 3:9 The Lord isn't really being slow about his promise to return, as some people think. No, he is being patient for your sake. He does not want anyone to perish, so he is giving more time for everyone to repent.

Jeremiah 29:13 In those days when you pray, I will listen. If you look for me in earnest, you will find me when you seek me. 14 I will be found by you," says the Lord.

Psalm 9:10 Those who know your name trust in you, for you, O Lord, have never abandoned anyone who searches for you.

1 Chronicles 28:9 For the Lord sees every heart and understands and knows every plan and thought. If you seek him, you will find him. But if you forsake him, he will reject you forever.

Matthew 7:7-8 Keep on asking, and you will be given what you ask for. Keep on looking, and you will find. Keep on knocking, and the door will be opened. [8]For everyone who asks, receives. Everyone who seeks, finds. And the door is opened to everyone who knocks.

Ezekiel 34:11 For this is what the Sovereign Lord says: "I myself will search and find my sheep.

Acts 10:34-35 Then Peter replied, "I see very clearly that God doesn't show partiality. [35]In every nation he accepts those who fear him and do what is right.

Romans 1:19-20 For the truth about God is known to them instinctively. God has put this knowledge in their hearts. [20]From the time the world was created, people have seen the earth and sky and all that God made. They can clearly see his invisible qualities–his eternal power and divine nature. So they have no excuse whatsoever for not knowing God.

Romans 2:14-16 Even when Gentiles, who do not have God's written law, instinctively follow what the law says, they show that in their hearts they know right from wrong. [15]They demonstrate that God's law is written within them, for their own consciences either accuse them or tell them they are doing what is right. [16]The day will surely come when God, by Jesus Christ, will judge everyone's secret life. This is my message.

Hebrews 11:6 So, you see, it is impossible to please God without faith. Anyone who wants to come to him must believe that there is a God and that he rewards those who sincerely seek him.

Study Questions

1. How would you respond to the person who says, "God is a loving God, so He won't judge anyone who hasn't heard of or responded to Him"?

2. "It is unfair for God to judge those who have not heard about Christ." This statement is built on the following false premises. Respond to each.

   • They are ignorant of God

   • They are ignorant of Sin

   • They are ignorant of a Solution

3. What are some of the biblical examples of God getting the message to those who had never heard?

4. How would you respond to people who continue to be more concerned about those who haven't heard than themselves?

Notes

QUESTION 8: IF CHRISTIANITY IS TRUE, WHY ARE THERE SO MANY HYPOCRITES?

Often-Asked Questions:

- The Christians I know are full of talk about love, but they are some of the most intolerant, selfish, and bigoted people I know. Why would I want anything to do with Christianity?

- Too many Christians I know are two-faced. If that's what Christianity is all about, why should I become a Christian?

- If Christians are really concerned about others, why don't they show it?

- Some non-Christians I know seem to live better lives than a lot of people who go to church—doesn't this show that Christianity isn't all it claims to be? How can people who profess to be Christians still be full of racial hatred, materialism, and social insensitivity?

- Many churchgoers seem to have holier-than-thou attitudes. Why should I join the ranks of the self-righteous?

For some, this is one of the most emotionally charged questions, right behind the question of Evil and Suffering. We need to listen well to hear whether this question is being asked because of the negative cultural stereotypes and historical blunders of Christians, or whether it is being asked because the person (or someone close to them) has been personally wronged by a supposed Christ-follower. In order to diffuse the anger that people feel about his issue, we must first empathize with them and admit that hypocrisy is an issue in the church.

Two Options

The underlying issue in this question is the implication that since Christians fall short, the truth claims of Christianity must also fall short. Does hypocritical behavior among those who profess to be Christians nullify the message about Christ? Some who have been disillusioned by the behavior of believers assume that it does, and they want no part of Christianity. The other possibility is that the truth of Christianity is not determined by the track record of adherents.

First Option: Hypocrisy Invalidates Christianity

Many delight in rehearsing the worst travesties perpetrated in the name of Christianity; for example, the Crusades, the Spanish Inquisition, or the Salem witch trials. They also turn to the present and point to examples of financial exploitation, adultery, and other forms of unethical behavior among church leaders. They conclude, therefore, that the entire church is full of all sorts of hypocrites, and they imply that Christianity is not true because it does not work.

Though we cannot agree that the church is *full* of hypocrites, we must acknowledge that there are some. We can't deny the abuses and inconsistencies mentioned above, and we should quickly admit that the church is not immune to this problem. In his *Pensees*, Blaise Pascal wrote, "Men never do evil so completely and cheerfully as when they do it from religious conviction."

Hypocrisy, then, is a problem in the church—*and everywhere else virtues are valued*. It would be wrong to condemn the medical profession because of wrong diagnoses and ineffective treatments, as well as certain instances of malpractice.

False assumptions. Three false assumptions are associated with this objection concerning the hypocrites, and they need to be exposed as such before the objection can be overcome. *The first false assumption* is that *all sin or* *bad behavior is hypocrisy*. While all hypocrisy is sin, not all sin is hypocrisy. Sin is a general term, and hypocrisy, like theft and slander, is a particular species of sin. In ancient Greece, the word *hypokrisis* referred to a "pretense" or an "outward show." Another word, *hypokrites*, meant "hypocrite, pretender" and was originally used to describe Greek actors who spoke through masks (the kind sometimes found on playbills and theater decorations) during their performances. Thus, the word came to be used of a person who was pretending to be something he was not. The hypocrite is living a lie because he makes a pretense of moral character that he does not possess. He carefully covers his faults so that others will have a higher opinion of him.

For a person to come to Christ on his terms, he must become the opposite of a hypocrite. That is, he must acknowledge his own lack of merit in God's sight and accept the unmerited favor (grace) that God has provided in his gift of Christ's righteousness to those who come to him. Before a person can embrace Christ as Savior, he must admit that he is a sinner. Jesus told the Pharisees, "It is not those who are healthy who need a physician, but those who are sick; I did not come to call the righteous, but sinners" (Mark 2:17). It is the man who thinks he is morally healthy before God apart from Christ who is the real hypocrite, because he considers himself righteous when he is in fact a transgressor of God's moral law. "If we say that we have no sin, we are deceiving ourselves, and the truth is not in us... If we say that we have not sinned, we make him a liar, and his Word is not in us" (1 John 1:8, 10). Thus, while all Christians sin (1 John 1:8, 10), not all Christians are hypocrites.

(2)   *The second false assumption is* that *profession means possession*. Many people take it for granted that whoever claims to be a Christian must therefore be a Christian. But there is a great deal of difference between Christianity and "churchianity"; many church members are not members of the body of Christ. Being religious is not synonymous with having a relationship. The Pharisees were highly religious, but many of them did not know God. Profession does not mean possession.

When this objection about the hypocrites surfaces, it is important to be sure we are talking about real Christians—that is, those who have admitted their sinfulness and turned to Christ as their Savior. Anything of genuine value like money, jewels, and art can and will be counterfeited. But the fact that counterfeit money exists does not mean we should stop using money. Similarly, reproductions or forgeries of great paintings do not lessen the value of the genuine paintings. Church attendance, high moral standards, and religious profession do not make someone a biblical Christian any more than going to a ballpark makes a person a baseball player. This can help alleviate the problem raised by the hypocrite question because many of the misdeeds associated with Christianity are not accomplished by genuine Christians.

(3)   *The third false assumption* is that *Christians claim to be perfect*. Some non-Christians put Christians in a lose-lose situation. On the one hand,

they impose a double standard, expecting Christians to behave on a level that they themselves never think of attaining. On the other hand, they are offended by righteous behavior because of their inward sense of guilt. When their Christian friends behave in a godly manner, they assume it must be a show and equate piety with pretense.

But ethical behavior does not have to mean self-righteousness; one can be moral without being moralistic. In fact, a true Christian should be the first to admit that he is not perfect in his practice. Christians do not claim to be sinless, but they do claim to be perfectly forgiven.

It is clear from such passages as Romans 7:14-25; Galatians 5:13-26; Philippians 3:12-16; and 1 John 1:5-10 that Christians have not arrived at a state of complete Christlikeness. Until we see Christ "just as he is" (1 John 3:2) and become like him, no believer will be immune to the pull of various kinds of sins. We will fail, but this does not invalidate Christianity; it simply means that for a time we withdraw from our walk with Christ.

Thus, the real issue is not perfection but progression. The quality of a Christian's life will fluctuate, but over a period of time it should progress toward increasing Christ-likeness. Unlike the hypocrite, this change is not an external veneer but is being wrought from the inside out.

So it is unwise to compare the life of one believer with the lives of others. It is more valid to compare what he is now with what he was before coming to Christ. If we met someone on the beach with an average physique who proudly told us about the terrific exercise program he has been following, we wouldn't be terribly impressed. But if we found out that he had been a 97-pound weakling (or a 300 pound couch potato) only a few months before, our assessment of his exercise program would suddenly change. Similarly, some non-Christians are better adjusted people than some Christians, but this does not mean that Christianity is ineffective. Non-Christians may point to inconsistencies in the lives of Christians they know, especially new believers. But if they take a closer look, they will probably find that some real changes have actually taken place when they compare the believer's present life with what it used to be before he became a Christian.

Even though the Spirit of God indwells and empowers believers, it is only too easy for us to "quench the Spirit" (1 Thessalonians 5:19) and grieve him (Isaiah 63:10; Ephesians 4:30). When a true Christian fails to progress in his faith and leads a life of inconsistency or hypocrisy, he will begin to experience the firm but loving discipline of his heavenly Father. "God deals with you as with sons; for what son is there whom his father does not discipline? But if you are without discipline, of which all have become partakers, then you are illegitimate children and not sons" (Hebrews 12:7-8). Because God loves his children, "he disciplines us for our good, that we may share his holiness" (Hebrews 12:10). This divine training is designed to yield "the peaceful fruit of righteousness" (Hebrews 12:11) which will attract others to Christianity rather than repel them.

Christ's view of hypocrisy. Only Christ used the word *hypocrite* in the New Testament, and he reserved his harshest words for those who fell into this category. Matthew 23 contains a frightening series of woes delivered by our Lord to the religious leaders of his day (the scribes and Pharisees) who made an outward display of godliness but inwardly did not know God. In their pomp and formalism, they sought the plaudits of men rather than the approval of God. Their self-righteousness prevented them from seeing their own sin. This is why Jesus told them, "You are like white-washed tombs which on the outside appear beautiful, but inside they are full of dead men's bones and all uncleanness. Even so you also appear outwardly righteous to men, but inwardly you are full of hypocrisy and lawlessness...You snakes! You brood of vipers! How will you escape being condemned to hell?" (Matthew 23:27-28, 33).

Today also there are religious pretenders in the church who are fooling others and, just as tragically, fooling themselves. But God, who searches men's hearts, cannot be deceived and will one day tell these modern-day Pharisees the awful words, "I never knew you; depart from me, you who practice lawlessness" (Matthew 7:23).

Christ uttered these stern words not only because of the self-deceiving pride involved in such hypocrisy but also because of the great damage that hypocrisy causes. When religious fraud is exposed in the lives of ministers, many people become disillusioned and disappointed. Hypocrisy causes people to stumble, and the effects can be far-reaching.

Not only is Jesus adamantly opposed to hypocrisy in all its forms but so is the entire Bible. The prophets of the Old Testament continually denounced religious orthodoxy and formalism that lacked inner reality. The Lord denounced Judah through the Prophet Isaiah saying, "This people draw near with their words and honor me with their lip service, but they remove their hearts far from me, and their reverence for me consists of tradition learned by rote" (Isaiah 29:13; also see Proverbs 26:23-26; Isaiah 1:13-17; Jeremiah 7:8-10; 9:8). Amos made this point abundantly clear in his oracle to the Northern Kingdom of Israel:

> I hate, I reject your festivals, nor do I delight in your solemn assemblies. Even though you offer up to me burnt offerings and your grain offerings, I will not accept them; and I will not even look at the peace offerings of your fatlings. Take away from me the noise of your songs; I will not even listen to the sound of your harps. But let justice roll down like waters and righteousness like

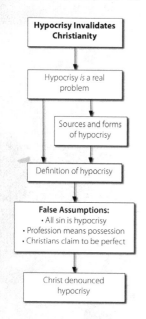

Hypocrisy Invalidates
Christianity

Hypocrisy *is* a real
problem

Sources and forms
of hypocrisy

Definition of hypocrisy

False Assumptions:
• All sin is hypocrisy
• Profession means possession
• Christians claim to be perfect

Christ denounced
hypocrisy

an ever-flowing stream (Amos 5:21-24).

New Testament authors are also united in their opposition to religious hypocrisy and pretense. Paul describes certain people as "holding to a form of godliness, although they have denied its power; avoid such men as these" (2 Timothy 3:5).

Writing to his coworker Titus, Paul says, "They profess to know God, but by their deeds they deny him, being detestable and disobedient, and worthless for any good deed" (Titus 1:16; also see Romans 2:1, 3, 17-29; Galatians 2:11-14; 1 Timothy 4:1-2; James 1:22-26; 2:14-26; 2 Peter 2:17, 19; 1 John 1:6; 4:20; Jude 12-13; Revelation 2:9).

So the non-Christian who is opposed to religious hypocrisy actually agrees with Christ and the Bible on this point.

Second Option: Hypocrisy Does Not Invalidate Christianity

Christians do not claim to be perfect, but they do claim to be forgiven by the One who is perfect, Jesus Christ. Because of human frailty, inconsistency, and rebellion against God, the performance of the Christian church through the centuries has been far from ideal. But Christianity really stands or falls on the person of Christ, not the performance of Christians. If Christ was a hypocrite, the whole structure of Christianity crumbles into a heap.

The officers who were sent out by the chief priests and the Pharisees to seize Jesus returned empty-handed and said of him, "Never did a man speak the way this Man speaks" (John 7:46). Jesus spoke the noblest words ever spoken, and the standards he raised were so high that they were humanly unattainable. But in the life of Jesus, his words and works were a seamless piece; his precepts were perfectly matched by his practice. He spoke of loving one another and displayed unmatched compassion for people on every level. He spoke of servanthood and became the model of servanthood. He spoke of obedience to the will of his Father and walked every moment in complete dependence and submission to the life and will of God. He was the humblest and wisest man who ever lived, and in his character he perfectly realized the fruit of the Spirit: love, joy, peace, patience, kindness, goodness, faithfulness, gentleness, self-control. He spoke the truth and lived the truth, and when he publicly asked, "Which one of you convicts me of sin?" no one was able to respond. His own disciples who lived with him day and night for more than three years declared him to be sinless (1 Peter 2:22; 1 John 3:5).

Jesus was against hypocrisy, and his life was the antithesis of hypocrisy. Our job is to help those who raise the question of hypocrisy see that they actually agree with us and with Jesus on this issue. We need to tell them, "Jesus strongly denounced the hypocrites of his day and was the opposite

Jesus strongly denounced the hypocrites of his day and was the opposite of a hypocrite in his own life and character. Why should you let these people come between you and Christ?

of a hypocrite in his own life and character. Why should you let these people come between you and Christ?" No one ought to miss out on a relationship with Jesus because of someone else's inconsistency and hypocrisy. He offers his perfect righteousness to imperfect people who repent and turn to him. It would be foolish to let resentment against hypocritical behavior prevent you from receiving this priceless gift. Christ said that the religious hypocrites will not "escape the sentence of hell" (Matthew 23:33). Why plan to spend an eternity with them by rejecting Christ?

A great way to illustrate this point is with the following story:

Suppose I walk into the gas station with a ski mask on and gun in the air. As I instruct the clerk to empty the cash drawer, I announce that I am under orders from you not to leave any witnesses. When the drawer am empty, I unload two bullets into the clerk and make my getaway.

The police arrive moments later and find the clerk on the floor covered in blood and gasping for air.

"Can you give a description of your assailant?" The officer asks.

With his final breaths, the clerk weakly replies, "All I know is that [you] sent him."

A few hours later four squad cars pull into your driveway and demand that you come out with your hands up. Totally disoriented, you demand an explanation. "Armed robbery and murder were committed in your name tonight at the gas station."

Would it be fair for you to be locked away for life for crimes done in your name? Crimes that you would never have approved? Many things have been done in the name of Christ that directly contradict everything he stood for. Is it fair to condemn Christianity or Jesus Christ because of the things done in his name?

Sometimes the issue of hypocrisy is raised as an excuse for rejecting Christianity or as a dodge for avoiding a confrontation with the claims of Christ. When this happens, the objector should be brought as quickly as possible to the realization that the real issue is not the performance of Christians but the person of Christ. Religious pretense and abuses done in the name of Christianity are a problem, but they cannot be blamed on Christ or used to avoid one's own problem of sin. That problem needs to be dealt with whether a person is troubled by hypocrites or not. The only solution to that problem is the work of Christ.

Summary

Many people have been disappointed and disillusioned by people who profess to be Christians but live ungodly lives. Some non-Christians claim that Christianity cannot be true because it doesn't work—the church is full

---

Key Illustration: Robbing a Gas Station

Hypocrisy Does Not Invalidate Christianity

Christianity stands on the person of Christ, not the performance of Christians

Don't let the sins of others keep you from Christ

of hypocrites. There is no question that hypocrisy is a real problem and that there are many sources and forms of hypocrisy. But on closer examination, the hypocrisy issue is not as devastating as it first appears. The word hypocrite applies to a person who pretends to be something he is not. But the prerequisite to becoming a genuine Christian is an open acknowledgment that one is sinful, not righteous.

being a sinner is a prerequisite

In addition, we must correct three false assumptions to alleviate this objection. First, not all who profess to be Christians are in fact Christians. Second, real Christians do not claim to live perfect lives. Third, though believers sin, not all sin is hypocrisy. Furthermore, Christ himself denounced hypocrisy, and so does the entire Bible. Christ's character was perfect, and this is the basis of Christianity, not the performance of Christians. We shouldn't let the hypocrisy of some people become a barrier between the one who raises this objection and Christ.

basis of Christ's character & credibility

Supplemental Reading

Hart, David Bentley. *Atheist Delusions: The Christian Revolution and Its Fashionable Enemies.* Yale Univ. Press, 2009.

Hill, Jonathan. *What Has Christianity Ever Done for Us? How it shaped the modern world.* IVP Academic, 2005.

Hitchens, Christopher, and Douglas Wilson. *Is Christianity Good for the World? A Debate.* Canon Press, 2008.

<u>Study Guide for If Christianity Is True, Why Are There So Many Hypocrites?</u>

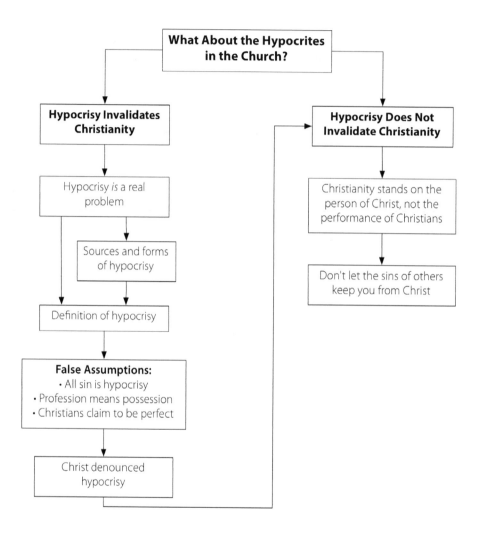

Key Verses

Matthew 23:23-36 "Woe to you, teachers of the law and Pharisees, you hypocrites! You give a tenth of your spices–mint, dill and cumin. But you have neglected the more important matters of the law, justice, mercy and faithfulness. You should have practiced the latter, without neglecting the former. [24]You blind guides! You strain out a gnat but swallow a camel.

[25]Woe to you, teachers of the law and Pharisees, you hypocrites! You clean the outside of the cup and dish, but inside they are full of greed and self-indulgence. [26]Blind Pharisee! First clean the inside of the cup and dish, and then the outside also will be clean.

[27]"Woe to you, teachers of the law and Pharisees, you hypocrites! You are like whitewashed tombs, which look beautiful on the outside but on the inside are full of dead men's bones and everything unclean. [28]In the same way, on the outside you appear to people as righteous but on the inside you are full of hypocrisy and wickedness.

[29]"Woe to you, teachers of the law and Pharisees, you hypocrites! You build tombs for the prophets and decorate the graves of the righteous. [30]And you say,'If we had lived in the days of our forefathers, we would not have taken part with them in shedding the blood of the prophets.' [31]So you testify against yourselves that you are the descendants of those who murdered the prophets. [32]Fill up, then, the measure of the sin of your forefathers!

[33]'You snakes! You brood of vipers! How will you escape being condemned to hell? [34]Therefore I am sending you prophets and wise men and teachers. Some of them you will kill and crucify; others you will flog in your synagogues and pursue from town to town. [35]And so upon you will come all the righteous blood that has been shed on earth, from the blood of righteous Abel to the blood of Zechariah son of Berekiah, whom you murdered between the temple and the altar. [36]I tell you the truth, all this will come upon this generation.

Isaiah 29:13 And so the Lord says, "These people say they are mine. They honor me with their lips, but their hearts are far away. And their worship of me amounts to nothing more than human laws learned by rote.

Matthew 7:21-23 "Not all people who sound religious are really godly. They may refer to me as 'Lord,' but they still won't enter the Kingdom of Heaven. The decisive issue is whether they obey my Father in heaven. [22]On judgment day many will tell me,'Lord, Lord, we prophesied in your name and cast out demons in your name and performed many miracles in your name.' [23]But I will reply,'I never knew you. Go away; the things you did were unauthorized.

Proverbs 26:23-26 Smooth words may hide a wicked heart, just as a pretty glaze covers a common clay pot. [24]People with hate in their hearts may sound pleasant enough, but don't believe them. [25]Though they pretend to be kind, their hearts are full of all kinds of evil. [26]While their hatred may be concealed by trickery,it will finally come to light for all to see.

Titus 1:16 Such people claim they know God, but they deny him by the way they live. They are despicable and disobedient, worthless for doing anything good..

1 John 1:8, 10 If we say we have no sin, we are only fooling ourselves and refusing to accept the truth... [10]If we claim we have not sinned, we are calling God a liar and showing that his word has no place in our hearts.

Key Illustrations

Robbing a Gas Station

Suppose I walk into the gas station with a ski mask on and gun in the air. As I instruct the clerk to empty the cash drawer, I announce that I am under orders from you not to leave any witnesses. When the drawer am empty, I unload two bullets into the clerk and make my getaway.

The police arrive moments later and find the clerk on the floor covered in blood and gasping for air.

"Can you give a description of your assailant?" The officer asks.

With his final breaths, the clerk weakly replies, "All I know is that [you] sent him."

A few hours later four squad cars pull into your driveway and demand that you come out with your hands up. Totally disoriented, you demand an explanation. "Armed robbery and murder were committed in your name tonight at the gas station."

Would it be fair for you to be locked away for life for crimes done in your name?

Study Questions

1. Give a good definition of the word hypocrite.

2. There are three false assumptions which cause people to conclude that hypocrisy invalidates Christianity. Respond to each.

   - All sin is hypocrisy

   - Profession means possession

   - Christians claim to be perfect

3. List a key passage which gives some of Jesus' feelings and descriptions about hypocrisy.

4. How can Jesus' view of hypocrisy help turn this objection into an opportunity?

5. If the validity of Christianity is not based on the performance of Christians, what is its basis?

Notes

QUESTION 9: WHAT ABOUT GOOD WORKS?

Often-Asked Questions:

- If people do their very best, won't God let them into heaven?

- I know many non-Christians who are far better people than most of the Christians I've met. Would God really refuse them?

- Doesn't God require me only to be better than the average human?

- Don't I have to have faith in Christ and live a good life if I want to go to heaven?

Two Options

The options for this question are quite straightforward. The first option holds that good works play an integral, if not the only, role in achieving heaven. The second option claims that salvation is attained solely through Christ's gift on our behalf.

The biblical perspective on this question is significant. Ten of the eleven major religions of the world teach salvation by good deeds. Christianity stands alone with its emphasis on grace rather than works for salvation.

First Option: Good Deeds Can Get Us To Heaven

People have sought for millenia to appease God by their own efforts. Knowing, however, that they could not achieve perfection, they devised various systems that called for degrees of goodness. They sought to elevate themselves toward God by performing a certain number or type of good deeds. These systems appeal to many people but, on close scrutiny, we find four major problems with them: they are arbitrary; they offer no assurance of salvation; they ask God to approve of evil; and they contradict the Bible.

(1) They are arbitrary. First, who determines which standard of works we should follow? Some would say we should follow the Ten Commandments. Others choose the Five Pillars of Islam and still more opt for the Golden Rule. See question 6 for further discussion on the incompatibility of the world's religious systems. Second, if we try to follow a system of works, how well do we have to do? What will be good enough for God to let us into heaven?

In a recent adult discussion group, someone asked, "What is good enough to get man to heaven?" Some people responded, "We must keep the Ten Commandments and follow the Golden Rule." The next question was, "How many keep those two things?" The answer: "Even though we don't keep them perfectly, we should all do our best." A third question immediately followed: "Do any of you do your best all the time?" No one could respond with a resounding yes, so the group lowered the standard again. They felt that if you tried your best *most* of the time, you could make it. But what does most of the time mean? Perhaps 51 percent? Or 85 percent? In the final round, the group admitted that it was unable to determine one level of commitment that would be necessary for salvation.

This becomes frustrating because we don't know how God grades our performance. Does he grade on a bell-shaped curve? Does he compare us against ourselves or against others? If it is against others, does he compare us with Jack the Ripper and the Boston Strangler or with Albert Schweitzer and Mother Teresa?

(2) They offer no assurance of salvation. Even though man's systems are

How good is good enough?

very arbitrary, it is amazing how many people hope they will make it. It's as though we put the human race on a ladder. The more good deeds a person does, the higher on the rungs he or she goes, with the lowest scoundrel on the bottom and the most saintly on the top. If we were to ask people to select the rung on which God would draw the line for salvation, most would respond that the cutoff point is just below their rung. But even though they might think they have made it, they have a nagging uncertainty. *They can't be sure.* Those who play a balancing scale game with their good versus their evil deeds cannot know the outcome until the end, when it is too late.

(3) They ask God to approve of evil. A system that demands less than perfection must allow some evil and, therefore, must ask God to approve of this evil. If God allowed imperfect people into heaven, then heaven would no longer be perfect. Heaven is without suffering and sin, not just a place where there is minimal suffering and sin (Revelation 21-22).

Imagine you are given a glass of cold, refreshing water. Just before you put the glass to your lips you are told that a small drop of cyanide has been added to the water. However, since it is such a small amount of cyanide, you needn't worry. What harm can such a small amount of poison do to a full glass of cool, clear water? *Great harm* is the correct answer, a small dose of poison contaminates the whole glass of water. In the same way, God cannot allow even a small amount of sin into heaven lest it contaminate the entire place.

This is why God must prohibit sin from his kingdom, for heaven would soon look like Earth if imperfect people were allowed in. God cannot approve of any evil. His flawless character demands that he judge all evil. God says that anyone less than perfect must be separated from him (Isaiah 59:2). Some object to this point and wonder *why* God must judge evil. Apart from the corruption of a perfect heaven, it might be helpful to look closer at the reality of sin. The concept that all sin is ultimately committed against God can be difficult to grasp. It may be helpful to observe that all sin also has a human cost. My selfish actions always cost someone else. Sometimes, such as with theft or violence, the costs are tangible. Other sins result in the intangible loss of potential, as when dishonesty robs a relationship of trust, or lust robs a relationship of intimacy. For God to casually overlook the sinful selfish choices, he must, in effect, say to the person wronged, "Get over it."

Take note that the topic of reincarnation sometimes comes to the surface here. The reincarnationist believes that good deeds will get one to a perfect state, and that selfish actions will meet justice, but only after a long series of transmigrations. After millions of lives, one can attain perfection, and thus become acceptable to God. We will deal more fully with reincarnation in the appendix to this chapter.

How much do we expect God to overlook?

All sin has a human cost, in addition to being against God. For God to casually overlook the sinful selfish choices, he must, in effect, say to the person wronged, "Get over it."

(4) They contradict the Bible. Any system of salvation by works clearly conflicts with the Bible. The scriptures plainly teach that the only way to overcome the gap between God and man is through faith in Christ, not good works.

> Because by the works of the Law no flesh will be justified in his sight; for through the Law comes the knowledge of sin (Romans 3:20).

> Now to the one who works, his wage is not reckoned as a favor, but what is due. But to the one who does not work but believes in him who justifies the ungodly, his faith is reckoned as righteousness (Romans 4:4-5).

> Now that no one is justified by the Law before God is evident; for, "The righteous man shall live by faith" (Galatians 3.11).

> He saved us, not on the basis of deeds which we have done in righteousness, but according to his mercy, by the washing of regeneration and renewing by the Holy Spirit (Titus 3:5).

The whole works-based system is rooted in the subtle sin of pride. Pride caused Satan and Adam to fall, and pride continues to keep mankind away from God's solution. By following a works-based system, a person seeks to give credit to themselves. If they trust in Christ for their salvation, only God can receive credit. There are many reasons why God chose to save man by grace, but the one Paul mentions is related to man's pride:

> For by grace you have been saved through faith; and that not of yourselves, it is the gift of God; not as a result of works, that no one should boast (Ephesians 2:8-9).

Some may question the testimony of the Bible, and at that juncture, we may need to go back and deal with the Bible's authority (see question 4). If works are not the means of salvation, what is the answer?

Second Option: Good Deeds Cannot Get Us To Heaven

God's Position

One of Christ's greatest discourses was the Sermon on the Mount where he gave God's standard for entering heaven: "Therefore you are to be perfect, as your heavenly Father is perfect" (Matthew 5:48). The standard is *perfection*. Note the qualifying phrase: "as your heavenly Father is perfect." He is holy and without blemish. Christ had already told the multitude that a perfection equal to that of their religious leaders would not be enough to save

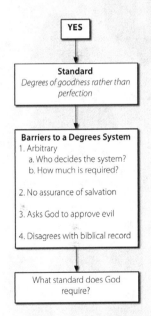

YES

Standard
Degrees of goodness rather than perfection

Barriers to a Degrees System
1. Arbitrary
   a. Who decides the system?
   b. How much is required?

2. No assurance of salvation

3. Asks God to approve evil

4. Disagrees with biblical record

What standard does God require?

Why justice? *Two illustrations that demonstrate why love is so dependent on justice.*

1. Sorry Criminal: *An Illustration to show that we yearn for justice, not just rehabilitation*

Imagine that I'm short on cash and I decide to rob a convenience store. In the midst of the robbery my mask falls off and knowing that he might identify me, I impulsively shoot and kill the clerk.

But as I read about the grieving widow and her four children, my remorse and guilt overwhelm me until I finally turn myself into the authorities and plead guilty at the trial. After I'm pronounced guilty and it is time for sentencing, let's imagine that I approach the bench and that you're the judge. "Your honor, I'm terribly sorry for what I have done. I want to do better with my life and I ask you for a pardon. Will you let me go free?"

Even if you are able to somehow supernaturally see inside me and know that I was truly sorry, and you could see into the future and know that I'd never commit that crime again. Will you let me go?

Suppose the widow and children aren't screaming for revenge. They're simply numb with pain over their irretrievable loss. Now will you let me go?

Something just doesn't seem right about letting me go free. Not because we're mean and vengeful, it's because we're caring and because we have a sense of justice. The fact that I'm sincerely sorry doesn't remove the need for justice.

2. Do I love my family: *An Illustration to show that love without justice is impossible*

"God is a loving God, so he won't judge those who have not heard of or responded to him"

I tell you that I love my wife and kids. I say that I could talk for hours about how much I love them. When I get home tonight, I discover that they've been involved in a terrible hit and run accident with a reckless/drunk driver. My son dies and my wife is paralyzed. The next week I discover the identity of the reckless/drunk driver and say, "I'm sure he didn't mean anything by it, we'll just let it go this time." The next time you and I talk and I tell you how much I love my family, do you believe me? No, in fact you might wonder whether I had hired the guy to take out my family. If I am not crying out for justice, then you have every right to doubt the love I claim for my family. Justice without love is cruel. Love without justice is not love at all.

God loves me too much not to impose justice on those who have hurt me. God loves those that I've hurt too much to allow me to escape justice.

them: "For I say to you, that unless your righteousness surpasses that of the scribes and Pharisees, you shall not enter the kingdom of heaven" (Matthew 5:20).

We must go back in time and recreate the atmosphere of Israel during the time of Christ. The religious leaders of the day had committed themselves to a good deeds system for salvation. The Pharisees had deceived themselves into believing that they had achieved perfection by observing their outward rituals. Christ exposed their sinful hearts by stating that God's standard was perfection not only in their actions but also in their attitudes. They may not have committed the act of murder, but they had the attitude of murder in their hearts (Matthew 5:21-22). They may not have committed the act of adultery, but they had the attitude of adultery in their hearts (Matthew 5:27-28). Christ went on to say:

> And if your right eye makes you stumble, tear it out, and throw it from you; for it is better for you that one of the parts of your body perish, than for your whole body to be thrown into hell. And if your right hand makes you stumble, cut it off, and throw it from you; for it is better for you that one of the parts of your body perish, than for your whole body to go into hell (Matthew 5:29-30).

Jesus was not advocating a new cult of self-mutilation, just graphically illustrating a point. The Pharisees were trying to earn their salvation by their good deeds, but God considered the heart condition as well as the external display. Even if they gouged out their eyes to keep from lusting, they could still have the attitude of lust. Christ made it quite clear that (1) salvation does not come to those who make an attempt at being perfect, but only to those who are perfect; and (2) man is imperfect, not only in his actions, but also in his attitudes.

Our Condition

How we illustrate imperfection is crucial, if we want to communicate the claims of Christ. When Christians talk of sin, they often think in *theological terms* and see all sin as equal. When an outsider feels accused of sin and imperfection, he or she thinks in *sociological terms* and notices vast differences in the sins of people. Our friends must understand that we are not saying that they are the most vicious people alive when we talk of how short they fall of God's standard of perfection.

You may want to use a variation of the following illustration as an aid in communicating this truth. Imagine all of humanity lined up around the rim of the Grand Canyon. The object is for each person to jump from one side of the rim to the other. Each person's ability to jump is directly proportional to how many good deeds he or she has performed. The first person to jump is a mass murderer who goes only one foot and plummets downward. The average person can bound for 8 to 10 feet, but this too is still pitifully short of the goal. An exceptionally self-sacrificing humanitarian out-distances most of humanity by going 150 feet away from the bank. But the same thing occurs to everyone who jumps; each falls short of the other bank. There are great differences among people as to their levels of goodness, but all of mankind fall short of perfection.

Or, you can illustrate this concept with a chart like the one in the sidebar.

The person represented by the long arrow might be inclined to compare their life with the lives of those around them and think that God will surely let them into heaven because of the relative quality of their life. But the standard God requires is absolute, not relative. It is nothing less than the perfect life of Christ. God will not and cannot lower his standards of righteousness and grade on a curve.

To be more accurate, the left line would actually be much further than portrayed in this diagram. On that scale, the relative differences in human works pale. (Similarly, if the earth could be reduced to the size of a basketball and held in your hands, your finger would not be able to tell the difference between Mt. Everest and low-lying hills.)

Paul tells us in Romans 3:23, "For all have sinned and fall short of the glory of God." This means that every human being is imperfect. Some people may not readily admit their lack of perfection, and when this happens, we introduce our 24-hour thought camera. We lightheartedly ask our friends if they would care to let us see all of their thoughts for the last 24 hours projected on the wall in living color. Then we remind them of Samuel Johnson's famous one-liner: "Every man knows that of himself which he dare not tell his dearest friend." It is important that we share with our friends that we don't want them to see our thoughts for the past 24 hours any more than they want us to see theirs. If not, this illustration could sound

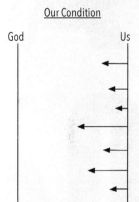

Our Condition

God   Us

snobbish and self-righteous.

James tells us how little it takes to become imperfect: "For whoever keeps the whole Law and yet stumbles in one point, he has become guilty of all" (James 2:10). Suppose you were dangling by a chain from a 2,000-foot precipice and one of the links in the chain breaks. It doesn't matter whether just one link breaks or they all break. The result is the same—you plummet to your death. So it is when man violates God's Law, whether there are numerous transgressions or just one.

The justice of God demands that a penalty be paid for this disobedience. The judgment for sin is eternal separation from the holy God. Isaiah tells us that our sins caused us to be separated from God: "But your iniquities have made a separation between you and your God" (Isaiah 59:2). Paul also describes the penalty in Romans 6:23: "For the wages of sin is death." God cannot change the penalty, for if he did, he would no longer be a just judge. The penalty must be paid. Either man pays for his own penalty, or someone else pays it. This is why it was necessary for God to bridge the gap, just like the updated illustration in the sidebar.

God's Provision

God's justice demands payment, and God's love offers us a substitute. Christ paid our debt on the cross of Calvary. "But God demonstrates his own love toward us, in that while we were yet sinners, Christ died for us" (Romans 5:8). We can rejoice that Paul didn't stop Romans 6:23 halfway through but finished the verse for us: "For the wages of sin is death, but the free gift of God is eternal life in Christ Jesus our Lord." Peter describes the beauty of Christ's sacrifice for us: "And he himself bore our sins in his body on the cross, that we might die to sin and live to righteousness; for by his wounds you were healed" (1 Peter 2:24). "For Christ also died for sins once for all, the just for the unjust, in order that he might bring us to God, having been put to death in the flesh, but made alive in the spirit" (1 Peter 3:18).

Consider the following story that depicts the interplay between justice and love that God displays to his creation. One day during the Great Depression, police hauled a frightened old man before the magistrate in a New York City night court. They charged him with petty larceny; he was starving and had stolen a loaf of bread. By coincidence, the mayor himself, Fiorello LaGuardia, was presiding over the court that night. LaGuardia sometimes sat in for judges as a way of keeping close to the citizens of the city. LaGuardia fined the old man $10. "The law is the law, and cannot be broken," the mayor pointed out. At the same time, he took a $10 bill out of his own wallet and told the man he would pay his fine for him. Then LaGuardia turned to the others in the courtroom and "cited" each of them

God's Provision

God   Us

Key Illustration: LaGuardia... (Justice & Love Demonstrated)

for living in a city that did not reach out and help its poor and elderly, tempting them unduly to steal. The mayor fined everyone in the audience $0.50 each, passed around his famous fedora to collect the fines, and turned over its contents to the amazed defendant. The hat contained almost $50. The old man left the courtroom with tears in his eyes.

Our Decision

God provided a solution to our problem, and freely offers it to us as a gift. Christ's death paid for everyone's sin, but each individual must decide if he wants Christ's payment or if he plans to pay the debt himself. Each person must personally receive this gift, and when he does, the payment that it provides is credited to his account. God can then reckon that person's debt of sin as "PAID IN FULL." The need for receiving Christ personally is mentioned by John: "But as many as received him, to them he gave the right to become children of God, even to those who believe in his name" (John 1:12). For a more detailed explanation of what is entailed in receiving Christ as Savior, see Question 11.

We solve our problem of separation from God by trusting in Christ's payment alone and not by seeking to pay the penalty with our own good deeds. While good works might make us better people, we will still fall far short of God's standard. Only through Christ can we be restored to a position of perfection before God. The moment we trust Christ, we appear as perfect before the Father. He no longer sees us in our sin but sees Christ in us.

One of the richest verses in scripture can be used to illustrate this concept. Paul wrote: "He [God] made him [Christ] who knew no sin to be sin on our behalf, that we might become the righteousness of God in him" (2 Corinthians 5:21). If I add up my own accomplishments in the flesh, words, deeds, thoughts, they add up to sin; but if the accomplishments of Christ are added up, the sum is righteousness. However, Christ placed *our* sin on his balance, and *his* righteousness on our balance.

Key Illustration: The Orange Balloon

An illustration concerning a young boy and his balloon casts light on the matter. The boy went into the house one day, peered at his father through the orange balloon, and cried, "Daddy, Daddy! You're an orange daddy, you're an orange daddy!"

The father smiled, removed the balloon, and said to his son, "Now, what do you see?"

The boy responded, "Aw, now you're just an ordinary daddy."

He quickly pressed his face flush against the balloon again and excitedly declared, "You're an orange daddy again!" The father asked him why he appeared to be orange. "Because I'm looking at you through my orange balloon," said the young boy.

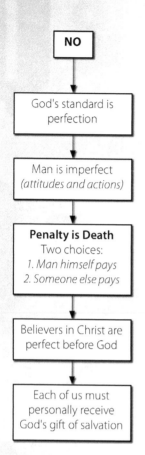

NO

God's standard is perfection

Man is imperfect
(attitudes and actions)

Penalty is Death
Two choices:
1. Man himself pays
2. Someone else pays

Believers in Christ are perfect before God

Each of us must personally receive God's gift of salvation

When we belong to Christ, God views us differently in him and sees perfect children. We call this *positional sanctification* (1 Corinthians 6:11). In Christ, we become new creatures (2 Corinthians 5:17). When we receive our resurrected bodies, we will be completely free from any blemish of sin (*ultimate sanctification*; Ephesians 5:26-27).

Christ's disciples were immersed in a society caught up with a salvation by works mentality. Early in his ministry, people came to Christ and asked what they must do to perform the works of God. Christ responded, "This is the work of God, that you believe in him whom he has sent" (John 6:29). John 14:6 tells us that it is through Christ alone that salvation is possible. (If someone has problems with Christ's credentials, remember the case for his Resurrection in Question 2.)

God will not accept our good deeds as payment for our sins. Even if we were 99 percent good most of the time, the 1 percent that was imperfect would be enough to disqualify us from heaven. In Ephesians 2:8-10, we learn how good works fit with salvation. Good works are not the *means* of salvation, they are the *results* of salvation. Having accepted Christ and his payment for us, we become children of God. As such, we seek to please him and become involved in good works for him.

Summary

We first considered the possibility of getting into heaven through good works. Most religious systems of works demand that we achieve certain degrees of goodness, since we cannot reach perfection. This appeals to many people raised in a society with a strong work ethic. But, for all its appeal, there are several barriers that render this option invalid:

The different work systems are arbitrary. Who decides which one is right?

We can never have assurance of salvation under a system of works. The standards change like shifting sands, and no one can be sure if his life is good enough.

The good deeds mentality is, in essence, asking God to approve of limited evil and assimilate it into his kingdom. (This relates to the question of reincarnation treated in the appendix to this chapter.) God is perfect, and he cannot "grade on a curve" by lowering his standard for salvation.

Finally, any system of salvation by works stands in direct disagreement with the scriptures.

So, if degrees of goodness are not the standard, what is? Christ has set the standard by being perfect himself. Man is imperfect, and the result of sin is separation from God. There are only two choices for paying the penalty for sin: (1) we can pay the penalty ourselves, or (2) we can allow someone else to pay the price for us.

Christ has paid our penalty, but we must personally accept Christ's payment because he will not force it on us. Those who receive Christ's gift become perfect in the sight of God, and are reconciled to him. Man cannot attain salvation by good deeds because the standard is perfection, and that is achievable only through Christ.

Appendix On Reincarnation

The theory of reincarnation may need to be examined when discussing the issue of good deeds as a means of getting to heaven. Reincarnation is the epitome of a works-based salvation.

The major tenet of all forms of reincarnation is a belief in a continuously rotating cycle of one's soul from body to body until it achieves a state of sinlessness. The soul passes from one life form to another at the point of death. In some versions the soul goes only into another human body, while other versions teach that the soul can pass into lower forms of life as well. Reincarnation, then, is a purification process whereby one attains salvation through his own merit and effort.

A person's progress through the cycles of life is determined by the law of karma. Karma is the moral law of cause and effect. A person's present fate, whether good or bad, is based on his actions in previous lives. This is the idea of reaping what you have sown. Sin cannot be forgiven but must be paid for by suffering in the next life. The reincarnationist believes that if we are suffering now, it is because of sins in our past life. The payment must be made by the individual who committed the sins, and it cannot be circumvented in any way. This system allows no room for grace or forgiveness.

However, reincarnation does solve some of man's basic questions and concerns. If a person sees good deeds as the means to heaven, he can become frustrated with his lack of progress toward perfection. But in reincarnation, man has many lives to better himself. This system allows an individual to solve the problem of his sin on his own.

Reincarnation can be appealing to a society raised on the notion that you get only what you pay for. And it explains the pain and suffering of the apparently innocent. People suffer because of the sins in their past lives, so God is not to blame. By requiring a man to stay on the treadmill of rebirth until he is sinless, reincarnation overcomes the problem of asking God to approve evil.

Granting that reincarnation solves some problems, when we look at it closely, it creates more problems than it solves.

First, since new souls are not created, life should be improving as man progresses through the purification process. The problem is that we see just as much, if not more, evil in the world today as there was 100 years ago.

Second, why is the population of the world increasing and not decreasing as the theory would lead us to think? The traditional reincarnationist answers this objection by saying that souls have been transmigrating not only in humans, but also in other living forms. It should follow that as the human population increases, the population of other life forms should decrease. But a study of nature does not reveal this to be true.

Third, if we were all to espouse reincarnation, our world would be virtually devoid of compassion and care for those who suffer. Remember, suffering comes as a result of sins in previous lives. Since karma never allows for the forgiveness of sin, but demands that payment always be made, we are actually robbing people of the opportunity to atone for their sins in this life if we ease their suffering now. The concept of karma allows no room for grace.

Fourth, how do lower forms of life like worms and mollusks build good karma? Will a roach be incarnated into a higher form if it stays out of people's kitchens? Morality requires the ability to make a conscious choice, and this is quite different from blind obedience to instinct.

The most difficult problem for reincarnation is that it contradicts scripture. In this chapter, we examined a number of passages that teach the impossibility of salvation through man's efforts. A review of these verses would be helpful. In addition, Christ repudiated the law of karma in John 9:1-3. If karma prevailed, the blind man's condition would have resulted from his own sin. But Christ said, "It was neither that this man sinned, nor his parents" (John 9:3). Also, 2 Corinthians 5:21 says that Christ substituted himself for us so that we could be made righteous through him.

This concept of forgiveness of sin is foreign to reincarnation. Karma demands payment and requires suffering, while Christ pays the penalty and offers forgiveness. What a contrast!

Hebrews 9:27 tells us, *"It is appointed for men to die once, and after this comes judgment."* This, as we learn in John 3:18, comes as a result of rejecting Christ and his payment. John 5:24 explains that by receiving Christ, one is removed from this judgment.

The famous Indian leader Gandhi expressed the frustration that millions face when they attempt to achieve perfection through their works. Near the end of a life of tirelessly giving himself for others, he confessed in his autobiography, *The Story of My Experiments with Truth:*

To attain to perfect purity one has to become absolutely passion free in thought, speech and action.... I know that I have not in me as yet that triple purity, in spite of constant ceaseless striving for it. That is why the world's praise fails to move me; indeed it very often stings me. To conquer the subtle passions seems to me harder far than the physical conquest of the world by the force of arms (pp. 504-5).

Study Guide for What About Good Works?

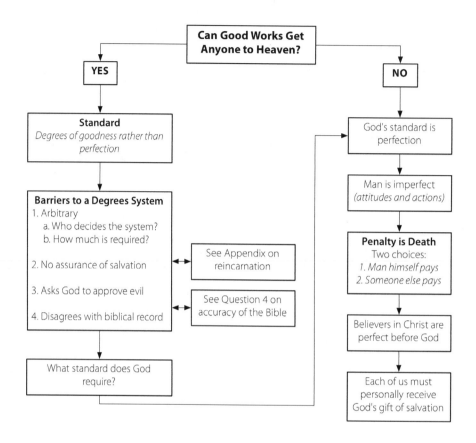

Key Illustrations

LaGuardia

Consider the following story that depicts the interplay between justice and love that God displays to his creation. One day during the Great Depression, police hauled a frightened old man before the magistrate in a New York City night court. They charged him with petty larceny; he was starving and had stolen a loaf of bread. By coincidence, the mayor himself, Fiorello LaGuardia, was presiding over the court that night. LaGuardia sometimes sat in for judges as a way of keeping close to the citizens of the city. LaGuardia fined the old man $10. "The law is the law, and cannot be broken," the mayor pointed out. At the same time, he took a $10 bill out of his own wallet and told the man he would pay his fine for him. Then LaGuardia turned to the others in the courtroom and "cited" each of them for living in a city that did not reach out and help its poor and elderly, tempting them unduly to steal. The major fined everyone in the audience $0.50 each, passed around

his famous fedora to collect the fines, and turned over its contents to the amazed defendant. The hat contained almost $50. The old man left the courtroom with tears in his eyes.

Orange Balloon

An illustration concerning a young boy and his balloon casts light on the matter. The boy went into the house one day, peered at his father through the orange balloon, and cried, "Daddy, Daddy! You're an orange daddy: you're an orange daddy!"

The father smiled, removed the balloon, and said to his son, "Now, what do you see?"

The boy responded, "Aw, now you're just an ordinary daddy."

He quickly pressed his face flush against the balloon again and excitedly declared, "You're an orange daddy again!" The father asked him why he appeared to be orange. "Because I'm looking at you through my orange balloon," said the young boy.

Sorry Criminal

Imagine that I'm short on cash and I decide to rob a convenience store. In the midst of the robbery my mask falls off and knowing that he might identify me, I impulsively shoot and kill the clerk.

But as I read about the grieving widow and her four children, my remorse and guilt overwhelm me until I finally turn myself into the authorities and plead guilty at the trial. After I'm pronounced guilty and it is time for sentencing, let's imagine that I approach the bench and that you're the judge. "Your honor, I'm terribly sorry for what I have done. I want to do better with my life and I ask you for a pardon. Will you let me go free?"

Even if you are able to somehow supernaturally see inside me and know that I was truly sorry, and you could see into the future and know that I'd never commit that crime again. Will you let me go?

Suppose the widow and children aren't screaming for revenge. They're simply numb with pain over their irretrievable loss. Now will you let me go?

Something just doesn't seem right about letting me go free. Not because we're mean and vengeful, it's because we're caring and because we have a sense of justice. The fact that I'm sincerely sorry doesn't remove the need for justice.

To Show That Love Without Justice Is Impossible

"God is a loving God, so he won't judge those who have not heard of or responded to him"

I tell you that I love my wife and kids. I say that I could talk for hours about how much I love them. When I get home tonight, I discover that they've been involved in a terrible hit and run accident with a reckless/drunk driver. My son dies and my wife is paralyzed. The next week I discover the identity of the reckless/drunk driver and say, "I'm sure he didn't mean anything by it, we'll just let it go this time." The next time you and I talk and I tell you how much I love my family, do you believe me? No, in fact you might wonder whether I had hired the guy to take out my family. If I am not crying out for justice, then you have every right to doubt the love I claim for my family. Justice without love is cruel. Love without justice is not love at all.

God loves me too much not to impose justice on those who have hurt me. God loves those that I've hurt too much to allow me to escape justice.

Key Verses

Romans 3:20 Because by the works of the Law no flesh will be justified in His sight; for through the Law comes the knowledge of sin.

Romans 4:4-5 Now to the one who works, his wage is not reckoned as a favor, but as what is due. 5But to the one who does not work, but believes in Him who justifies the ungodly, his faith is reckoned as righteousness,

Romans 5:8 But God demonstrates his own love for us in this: While we were still sinners, Christ Died for us.

Romans 6:23 The wages of sin is death, but the gift of God is eternal life

Galatians 3:11 Now that no one is justified by the Law before God is evident; for,"THE RIGHTEOUS MAN SHALL LIVE BY FAITH."

Ephesians 2:8-9 It is by grace you have been saved, through Faith – and this is not from yourselves, it is the gift of God – not by works so that no one can boast.

James 2:10 For whoever keeps the whole law and yet stumbles at one point is guilty of breaking all of it.

1 Peter 2:24 And He Himself bore our sins in His body on the cross, that we might die to sin and live to righteousness; for by His wounds you were healed.

Matthew 5 (selected verses)

20For I say to you that unless your righteousness surpasses that of the scribes and Pharisees, you will not enter the kingdom of heaven. 21You have heard that the ancients were told,'You shall not commit murder' and 'Whoever commits murder shall be liable to the court.' 22But I say to you that everyone who is angry with his brother shall be guilty before the court; and whoever says to his brother,'You good-for-nothing,' shall be guilty before the supreme court; and whoever says,'You fool,' shall be guilty enough to go into the fiery hell.

27You have heard that it was said,'You shall not commit adultery'; 28but I say to you that everyone who looks at a woman with lust for her has already committed adultery with her in his heart. 29If your right eye makes you stumble, tear it out and throw it from you; for it is better for you to lose one of the parts of your body, than for your whole body to be thrown into hell. 30If your right hand makes you stumble, cut it off and throw it from you; for it is better for you to lose one of the parts of your body, than for your whole body to go into hell.

43You have heard that it was said,'You shall love your neighbor and hate your enemy.' 44But I say to you, love your enemies and pray for those who persecute you, 45so that you may be sons of your Father who is in heaven; for He causes His sun to rise on the evil and the good, and sends rain on the righteous and the unrighteous.

46For if you love those who love you, what reward do you have? Do not even the tax collectors do the same? 47If you greet only your brothers, what more are you doing than others? Do not even the Gentiles do the same? 48Therefore you are to be perfect, as your heavenly Father is perfect.

Study Questions

1. Describe the system (way) most people believe leads to heaven.

2. There are four problems with any works-based system. Elaborate on each problem.

- It's arbitrary.

- It offers no assurance of salvation.

- It asks God to approve of evil.

- It contradicts the Bible.

3. Describe Christ's standard, and give scriptural support.

4. What is the difference between the theological and sociological view of sin? Give an illustration to explain the difference.

5. What is the problem with comparing one's good works against another's? Give an illustration.

Notes

QUESTION 10: ISN'T SALVATION BY FAITH TOO EASY?

Often-Asked Questions:

- Isn't just believing too easy?

- You don't get something for nothing. Why should it be any different with salvation?

- Doesn't the Bible say, "God helps those who help themselves?"

- What happens to the incentive for being good?

- Why would anyone appreciate salvation if it were free?

Two Options

There are two options for salvation. First, some balk at the idea that all a person has to do to obtain the gift of salvation is receive Jesus Christ and his payment for sin. They argue that this is too easy or too cheap; just believing is not enough. Salvation must be earned if it is to be appreciated. The second option, affirmed by the scriptures, is that while salvation is free to us, it is neither cheap nor easy.

First Option: Salvation By Faith Is Too Easy

There are many who shudder at the concept of salvation being a gift. Salvation must be earned, they think, for everyone knows you never get something for nothing. If your friends stress that salvation must be earned, then you must first deal with the question of good works (see question 9).

Behind this position is the notion that nothing of value is ever truly free. But something could be of value and free to us if it was paid for by someone else. When a son gets a new car for a graduation gift, it is free to him. But his parents had to pay the price.

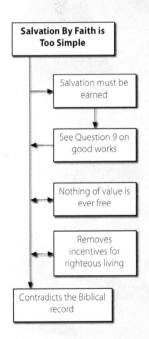

Another argument for this position says that if salvation is ours for the taking, it would remove all incentive for righteous living. Why not receive Christ and then go out and live any way we want, indulging any whim? Paul addresses this very issue in Romans 6:1-2. He has just developed the theme that salvation is by grace, not by works. Realizing that some may question a man's motives once he is guaranteed salvation, Paul queries, "What shall we say then? Are we to continue in sin that grace might increase?" His response: "May it never be! How shall we who died to sin still live in it?" When a person understands the greatness of God's salvation and the riches of his mercy, he will not seek ways to violate his relationship with God. Rather, he will want to cultivate his relationship with God. This idea is further explored in question 12.

The big problem with the idea that salvation must be earned is that it contradicts the biblical record. Ephesians 2:8-9 clearly states, "For by grace you have been saved through faith; and that not of yourselves, it is the gift of God; not as a result of works, that no one should boast."

For a more detailed scriptural refutation of this untenable view, review question 9.

Second Option: Salvation By Faith Is Not Too Easy

The gift of salvation had to be free, because the goal of achieving salvation through good works is not difficult—it's impossible. Christ made this clear in Matthew 5:48: "Therefore you are to be perfect, as your heavenly Father is perfect." Paul tells us that "all have sinned and fall short of the glory of

God" (Romans 3:23).

Free is not the same as easy, however. The plan of salvation was not easy for the Father. He had to separate himself from his Son (Matthew 27:46). The plan of salvation was not easy for the Son. He humbled himself (Philippians 2:5-8), paid the penalty for our sins (2 Corinthians 5:21), and was separated from the Father. And the plan of salvation is not easy for us. We have to give up our pride and admit there is nothing we can do to make ourselves worthy before the Father (Titus 3:5).

Objection: "Faith Alone" Removes Incentive For Being Good.

Unless someone asks the question, "Why should I be good if salvation is based on faith alone," then they don't truly understand the radical offer of the gospel. The Bible offers other motives for doing good deeds.

(1) Gratitude to God for his indescribable gift.

(2) A desire to serve and obey the one who loves me so much.

(3) A realization that since God loves me that much, he must want the best for me. And since he's all-knowing, he knows what's best. Therefore, his commands are for my joy, his prohibitions are for my protection. I do God's will because I want God's joy and blessing on my life, which is true success. I also do his will because I want to avoid getting hurt unnecessarily by disobeying his will. Living God's way leads to a generally better life and avoids much of the world's avoidable pain.

An illustration of this idea comes from the rules that good parents set for their kids—When our children were just learning to walk, we would forbid them to walk out into the street. Why? Because we're mean and selfish parents who want to deprive our children of any possible kind of fun? No, because we love them greatly and we want to protect them from the great danger on the road that they may not even be aware of, and which could have tragic consequences.

(4) A desire to avoid the discipline of a loving Father. Hebrews 12:5-7 says that God may have to discipline us if we disobey him, not out of anger, but out of his great love for us.

(5) Rewards in heaven. Passages such as 1 Corinthians 3:10-15, 2 Corinthians 5:10 and 2 Timothy 4:8 teach us that it is God's desire to reward us for faithful service to him. This is one of the great demonstrations of his love and grace.

Appendix on "Faith"

The Greek word *pisteuo* is usually translated "believe" or "faith" in key passages about salvation (see John 1:12; Acts 16:31; Romans 4:3). The New Testament repeatedly emphasizes that faith in Christ is the only condition for salvation. Here are just some of the passages that teach this:

Luke 7:48 Then Jesus said to her, "Your sins are forgiven." 7:49 But those who were at the table with him began to say among themselves, "Who is this, who even forgives sins?" 7:50 he said to the woman, "Your faith has saved you; go in peace."

Luke 8:11 "Now the parable means this: The seed is the word of God. 8:12 Those along the path are the ones who have heard; then the devil comes and takes away the word from their hearts, so that they may not believe and be saved.

John 1:12 1:12 But to all who have received him—those who believe in his name—he has given the right to become God's children

John 3:14 Just as Moses lifted up the serpent in the wilderness, so must the Son of Man be lifted up, 3:15 so that everyone who believes in him may have eternal life." 3:16 For this is the way God loved the world: he gave his one and only Son, so that everyone who believes in him will not perish but have eternal life. 3:17 For God did not send his Son into the world to condemn the world, but that the world should be saved through him. 3:18 The one who believes in him is not condemned. The one who does not believe has been condemned already, because he has not believed in the name of the one and only Son of God. 3:36 The one who believes in the Son has eternal life. The one who rejects the Son will not see life, but God's wrath remains on him.

John 6:28 So then they said to him, "What must we do to accomplish the deeds God requires?" 6:29 Jesus replied, "This is the deed God requires—to believe in the one whom he sent."

John 6:35 Jesus said to them, "I am the bread of life. The one who comes to me will never go hungry, and the one who believes in me will never be thirsty.

John 6:40 For this is the will of my Father—for everyone who looks on the Son and believes in him to have eternal life, and I will raise him up at the last day."

John 6:47 I tell you the solemn truth, the one who believes has eternal life.

John 7:37 "If anyone is thirsty, let him come to me, and 7:38 let the one who believes in me drink. Just as the scripture says, 'From within him will flow rivers of living water.'" 7:39 (Now he said this about the Spirit, whom those who believed in him were going to receive, for the Spirit had not yet been given, because Jesus was not yet glorified.)

John 8:24 Thus I told you that you will die in your sins. For unless you believe that I am he, you will die in your sins."

John 9:35 Jesus heard that they had thrown him out, so he found the man and said to him, "Do you believe in the Son of Man?" 9:36 The man replied, "And who is he, sir, that I may believe in him?" 9:37 Jesus told him, "You have seen him; he is the one speaking with you." [9:38 he said, "Lord, I believe," and he worshiped him.

John 11:25 Jesus said to her, "I am the resurrection and the life.

The one who believes in me will live even if he dies,11:26 and the one who lives and believes in me will never die.

John 12:36 While you have the light, believe in the light, so that you may become sons of light."

John 12:46 I have come as a light into the world, so that everyone who believes in me should not remain in darkness.

John 14:1 "Do not let your hearts be distressed. You believe in God; believe also in me.

John 17:21 I pray that they will be in us, so that the world will believe that you sent me.

John 20:29 Jesus said to him, "Have you believed because you have seen me? Blessed are the people who have not seen and yet have believed." 20:30 Now Jesus performed many other miraculous signs in the presence of the disciples, which are not recorded in this book. 20:31 But these are recorded so that you may believe that Jesus is the Christ, the Son of God, and that by believing you may have life in his name.

Acts 8:12 But when they believed Philip as he was proclaiming the good news about the kingdom of God and the name of Jesus Christ, they began to be baptized 10:43

Acts 11:17 Therefore if God gave them the same gift as he also gave us after believing in the Lord Jesus Christ, who was I to hinder God?",

Acts 11:21 The hand of the Lord was with them, and a great number who believed turned to the Lord. Acts

Acts 13:38 Therefore let it be known to you, brothers, that through this one forgiveness of sins is proclaimed to you, 13:39 and by this one everyone who believes is justified from everything from which the law of Moses could not justify you.

Acts 15:7 After there had been much debate, Peter stood up and said to them, "Brothers, you know that some time ago God chose me to preach to the Gentiles so they would hear the message of the Gospel and believe. 15:8 And God, who knows the heart, has testified to them by giving them the Holy Spirit just as he did to us, 15:9 and he made no distinction between them and us, cleansing their hearts by faith.

Acts 16:30 Then he brought them outside and asked, "Sirs, what must I do to be saved?" 16:31 They replied, "Believe in the Lord Jesus and you will be saved, you and your household."

Acts 18:27 When Apollos wanted to cross over to Achaia, the brothers encouraged him and wrote to the disciples to welcome him. When he arrived, he assisted greatly those who had believed by grace,

Acts 19:4 Paul said, "John baptized with a baptism of repentance, telling the people to believe in the one who was to come after him, that is, in Jesus."

Acts 26:18 to open their eyes so that they turn from darkness to light and from the power of Satan to God, so that they may receive forgiveness of sins and a share among those who are sanctified by faith in me.'

Romans 1:16 For I am not ashamed of the Gospel, for it is God's power for salvation to everyone who believes, to the Jew first and also to the Greek. 1:17 For the righteousness of God is revealed in the Gospel from faith to faith, just as it is written, "The righteous by faith will live."

Romans 4:3 For what does the scripture say? "Abraham believed God, and it was credited to him as righteousness." 4:4 Now to the one who works, his pay is not credited due to grace but due to obligation. 4:5 But to the one who does not work, but believes in the one who declares the ungodly righteous, his faith is credited as righteousness.

Romans 4:23 But the statement it was credited to him was not written only for Abraham's sake, 4:24 but also for our sake, to whom it will be credited, those who believe in the one who raised Jesus our Lord from the dead. 4:25 he was given over because of our transgressions and was raised for the sake of our justification.

Romans 5:1 Therefore, since we have been declared righteous by faith, we have peace with God through our Lord Jesus Christ, 5:2 through whom we have also obtained access by faith into this grace in which we stand, and we rejoice in the hope of God's glory.

Romans 9:30 What shall we say then?—That the Gentiles who did not pursue righteousness obtained it, that is, a righteousness that is by faith, 9:31 but Israel even though pursuing a law of righteousness did not attain it. 9:32 Why not? Because they pursued it not by faith but (as if it were possible) by works.

Romans 10:4 For Christ is the end of the law, with the result that there is righteousness for everyone who believes.

Romans 10:9 because if you confess with your mouth that Jesus is Lord and believe in your heart that God raised him from the dead, you will be saved. 10:10 For with the heart one believes and thus has righteousness and with the mouth one confesses and thus has salvation. 10:11 For the scripture says, "Everyone who believes in him will not be put to shame." 10:12 For there is no distinction between the Jew and the Greek, for the same Lord is Lord of all, who richly blesses all who call on him. 10:13 For everyone who calls on the name of the Lord will be saved

Romans 11:20 Granted! They were broken off because of their unbelief, but you stand by faith. Do not be arrogant, but fear!

1 Corinthians 1:21 For since in the wisdom of God the world by its wisdom did not know God, God was pleased to save those who believe...

Galatians 2:16 yet we know that no one is justified by the works of the law but by the faithfulness of Jesus Christ. And we have come to believe in Christ Jesus, so that we may be justified by the faithfulness of Christ and not by the works of the law, because by the works of the law no one will be justified.

Galatians 3:2 The only thing I want to learn from you is this: Did you receive the Spirit by doing the works of the law or by believing what you heard? 3:3 Are you so foolish? Although you began with the Spirit, are you now trying to finish by human effort? 3:4 Have you suffered so many things for nothing?—If indeed it was for nothing. 3:5 Does God then give you the Spirit and work miracles among you by your doing the works of the law or by your believing what you heard? 3:6 Just as Abraham believed God, and it was credited to him as righteousness, 3:7 so then, understand that those who believe are the sons of Abraham. (The rest of the chapter continues this theme)

Ephesians 1:13 And when you heard the word of truth (the Gospel of your salvation)—when you believed in Christ—you were marked with the seal of the promised Holy Spirit, 1:14 who is the down payment of our inheritance, until the redemption of God's own possession, to the praise of his glory.

Ephesians 2:8 For by grace you are saved through faith, and this is not from yourselves, it is the gift of God; 2:9 it is not from works, so that no one can boast.

2 Thessalonians 1:10 when he comes to be glorified among his saints and admired on that day among all who have believed—and you did in fact believe our testimony.

1 Timothy 1:15 This saying is trustworthy and deserves full acceptance: "Christ Jesus came into the world to save sinners"—and I am the worst of them! 1:16 But here is why I was treated with mercy: so that in me as the worst, Christ Jesus could demonstrate his utmost patience, as an example for those who are going to believe in him for eternal life.

2 Timothy 1:12 Because of this, in fact, I suffer as I do. But I am not ashamed, because I know the one in whom my faith is set and I am convinced that he is able to protect what has been entrusted to me until that day.

2 Timothy 3:15 and how from infancy you have known the holy writings, which are able to give you wisdom for salvation through faith in Christ Jesus.

Hebrews 4:2 For we had good news proclaimed to us just as they did. But the message they heard did them no good, since they did not join in with those who heard it in faith. 4:3 For we who have believed enter that rest,

1 Peter 1:3 Blessed be the God and Father of our Lord Jesus Christ! By his great mercy he gave us new birth into a living hope through the resurrection of Jesus Christ from the dead, 1:4 that is, into an inheritance imperishable, undefiled, and unfading. It is reserved in heaven for you, 1:5 who by God's power are protected through faith for a salvation ready to be revealed in the last time.

1 Peter 2:6 For it says in scripture, "Look, I lay in Zion a stone, a chosen and priceless cornerstone, and whoever believes in him will never be put to shame."

1 John 5:1 Everyone who believes that Jesus is the Christ has been born of God, and everyone who loves the Father loves whoever has been born of him 5 Who is it that overcomes the world except the one who believes that Jesus is the Son of God?

Study Guide for Isn't Salvation by Faith Too Easy?

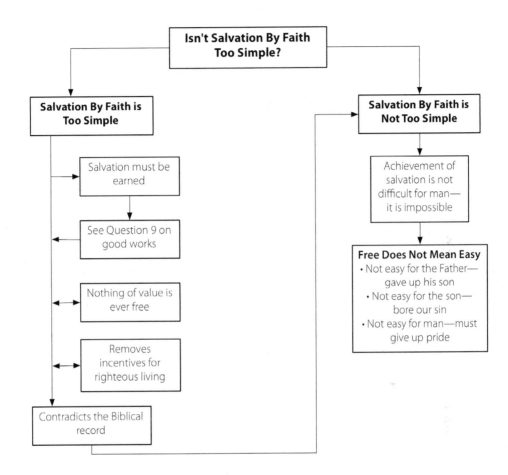

Key Verses

Matthew 19:16-26 [16]And behold, one came to Him and said,"Teacher, what good thing shall I do that I may obtain eternal life?" [17]And He said to him,"Why are you asking me about what is good? There is only One who is good; but if you wish to enter into life, keep the commandments." [18]He said to Him,"Which ones?"And Jesus said,"YOU SHALL NOT COMMIT MURDER; YOU SHALL NOT COMMIT ADULTERY;YOU SHALL NOT STEAL;YOU SHALL NOT BEAR FALSE WITNESS; [19]HONOR YOUR FATHER AND MOTHER; and YOU SHALL LOVE YOUR NEIGHBOR AS YOURSELF." [20]The young man said to Him, "All these things I have kept; what am I still lacking?" [21]Jesus said to him,"If you wish to be complete, go and sell your possessions and give to the poor, and you shall have treasure in heaven; and come, follow me." [22]But when the young man heard this statement, he went away grieved; for he was one who owned much property.

[23]And Jesus said to His disciples,"Truly I say to you, it is hard for a rich man to enter the kingdom of heaven. [24]"And again I say to you, it is easier for a camel to go through the eye of a needle, than for a rich man to enter the kingdom of God." [25]And when the disciples heard this, they were very astonished and said,"Then who can be saved?" [26]And looking upon them Jesus said to them,"With men this is impossible, but with God all things are possible."

Ephesians 2:8-9 It is by grace you have been saved, through Faith – and this is not from yourselves, it is the gift of God – not by works so that no one can boast.

John 20:31 But these are written so that you may believe that Jesus is the Messiah, the Son of God, and that by believing in him you will have life.

Study Questions

1. Respond to the following reasons for assuming salvation by faith is too easy. It must be earned.

   • Nothing of value is ever free.

   • It removes incentive for righteous living.

2. Differentiate between the concepts of "Free" and "Easy", and then respond to why salvation must be free in order to be attainable.

3. What are the incentives for being good if salvation is a free gift?

Notes_____

QUESTION 11: WHAT DOES THE BIBLE MEAN BY BELIEVE?

Often-Asked Questions:

- How much faith do you have to have?

- Doesn't everyone believe in Christ and his existence?

- What if I want to believe but still have doubts?

- Don't you have to stop sinning to believe in Christ?

There are more than 14,000 meanings for the 500 most commonly used words. With so many meanings for so few words, there is a lot of opportunity for miscommunication. It is therefore important when we seek to communicate with others that all parties involved are on the same page. This is particularly important when talking about the essence of the salvation message. Religious words like "faith" and "believe" can mean many things to many people, so we must be able to clearly explain them in the context of salvation.

Two Options

The first option for the word *believe* defines it as an intellectual acknowledgment of a set of facts. The second option calls not only for an intellectual acknowledgment but also for a personal acceptance of the truth.

First Option: Intellectual Acknowledgment

If we followed common usage, the sentence *"I believe in tornadoes"* would mean that we give intellectual acknowledgment to the existence of tornadoes. If we say we believe in George Washington or Susan B. Anthony, we are giving intellectual acknowledgment that they existed. This is a belief about someone or something. But James tells us that a belief that encompasses only intellectual assent is not enough. The demons have this type of belief (James 2:19). They recognize the existence of Christ and all the works he performed, but this belief does not save them.

The New Testament usage of the term *believe* carries the concept further than the popular usage of the term. John 1:12 says, *"But as many as received him, to them he gave the right to become children of God, even to those who believe in his name."* A biblical belief not only involves intellectual assent but also personal acceptance. It is not just believing *about* Christ; it is believing *in* Christ or, more accurately, believing *into* Christ. Biblical belief, then, is more than an acknowledgment of Christ's existence and death. It requires a trusting of oneself to Jesus. A person believes in Christ if he personally receives Christ's payment for his sin. This means a change in attitude so that he no longer relies on his own efforts to obtain salvation but trusts in Jesus Christ alone as his only hope of reconciliation with God.

Where is the crossover from one type of belief to the other? Perhaps the following illustration will help. Once a country boy ventured into the big city of Knoxville, Tennessee. He wanted to visit a friend in Memphis and decided to go by plane. He had never flown before, and this was his first trip to an airport. When he arrived, he looked over the departures and arrivals board and noticed that the plane for Memphis left Knoxville at 10:30 A.M. and arrived at its destination at 10:30 A.M. Not realizing the time zone change between the two cities, he was really puzzled by the departure and arrival times, so he asked the ticket agent if the times were correct. "Oh, yes," she said. "Would you like to purchase a ticket?" He said, "No, not yet," and went to a window to observe the planes. A little while later he noticed a different agent at the counter, so he went and asked again. The second person concurred that the times were correct and asked if he wanted to buy a ticket. His quick reply was, "No, ma'am, I'd just like to be around when that thing takes off!"

He believed what was said *about* the plane was true. He had an intellectual acknowledgment that the plane would do what the departure board said it would. But he was unwilling to believe in the plane and purchase a ticket for himself.

During the Middle Ages, three words were used to describe the different levels of belief: (1) *noticia* (notice)—observe the facts objectively; (2) *assentia* (assent)—acknowledge this truth intellectually; and (3) *fiducia* (faith)—receive the solution personally. Let's apply these words to the Gospel message. On the first level, we notice the facts to be believed. We are sinners, and the penalty for our sin is death and separation from God. On the cross, Christ paid the penalty for our sins and made the gift of eternal life available to us. On the second level, we not only notice the facts but also acknowledge their truth intellectually. Up to this point we still just believe *about* Christ. For us to believe in Christ, we need to move on to our third concept, *fiducia*. We must now place our trust in Christ alone for the forgiveness of our personal sins. When we go to level three, we have received the free gift of salvation from Christ, but not before. Salvation comes not from an intellectual acknowledgment, but from a belief that personally receives Christ's offer.

Believe =

Receive =

Trust =

Faith

Second Option: Personal Acceptance

As we saw in our examination of John 1:12, believe equals receive. The concept of receiving Christ is consistent with several other passages in scripture.

"Now I make known to you, brethren, the Gospel which I preached to you, which also you *received*, in which also you stand" (1 Corinthians 15:1). "For I delivered to you as of first importance what I also *received*, that Christ died for our sins according to the scriptures" (1 Corinthians 15:3). "As you therefore have *received* Christ Jesus the Lord, so walk in him" (Colossians 2:6). "And with all the deception of wickedness for those who perish, because they did not *receive* the love of the truth so as to be saved" (2 Thessalonians 2:10). The notion that biblical belief equals receiving Christ is further substantiated by the way salvation is described as *a gift* in several passages (Romans 5:17; 6:23; Ephesians 2:8-9).

Inherent in the idea of a gift is that it must be received from the giver, and this is true of the gift of salvation. Biblically, believing and receiving are synonymous, and John 1:12 uses both terms with the clear intent of equating the two actions. Imagine parents who want to give a gift to their young son. As they hold it in their hands, their son gazes at it, overwhelmed by his parents' love, and profusely thanks them for the gift. Yet the gift remains in the parents' hands. What's the problem? The son has done everything but receive the gift by reaching out and appropriating it from his parents. So it is with the gift of salvation—God extends his gift, and every individual must personally receive it from him.

A person can doubt Christ and his credentials or he can believe that Christ was who he said he was. But until he claims Christ's offer for himself, he is no better off than the person who doesn't believe at all.

A man and a woman came before a clergyman to be married. The clergyman asked the bride, "Will you take this man to be your lawfully wedded husband?"

Key Illustration: Marriage Vows

"Oh," she answered, "He's really handsome, isn't he?"

So the clergyman tried again, "Will you take this man as your husband?"

"Oh, I think he's so nice," she replied, and then added, "I think he'll be a wonderful husband and provider."

It's obvious here that the bride needs to say "I do." When she has said "I do," the groom becomes her husband, but not before. She must accept him, just as each person must go beyond mere acknowledgment of Jesus Christ. Each individual must receive Christ not just as the Savior of the world but as his personal Savior.

Picture a man who falls from a cliff. As he plunges down, he reaches out and grabs a small limb. He hangs on, looks up, and sees the sheer precipice above. He looks down and sees jagged peaks reaching up for his straining body, and begins to despair. Suddenly, he sees an angel above him and begins to scream, "Save me!"

Key Illustration: The Cliffhanger

"Do you believe I *can* save you?" the angel asks. The man sees the strong wings, the mighty arms. He says, "Yes, I believe you can save me."

"Do you believe I *will* save you?"

The man sees the compassionate, merciful face. "Yes, yes, I believe!" He cries.

"Then," says the angel, "LET GO!"

Still clinging, the man yells, "Is there anybody else up there?"

You see, you may believe that Jesus *can* save you. That's essential, but it is not enough. You may be confident that he *will* save you. That's also necessary, but it is not real belief. To trust in Jesus Christ is to let go of every other confidence, of every other trust, and of every other security,

Key Illustration: Blondin
Tightrope Walker

and to cast yourself on him as your only hope of salvation. Charles Blondin, a Frenchman, was one of the world's finest tightrope walkers. In 1860 he successfully crossed the treacherous river above Niagara Falls (approximately a 1,000-foot span, 160 feet above the raging waters) on a tightrope. He then turned to the gathered crowd that was awestruck by this incredible feat and asked how many believed he could traverse the tightrope a second time pushing a wheelbarrow. The enthusiastic crowd cheered, acknowledging their belief in Blondin. Blondin succeeded, and then addressed the astonished crowd again, "Does anyone believe enough in me to get in the wheelbarrow and cross Niagara Falls with me?" No one volunteered! Finally, Blondin's manager climbed on Blondin's back, and they crossed the great chasm together. Christ said that there is a great chasm between man and God, and the only way to get from one side to the other is through him.

Key Illustration: The
Appendectomy

Sometimes it helps to use a frivolous illustration to get the point across. For example, there is the story about a man who was afflicted with an acute pain in his right side. The doctor's diagnosis was appendicitis, and he felt it was absolutely necessary for the patient to have an emergency appendectomy. The patient was skeptical of the doctor's abilities, so he asked the doctor if he had any proof to support his diagnosis. It just so happened that the doctor was having a reunion of all his past appendectomy patients.

The nurse wheeled the sick man down the corridor in front of the doctor's previous patients, and all of them enthusiastically testified that the doctor had successfully cured them of the same kind of pain by performing appendectomies.

"OK," the man said, "I believe, Doctor, that you are capable of removing my appendix and eliminating the pain."

"Fine," the doctor replied. "Now please sign this consent form right here."

"Oh, no, you're not going to cut me open!"

The patient's belief was not true belief if he didn't allow the doctor to operate. We can believe that Christ diagnosed our problem correctly, and we can even believe that he has a 100 percent cure rate, but if we don't allow him to operate on us, our belief is not a saving one.

When we tell others about Christ, it is important that we clearly communicate the biblical concept of belief. One of the easiest ways Satan can keep people from trusting Christ is to have God's servants distort this concept. We should watch two things very carefully here:

The first is *doubt*. Some feel they can't decide for Christ until all their doubts are removed. It is imperative that we dispel this roadblock to Christ. Faith is not the absence of doubt; it is a decision based on the evidence at hand. A person can have some doubts about doing something and still make the decision to do it. Suppose two men have equal doubts about the safety of flying. A special opportunity arises for both men, but it means they must fly. Both continue to have their doubts, but one man decides to get on the plane while the other stays behind. So it is with Christianity; doubt doesn't have to inhibit a person from receiving Christ. It is a matter of choice. A step taken in spite of doubts.

The second thing we need to watch is *commitment*. Some people have labored over receiving Christ as their Savior because they felt that a promise to subject every area of their lives to the control of God forever had to go hand in hand with the decision. It is true that biblical belief requires commitment, but this is not so much a commitment to what we are going to do in the future as it is a commitment to what Jesus Christ has done in the past. In many cases, an understanding of total commitment to the lordship of Christ is not achieved until some time after salvation. It is an unfortunate reality that many Christians acknowledge that Jesus is Lord and Master but still try to run their own lives.

To "believe in Christ" is to understand who Jesus Christ is and what he did for you, to agree with God that you need him alone as your substitute for your sin, and to invite him to personally enter your life (John 5:24).

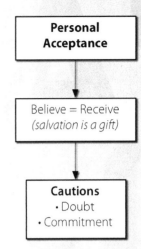

Summary

We first considered the idea that biblical belief means an intellectual acknowledgment of the facts of Christ and his work. But demons have that much belief, so we delved into scripture for further insight into the term *believe*. The biblical term means more than mere belief *about* something; it means belief *in* something or someone. It is an intellectual acknowledgment that leads to a personal reception of Christ and his offer of salvation.

Second, we defended the idea that *believe* equals *receive*, and we looked at corollary passages to John 1:12. Salvation is depicted in scripture as a gift, and we are called to receive that gift. We offered a few illustrations to help clarify the definition of *believe*, and stressed two cautions at the end: First, faith is not the absence of doubt. You can have doubts and still receive Christ. Second, the commitment made in accepting Christ is not a commitment to what we are going to do in the future. It is a commitment to what he has done for us in the past.

Study Guide for What Does the Bible Mean by Believe?

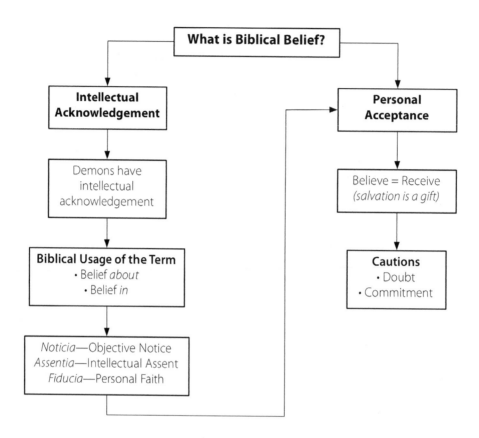

Key Illustrations

Marriage Vows

A man and a woman came before a clergyman to be married. The clergyman asked the bride, "Will you take this man to be your lawfully wedded husband?"

"Oh," she answered, "He's really handsome, isn't he?"

So the clergyman tried again, "Will you take this man as your husband?"

"Oh, I think he's so nice," she replied, and then added, "I think he'll be a wonderful husband and provider."

It's obvious here that the bride needs to say "I do." When she has said "I do," the groom becomes her husband, but not before. She must accept him, just as each person must go beyond mere acknowledgment of Jesus Christ. Each individual must receive Christ not just as the Savior of the world but as his personal Savior.

The Cliffhanger

Picture a man who falls from a cliff. As he plunges down, he reaches out and grabs a small limb. He hangs on, looks up, and sees the sheer precipice above. He looks down and sees jagged peaks reaching up for his straining body, and begins to despair. Suddenly, he sees an angel above him and begins to scream, "Save me!"

"Do you believe I *can* save you?" the angel asks. The man sees the strong wings, the mighty arms. He says, "Yes, I believe you can save me."

"Do you believe I *will* save you?"

The man sees the compassionate, merciful face. "Yes, yes, I believe!" he cries.

"Then," says the angel, "LET GO!"

Still clinging, the man yells, "Is there anybody else up there?"

Blondin Tightrope Walker

Charles Blondin, a Frenchman, was one of the world's finest tightrope walkers. In 1860 he successfully crossed the treacherous river above Niagara Falls (approximately a 1,000-foot span, 160 feet above the raging waters) on a tightrope. He then turned to the gathered crowd that was awestruck by this incredible feat and asked how many believed he could traverse the tightrope a second time pushing a wheelbarrow. The enthusiastic crowd cheered, acknowledging their belief in Blondin. Blondin succeeded, and then addressed the astonished crowd again, "Does anyone believe enough in me to get in the wheelbarrow and cross Niagara Falls with me?" No one volunteered! Finally, Blondin's manager climbed on Blondin's back, and they crossed the great chasm together. Christ said that there is a great chasm between man and God, and the only way to get from one side to the other is through him.

The Appendectomy

Sometimes it helps to use a frivolous illustration to get the point across. For example, there is the story about a man who was afflicted with an acute pain in his right side. The doctor's diagnosis was appendicitis, and he felt it was absolutely necessary for the patient to have an emergency appendectomy. The patient was skeptical of the doctor's abilities, so he asked the doctor if he had any proof to support his diagnosis. It just so happened that the doctor was having a reunion of all his past appendectomy patients.

The nurse wheeled the sick man down the corridor in front of the doctor's previous patients, and all of them enthusiastically testified that the doctor had successfully cured them of the same kind of pain by performing appendectomies.

"OK," the man said, "I believe, Doctor, that you are capable of removing my appendix and eliminating the pain."

"Fine," the doctor replied. "Now please sign this consent form right here."

"Oh, no, you're not going to cut me open!"

The patient's belief was not true belief if he didn't allow the doctor to operate. We can believe that Christ diagnosed our problem correctly, and we can even believe that he has a 100 percent cure rate, but if we don't allow him to operate on us, our belief is not a saving one.

Key Verses

Ephesians 2:8-9 It is by grace you have been saved, through Faith – and this is not from yourselves, it is the gift of God – not by works so that no one can boast.

John 1:12 Yet to all who received him, to those who believed in his name, he gave the right to become children of God.

1 Corinthians 15:1 Now I make known to you, brethren, the Gospel which I preached to you, which also you received, in which you stand.

Colossians 2:6 As you therefore have received Christ Jesus the Lord, so walk in Him.

2 Thessalonians 2:10 He will use every kind of wicked deception to fool those who are on their way to destruction because they refuse to believe the truth that would save them.

Study Questions

1. Identify and differentiate between the three terms used during the Middle Ages to describe the levels of belief.

2. What is a good synonym for "believe"? Give a passage for support.

3. How would you illustrate the difference between intellectual assent and personal acceptance?

4. How would you respond to the following issues?

   • "I still have some doubts."

   • "I am afraid of making a commitment."

Notes

QUESTION 12: CAN A PERSON BE SURE OF THEIR SALVATION?

Often-Asked Questions:

- Can't a Christian simply stop believing in Christ?

- Aren't there certain sins that could cause a person to lose his salvation?

- Will God let someone into heaven who claims to believe in Jesus but lives an immoral life?

- Salvation is appropriated by faith, but doesn't a person need to maintain it?

- Don't some verses teach that a Christian can "fall from grace"?

This is a question raised most often by Christians struggling with doubt, or by people who grew up in a culturally Christian setting where they were taught that salvation depended on rule-keeping or being good.

Two Options

If getting into heaven depended on our good works as well as our faith in Christ, none of us could say with any confidence that we know we are going to heaven. This is the first option. We could never be sure if we were working enough or sinning too much. No Christian could rest in the finished work of Christ, because, somehow, it would not be sufficient. Charity and church work would be prompted at least partly out of a desire to maintain that which otherwise could be lost. In contrast, the other option affirms that the believer *can* be assured of eternal life, because it is based solely upon the redemptive work of Christ, not our performance.

First Option: We Cannot Be Sure Of Eternal Life

When people gain some understanding of what it means to believe in Christ (Question 11), they will sometimes raise the question of assurance. In most cases, this question is not so much an objection to Christianity as it is a request for clarification of the Gospel. This very common position (we cannot be sure of salvation) often results from a misunderstanding of the nature of *faith*, *sin*, or *good works*, The real issue is what God's Word says about the matter of assurance, and not how we feel about it. An explanation of the meaning of God's **gift of eternal life**, along with a few biblical passages, may be all that is necessary to answer this question. But sometimes people will have specific objections to the idea of assurance, and when this happens, these objections will have to be met.

Faith (Can't a person stop believing?)

One of these objections has to do with the nature of *faith*. Can't someone stop believing in Christ, and wouldn't this cause him to lose his salvation? It is not uncommon to hear someone say, "I tried Christianity once, but it just didn't work." But was it really a Biblical faith in Jesus Christ that they tried? For others, church was a prominent part of their lives as they were growing up. They appeared to be zealous Christians, but they discarded their faith in college as just another religious delusion, and never returned. In cases like these, it may be that they never had real faith. They did not lose their salvation if they did not have it to begin with.

This does not mean that a genuine Christian will not stop believing. There may be times when believers experience profound doubts due to circumstances or intellectual problems. It can be healthy to wrestle with honest doubts about their faith, because this process can strengthen their understanding. The Christian who never consciously wonders, "Is all of this really true? How do I know I'm not deluding myself?" will probably not have as firm a grasp of the basis for his faith as the one who struggles through these questions.

When doubts arise, they do not put a Christian's salvation in jeopardy. Jesus did not condemn doubts, rather, he invited investigation. He asked the skeptics to evaluate his works, he exhorted the disciples to remember the miracles, and he offered Thomas the very evidence he asked for in order to believe in the resurrection (John 20).

Christ not only *saves* us but also *sustains* us. When a father holds the hand of his little girl as they walk together, he guides her and keeps her from the danger of the street. Because she is not yet proficient at walking, she may begin to trip several times, and she may try to wander off the curb, but his grip is sufficient to keep her from falling. What father would hold a child's hand while she is safe but let loose the moment she began to fall? Keep that image in mind when reading John 10:28-29: *I give them eternal life, and they will never perish; no one will snatch them from my hand. My Father, who has given them to me, is greater than all, and no one can snatch them from my Father's hand.* Our hands are firmly held by him who loves us to the end. Salvation is based on God's ability, not ours.

Sin (Don't Some Sins Disqualify A Person?)

Another objection relates to the nature of sin. Can't a person lose their salvation by committing certain sins?

The problem here is that most people make an artificial distinction between "big" and "little" sins that reflects human law codes more than God's attitude. In our system, murder and armed robbery are far more serious offenses than lying and cheating, while greed and arrogance count as nothing. But God regards the intent to murder or commit adultery as seriously as the acts themselves: *"You have heard that it was said, `You shall not commit adultery'; but I say to you, that everyone who looks on a woman to lust for her has committed adultery with her already in his heart"* (Matthew 5:27-28). John wrote in his first epistle, *"Everyone who hates his brother is a murderer"* (1 John 3:15). In God's sight, sins like jealousy, anger, malice, slander, pride, bitterness, and envy are not minor offenses. Thus, if any sins can disqualify someone from heaven, all of us would be disqualified.

An alternate way of approaching this objection is to ask, "What is good enough to get you into heaven, and what is bad enough to keep you out of heaven?" If God held some kind of scale that weighed our good works against our bad, a "score" of 51 percent good would make it. People who are up to 49 percent evil would be allowed into his presence. In his Sermon on the Mount, Jesus said, *"Therefore you are to be perfect, as your heavenly Father is perfect"* (Matthew 5:48). God will accept nothing less than perfection. As we saw in Question 9 (Good Works), he does not (and cannot) grade on a curve. Our only hope of salvation, then, is the perfect righteousness of Jesus Christ, which is imparted to those who trust in him. As perfection is required for salvation, anything less disqualifies us. Any sin of action *or inaction* would cause us to fall short.

Some object, "Of course all of my past sins can be forgiven when I trust Christ for my salvation. But what about my future sins?" When Christ paid for our sins almost 2,000 years ago, he knew us though we did not yet exist. At that point, ***all our sins were future events***, but he knew them all and paid for them all. It doesn't make any sense to say that he paid only for those sins which we would commit prior to believing in him but not for those sins which we would commit after believing in him. A simple way to point this out is to ask the doubter, "How many of your sins were in the future when Jesus died for them?" Either he paid for them all or he paid for none; a partial redemption is no redemption in God's sight.

How many of your sins were in the future when Jesus died for them?

Good Works (Doesn't Salvation Need To Be Maintained?)

Yet another objection relates to the nature of *works*. Doesn't a Christian have to *maintain* his relationship to God and thus his salvation? No, because salvation is a gift by God's grace; it must be by grace since no one deserves it. It is maintained by his power, not by our performance. Jude's doxology is addressed *"to him who is able to keep you from stumbling, and to make you stand in the presence of his glory blameless with great joy"* (Jude 24). He is the one who keeps us from stumbling, because we could not otherwise keep ourselves blameless. Titus 3:4-7 is one of the clearest biblical portraits of God's grace on our behalf:

> But when the kindness of God our Savior and his love for mankind appeared, he saved us, not on the basis of deeds which we have done in righteousness, but according to his mercy, by the washing of regeneration and renewing by the Holy Spirit, whom he poured out upon us richly through Jesus Christ our Savior, that being justified by his grace we might be made heirs according to the hope of eternal life.

Christ's righteousness has been imputed to us—placed, as it were, on our account. This is *his* righteousness, and by his grace, it has become ours; it is not jeopardized by our behavior. Speaking of the Father and the Son, Paul stated, *"He made him who knew no sin to be sin on our behalf, that we might become the righteousness of God in him"* (2 Corinthians 5:21). It is evident from

224

I'm Glad You Asked

passages like these that not only salvation but also sanctification is achieved by faith. Any good works that follow should be a product of this living faith, accomplished by the Spirit. Indeed, belief should lead to behavior, and if we do not see any qualitative changes in a person's life, we might wonder whether that person's faith is real (see James 2:14-26). There is a danger, however, of falling into the mindset that salvation is achieved by the principle of grace and maintained by the principle of works. Paul denounced the Galatians for this type of thinking when he wrote, *"Are you so foolish? Having begun by the Spirit, are you now being perfected by the flesh?"* (Galatians 3:3)

Key Illustration: Mortgage

If someone decided to pay off the mortgage on your house, you would be notified to that effect, and your monthly house payment would be returned if it reached the bank after the note had been paid. It would be absurd for the bank to take your check and send you a letter stating that even though the mortgage had been paid off, you must still pay it because it was your mortgage. When a debt has been paid in full, it no longer exists.

The Nature Of A Gift.

Salvation is a gift, not a wage.

Salvation is described as a gift throughout the New Testament (John 3:16; Romans 5:15-16; Ephesians 2:8-9, 2 Corinthians 9:15). Gifts cannot be earned, but must be accepted with empty hands. God paid our debt in full, and we have been set free from our bondage. Nothing more remains to be paid.

If a friend gave you a book as a birthday present, you would not offer to pay him back—only a word of gratitude would be appropriate. An attempt to pay for a present would defeat the whole concept of a gift, and could even insult the giver. If you pay for something, it can no longer be regarded as a gift.

In addition, when a gift is received, the recipient should not have to work to keep it. If a father gave his son some camping equipment as a gift and later took it away because he did not clean his room, it was not a gift after all. Instead, it was a wage that was conditioned on the fulfillment of certain tasks. God's gift of salvation is different, because the sole condition is that a person must reach out and take it by an act of faith (Question 11). Because it is a gift, it is not maintained by our works. Nor is it the kind of gift that can be given back. The gift of forgiveness and acceptance cannot be received and then returned. When Christ's righteousness is placed on our account, it is there to stay.

People frequently object to this concept of an unconditional gift: "If a Christian doesn't have to maintain his salvation, why can't he go off and sin as much as he wants?" Another variation is the hypothetical "What if?" scenario—"What if a person believes in Christ and then commits 20 murders? Are you going to tell me that God would still let him into heaven?" Sometimes people really want to press their point by using the worst example they can think of: "Do you mean that if Adolph Hitler had repented and received Christ, God would have let him off the hook for **his** atrocities?"

To answer this kind of objection, stress that it is never wise to build a doctrine on hypothetical situations. It is theoretically possible that the roof may cave in on your house next week, but that is no basis for moving your family out. We need to build on reality, not idle speculation. How many people do you know who have trusted in Christ and then committed 20 murders? It is helpful to look at the *real* effect that knowing Jesus has on people's lives. When a person makes a genuine commitment to Christ, things gradually begin to change. Paul wrote that *"if any man is in Christ, he is a new creature; the old things passed away; behold; new things have come"* (2 Corinthians 5:17). New interests and desires begin to surface, and the believer finds that he or she can no longer indulge in old sinful patterns without conviction by the Spirit. When they do get enmeshed in sin, they will be disciplined by their heavenly Father, who loves them too much to allow them to stray very far without consequences. *"For those whom the Lord loves he disciplines, and he scourges every son whom he receives"* (Hebrews 12:6).

When a person becomes a Christian, they acknowledge their sin and turn to Christ for forgiveness. They do not say, "Well, now that I've got my fire and life insurance, I can sin with impunity." Paul wrote that *"where sin increased, grace abounded all the more"* (Romans 5:20), but was quick to add that no Christian should ever abuse the grace of God: *"What shall we say then? Are we to continue in sin that grace might increase? May it never be! How shall we who died to sin still live in it?"* (Romans 6:1-2) Paul added that *"our old self was crucified with him, that our body of sin might be done away with, that we should no longer be slaves to sin"* (Romans 6:6).

Sin is incompatible with the believer's new self, and one does not have to succumb to it. But when someone does, they will find that sin still has its consequences. As a person matures in Christ, they discover that what previously had been imagined to be a dreary life turns out to be the greatest adventure of all. A life of abiding in Christ is so much more abundant (John 10:10) than a life of putting self first.

Key Illustration:
Unconditional Love vs.
Jeopardy

This perspective becomes more obvious if we look at it in the context of parents and children. Imagine two families that set up an identical list of rules for their children. One communicates unconditional love for their daughter. If she breaks one of the rules, the parents discipline her lovingly, all the while assuring her of their love. She's never even considered the possibility that breaking one of the rules could get her expelled from the family.

Now imagine that the other family, while agreeing on the rules, takes a

different approach on consequences. They constantly threaten the children with expulsion or disinheritance.

Which approach will produce better or worse results if the goal is to raise healthy, productive, contributing people and citizens to society? God offering us eternal life, true security, actually promotes better behavior, not worse.

Thus, when someone becomes a Christian, there should be some changes in his or her life. If, after a number of months, there are no qualitative changes in his actions or attitudes, he may just be professing but not possessing a relationship with Jesus Christ.

Eternal Life

We saw that a gift cannot be purchased or earned or conditionally maintained. If any of these things were necessary, it would no longer be free. The meaning of eternal life is also important to the issue of assurance of salvation. Eternal life cannot be lost, because it is unlimited. If a person could somehow lose it, what he had was limited life, not eternal life. Christ says that eternal life is the present possession of each believer: *"Truly, truly, I say to you, he who hears My word, and believes him who sent Me, has eternal life, and does not come into judgment, but has passed out of death into life"* (John 5:24).

Second Option: We Can Be Sure Of Eternal Life

What about feelings?

Many people definitely have trusted in Jesus Christ but have no feelings of assurance of eternal life. Romans 8:16 says that the Holy Spirit should bear witness to our spirit that we are a child of God. In other words, the Holy Spirit should be the primary source for a sense or a feeling of assurance. One possible reason that this witness may be absent is because a person has never really trusted Christ. (See **Profession vs. Possession** in Question 8).

In the case of genuine believers, another reason may be inferred from Ephesians 4:30. Paul says that we can grieve the Holy Spirit, and perhaps in **grieving the Holy Spirit** with some hidden (or not-so-hidden) sin, the Spirit may not be providing the person with feelings of assurance.

A third reason for lacking a sense of assurance may be **ignorance of the biblical teaching** on assurance. As a result, they fall into one or more of the misunderstandings we just discussed (the nature of faith, sin, works, gifts, or eternal life). But doubts and depressed feelings do not change what God says is true. It is imperative that we reason from the truth of God's Word rather than our feelings. Our responsibility is to choose by faith to believe what God says; and when we honor God in this way, we create an environment in which his Spirit can gradually conform our feelings to the truth. Reasoning from man (our practice) to God will lead to insecurity and fear, but reasoning from God (our position) to man will lead to confidence and peace.

Biblical Passages On Assurance

Numerous biblical verses affirm the security of the child of God. Here are 12, listed in New Testament order:

John 3:16: *"For God so loved the world, that he gave his only begotten Son, that whoever believes in him should not perish, but have eternal life."* The only condition for eternal life is faith in Christ.

John 5:24: *"Truly, truly, I say to you, he who hears my word, and believes him who sent Me, has eternal life, and does not come into judgment, but has passed out of death into life."* Jesus promises three things to those who believe in him: (a) the present possession of eternal life, (b) exemption from a judgment of condemnation, and (c) a new position of spiritual life before God. A contract is no better than the people behind it—if we can believe men, why not Christ? Having believed in him, the fulfillment of his promises depends on him, not us.

John 6:37, 44: *"All that the Father gives me shall come to me, and the one who comes to me I will certainly not cast out.... No one can come to me, unless the Father who sent me draws him; and I will raise him up on the last day."* Everyone who comes to Christ has been drawn by the Father and given to the Son.

John 10:28-29: *"And I give eternal life to them, and they shall never perish; and no one shall snatch them out of my hand. My Father, who has given them to me, is greater than all; and no one is able to snatch them out of the Father's hand."* Christ's sheep are held securely in his hands and in the Father's hands. No force, including ourselves, can remove us from his grasp.

Romans 8:1, 16: *"There is therefore now no condemnation for those who are in Christ Jesus.... The spirit himself bears witness with our spirit that we are children of God."* The believer should have a spirit of adoption as one who knows he is a child of God.

Romans 8:29-35, 38-39: *"For whom he foreknew, he also predestined to become conformed to the image of his son, that he might be the firstborn among many brethren; and whom he predestined, these he also called; and whom he called, these he also justified; and whom he justified, these he also glorified. What then shall we say to these things? If God is for us, who is against us? He who did not spare his own Son, but delivered him up for us all, how will he not also with him freely give us all things? Who will bring a charge against God's elect? God is the one who justifies; who is the one who condemns? Christ Jesus is he who died, yes, rather who was raised, who is at the right hand of God, who also intercedes for us. Who shall separate us from the love of Christ? Shall tribulation, or distress,* *or persecution, or famine, or nakedness, or peril, or sword? ... For I am convinced that neither death, nor life, nor angels, nor principalities, nor things present, nor things to come, nor powers, nor height, nor depth, nor any other created thing, shall be able to separate us from the love of God, which is in Christ Jesus our Lord."* This magnificent passage tells us that once a person is in Christ, nothing at all (including himself) can separate him from Christ. This relationship becomes timeless and irrevocable.

Ephesians 1:4: *"Just as he chose us in him before the foundation of the world, that we should be holy and blameless before him."* God knew us even before the creation of the cosmos and planned that believers would become perfectly conformed to the image of his Son.

Ephesians 1:13-14: *"In him, you also, after listening to the message of truth, the Gospel of your salvation—having also believed, you were sealed in him with the Holy Spirit of promise, who is given as a pledge of our inheritance, with a view to the redemption of God's own possession, to the praise of his glory."*

Key Illustration: Empire State Building ⇨

Every Christian is sealed with the Holy Spirit, and this divine seal will not be removed until we obtain our heavenly inheritance. A visitor in Manhattan may decide to take the elevator up to the upper observation floor of the Empire State Building. When he steps on and the elevator begins to move, he has made an irrevocable decision that commits him to the whole quarter-mile vertical journey. He may be gripped with a sudden panic after 30 seconds and 55 floors, fully convinced that the cable will break. But this does not change the fact that he will safely arrive at the 102nd floor. Similarly, coming to Christ does not involve intellectual assent alone but a willful choice to place one's eternal destiny in the hands of the Savior. The choice needs to be made only once; then regardless of how we feel, he will bring us safely to our destination.

Colossians 1:12-14: *"Giving thanks to the Father, who has qualified us to share in the inheritance of the saints in light. For he delivered us from the domain of darkness, and transferred us to the kingdom of his beloved Son, in whom we have redemption, the forgiveness of sins."* Believers have already been placed in Christ's kingdom; his redemptive work has already been accomplished.

1 Peter 1:3-4: *"Blessed be the God and Father of our Lord Jesus Christ, who according to his great mercy has caused us to be born again to a living hope through the resurrection of Jesus Christ from the dead, to obtain an inheritance which is imperishable and undefiled and will not fade away, reserved in heaven for you."* As believers, our incorruptible inheritance is reserved for us by God.

1 John 2:1: *"My little children, I am writing these things to you that you may not sin. And if anyone sins, we have an Advocate with the Father, Jesus Christ the righteous; and he himself is the propitiation for our sins; and not for ours only, but also for those of the whole world."* When believers sin, Christ stands as our

Advocate and satisfies the Father because of his once-for-all sacrifice.

1 John 5:13: *"These things I have written to you who believe in the name of the Son of God, in order that you may know that you have eternal life."* Believers can know for sure.

For another list of passages that teach faith or belief as the only condition for salvation, see the appendix in Question 10.

Passages commonly used to refute Assurance

Doctrine should always be built on the clearest passages of scripture, but some people choose to ignore the obvious implications of the passages cited above, camping instead on unclear and disputed verses. The four passages that are most commonly used to dispute the assurance of the believer are John 15:6; Galatians 5:4; Hebrews 6:4-6; and James 2:18-26.

John 15:6: *"If anyone does not abide in me, he is thrown away as a branch, and dries up; and they gather them, and cast them into the fire, and they are burned."* In this context, Jesus is addressing believers on the issue of spiritual fruit, not salvation. The things that are burned are the dead works done by a believer who is not abiding in Christ. The Greek text uses the neuter gender (not masculine or feminine) for what is burned, and this cannot refer to the believer. A comparison with 1 Corinthians 3:11-15 illuminates this verse—the work that a believer does in the flesh will be burned at the Judgment Seat of Christ: *"If any man's work is burned up, he shall suffer loss; but he himself shall be saved, yet so as through fire"* (1 Corinthians 3:15).

Galatians 5:4: *"You have been severed from Christ, you who are seeking to be justified by law; you have fallen from grace."* Paul told the Galatians that Christ has set us free from the yoke of the Law (Galatians 5:1). Justification by grace is utterly incompatible with justification by law; the former is accomplished by God, and the latter cannot be achieved by man. If a person seeks to be justified by keeping the Law, he removes himself from the principle of grace and thus abandons or falls away from grace.

Hebrews 6:4-6: *"For in the case of those who have once been enlightened and have tasted of the heavenly gift and have been made partakers of the Holy Spirit, and have tasted the good word of God and the powers of the age to come, and then have fallen away, it is impossible to renew them again to repentance, since they again crucify to themselves the Son of God and put Him to open shame."* This is a very difficult passage, and many interpretations have been offered to explain it. There are some who take it to mean that a believer can lose his salvation, but few of these people realize that if the passage teaches this, it also teaches that those who lose their salvation can never get it back (and very few would want to go that far). The phrases used in verses 4 and 5 evidently refer to believers, and in the broader context here (5:11-6:3), the author of Hebrews

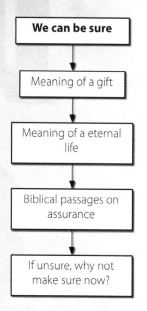

We can be sure

Meaning of a gift

Meaning of a eternal life

Biblical passages on assurance

If unsure, why not make sure now?

is making the case that we can only experience coming to Christ one time. His description of those falling away is given sarcastically to demonstrate the impossibility of such a scenario. Instead, the person should continue on towards Christian maturity.

James 2:18-26. It may appear that James is contradicting Paul's teaching on justification by faith (Romans 4) when he says that "a man is justified by works, and not by faith alone" (James 2:24). However, two observations clear up the problem: (1) Paul spoke of justification before God in Romans, and this is accomplished by faith alone. James, on the other hand, is referring to the evidence before other men that one is justified, and the only real evidence would be works, not profession of faith. (2) A saving faith is a faith that works; if there are no changes in a person's life, his may be a dead faith (James 2:26).

People who have no assurance of salvation may be walking by feelings and not by faith in God's promises. But a lack of assurance may also mean that a person never really became a biblical Christian in the first place. If the Holy Spirit does not bear witness with his spirit that he is a child of God (Romans 8:16), this witness may be absent because he is not a child of God. Therefore, it is unwise to give assurance to a person unless it is obvious that he is a genuine believer. Usually, if someone is unsure of where he stands with the Savior, the best approach is to ask, "Why not make sure right now?" and invite him to pray with you to receive Christ. Even if he already knew Christ, this can be beneficial in solidifying his commitment.

Summary

When people understand the Gospel, it may seem too good to be true, and they often doubt that anyone could really be sure of their salvation.

Three objections to the idea of security often come up: First, can't a person stop believing? This represents a deficient understanding of the nature of faith in Christ. Second, won't certain sins disqualify a Christian? Here the confusion has to do with the nature of sin. Third, don't we have to maintain our salvation? The misunderstanding here relates to the nature of works.

The solution to the problem of assurance is to reason from what God's Word says about us, not from our feelings. Salvation is a free gift that cannot be paid for, earned, or maintained. Eternal life knows no limits, and once a person has received the life of Christ, the scriptures are abundantly clear that no force or person can remove it from him. Some have argued from a few debated passages that salvation can be lost, but a closer analysis of these passages in their contexts reveals that they do not conflict with the clear testimony of the rest of scripture. If the matter of his or her own assurance troubles someone, they can overcome this uncertainty by making sure they are trusting in Christ alone for their salvation today. Write a note in the front cover of a bible, or on a card kept in a wallet, along the lines of this: "As of [today's date], I admit that I am a sinner and I understand that my sin separates me from God. I believe that Jesus, being God, paid the penalty for all my sins when he died on the cross and rose from the dead. As of today, I am trusting in him as my Savior. Thank you God for loving and forgiving me and giving me the gift of eternal life.

Supplemental Reading for Q9-12

Stanley, Andy. *How Good is Good Enough?* Multnomah Books, 2003.

Bing, Charles. *Simply by Grace: An Introduction to God's Life-Changing Gift.* Kregel, 2009.

Chafer, Lewis Sperry. *Salvation: God's Marvelous Work of Grace.* Reprint. Kregel Classics, 1917, 1991.

Demarest, Bruce. *The Cross and Salvation.* Crossway Books, 1997.

Ediger, Edwin Aaron. *Faith in Jesus: What Does It Mean To Believe in Him?* WestBow Press, 2012.

Gromacki, Robert Glenn. *Salvation Is Forever.* Regular Baptist Press, 1973, 1989, 2007.

Lloyd-Jones, D. Martyn. *The Assurance of Our Salvation.* Good News Publishing, 2000.

Moyer, R. Larry. *Free and Clear: Understanding & Communicating God's Offer of Eternal Life.* Kregel, 1997, 2009.

Pinson, J. Matthew, ed. *Four Views on Eternal Security.* Zondervan, 2002.

Radmacher, Earl. *Salvation.* Thomas Nelson, 2000.

Ryrie, Charles C. *So Great Salvation: What It Means To Believe in Jesus Christ.* Victor Books, 1989.

Schreiner, Thomas R., and Ardel B. Caneday. *The Race Set Before Us: A Biblical Theology of Perseverance and Assurance.* InterVarsity, 2001.

Stanley, Charles. *Eternal Security: Can You Be Sure?* Thomas Nelson, 1990.

Swindoll, Charles R. *The Grace Awakening.* Thomas Nelson, 1990, 1996, 2003, 2010.

Yancey, Philip. *What's So Amazing about Grace?* Zondervan, 2000.

Study Guide for Can a Person Be Sure of Their Salvation?

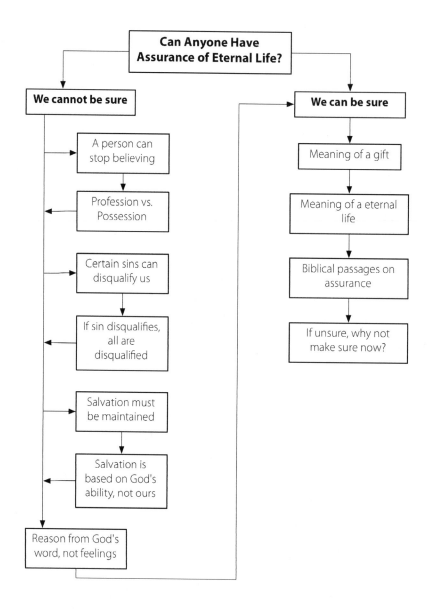

Key Illustrations

Mortgage

If someone decided to pay off the mortgage on your house, you would be notified to that effect, and your monthly house payment would be returned if it reached the bank after the note had been paid. It would be absurd for the bank to take your check and send you a letter stating that even though the mortgage had been paid off, you must still pay it because it was your mortgage. When a debt has been paid in full, it no longer exists.

Unconditional Love vs. Jeopardy

This perspective becomes more obvious if we look at it in the context of parents and children. Imagine two families that set up an identical list of rules for their children. One communicates unconditional love for their daughter. If she breaks one of the rules, the parents discipline her lovingly, all the while assuring her of their love. She's never even considered the possibility that breaking one of the rules could get her expelled from the family.

Now imagine that the other family, while agreeing on the rules, takes a different approach on consequences. They constantly threaten the children with expulsion or disinheritance.

Which approach will produce better or worse results if the goal is to raise healthy, productive, contributing people and citizens to society? God offering us eternal life, true security, actually promotes better behavior, not worse.

Empire State Building

A visitor in Manhattan may decide to take the elevator up to the upper observation floor of the Empire State Building. When he steps on and the elevator begins to move, he has made an irrevocable decision that commits him to the whole quarter-mile vertical journey. He may be gripped with a sudden panic after 30 seconds and 55 floors, fully convinced that the cable will break. But this does not change the fact that he will safely arrive at the 102nd floor.

Key Verses

John 3:16 For God so loved the world that he gave his only begotten son, that whosoever believes in him should not perish, but have eternal life.

John 5:24 Truly I say to you, he who hears my word, and believes him who sent me, has eternal life, and does not come into judgment, but has passed out of death into life.

John 6:37, 44 All that the father gives me shall come to me, and the one who comes to me I will surely not cast out... No one can come to me, unless the Father who sent me draws him; and I will raise him on the last day.

John 10:28-29 And I give eternal life to them, and they shall never perish, and no one shall snatch them out of my hand. My Father, who has given them to me, is greater than all; and no one is able to snatch them out of the Father's hand.

Romans 8:1 There is therefore no condemnation for those who are in Christ.

Romans 8:29-39 The Security Passage.

Ephesians 1:13-14 In Him, you also, after listening to the message of truth, the gospel of your salvation–having also believed, you were sealed in him with the Holy Spirit of Promise, who is given as a pledge of our inheritance, with a view to the redemption of God's own possession, to the praise of his glory.

Colossians 1:12-14 Joyously giving thanks to the Father, who has qualified us to share in the inheritance of the saints in light. He Delivered us from the domain of darkness, transferred us to the kingdom of his beloved Son, in whom we have redemption, the forgiveness of sins;

1 Peter 1:3-4 Blessed be the God and Father of our Lord Jesus Christ, who according to his great mercy has caused us to be born again to a living hope through the resurrection of Jesus Christ from the dead, to obtain an inheritance which is imperishable and undefiled and will not fade away, reserved in heaven for you.

1 John 2:1-2 And if anyone sins, we have an Advocate with the Father, Jesus Christ the Righteous, and he himself is the propitiation of our sins; and not for ours only, but also for those of the whole world.

1 John 5:13 These things I have written to you who believe in the name of the Son of God, in order that you may know that you have eternal life.

Study Questions

1. Why is it that most people are unsure about whether or not they will get to heaven?

2. There are five common misconceptions that cause people to doubt their salvation. How would you respond to each.

> The Nature of...
>
>> ...Faith
>>
>> ...Sin
>>
>> ...Works
>>
>> ...God's Gift
>>
>> ...Eternal Life

3. If you can accept "the gift" and be sure of salvation regardless of what you do, then what is the incentive for righteous living?

4. Below is a list of disputed passages concerning eternal security. Explain how you would respond to each.

- John 15:6
- Galatians 5:4
- Hebrews 6:4-6
- James 2:18-26

Notes

SUGGESTED READING LIST

General Apologetics

Introductory Level

Beckwith, Francis J., William Lane Craig, and J. P. Moreland, eds. **To Everyone An Answer**: *A Case for the Christian Worldview. Essays in Honor of Norman L. Geisler.* Downers Grove: InterVarsity Press, 2004.

Chamberlain, Paul. **Why People Don't Believe**: *Confronting Seven Challenges to Christian Faith.* Grand Rapids: Baker Books, 2011.

Cowan, Steven B., ed. **Five Views on Apologetics**. Zondervan, 2000.

Craig, William L. **On Guard**: *Defending Your Faith with Reason and Precision.* Colorado Springs: David C. Cook, 2010.

___, and Joseph E. Gorra. **A Reasonable Response**: *Answers to Tough Questions on God, Christianity and the Bible.* Chicago: Moody

Publishers, 2013.

Feinberg, John S. **Can You Believe It's True?** *Christian Apologetics in a Modern and Postmodern Era.* Wheaton: Crossway, 2013.

Geisler, Norman L., and Patrick Zuckeran. **The Apologetics of Jesus**: *A Caring Approach to Dealing with Doubters.* Grand Rapids: Baker Books, 2009.

Hazen, Craig J. **Five Sacred Crossings**: *A Novel Approach to a Reasonable Faith.* Eugene, OR: Harvest House, 2008.

Hindson, Ed, and Ergun Caner, eds. **The Popular Encyclopedia of Apologetics**: *Surveying the Evidence for the Truth of Christianity.* Eugene, OR: Harvest House, 2008.

Keller, Tim. **The Reason for God**: *Belief in an Age of Skepticism.* New York: Dutton, 2008.

Koukl, Gregory. **Tactics**: *A Game Plan for Discussing Your Christian Convictions.* Grand Rapids: Zondervan, 2009.

Kreeft, Peter, and Ronald K. Tacelli. **Handbook of Christian Apologetics**. Downers Grove: InterVarsity, 1994.

Lewis, C. S. **Mere Christianity**. Rev. ed. New York: HarperCollins, 1943, 1945, 1952, 1980, 2009.

Little, Paul E. **Know Why You Believe**. Fourth edition. Revised by Marie Little. Downers Grove: InterVarsity, 1967, 1968, 1988, 2000.

McDowell, Sean, ed. **Apologetics for a New Generation**: *A Biblical & Culturally Relevant Approach to Talking about God.* Eugene, OR: Harvest House, 2009.

McGrath, Alister E **Mere Apologetics**: *How To Help Seekers and Skeptics Find Faith.* Grand Rapids: Baker Books, 2012.

Metaxas, Eric, ed. **Life, God, and Other Small Topics**: *Conversations from Socrates in the City.* New York: Plume/Penguin, 2011, 2012.

Mittelberg, Mark. **Confident Faith**: *Building a Firm Foundation for Your Beliefs* (formerly, *Choosing in a World of Spiritual Options*).Revised Edition. Carol Stream, IL: Tyndale House, 2008, 2013.

___. **The Questions Christians Hope No One Will Ask** (*with answers*). Carol Stream, IL: Tyndale House, 2010.

___. **The Reason Why**: *Faith Makes Sense.* Carol Stream, IL: Tyndale House, 2011.

Moreland, J. P. **Love Your God With All Your Mind**. Rev. 15th Anniv. Ed. Colorado Springs: NavPress, 1997, 2012.

Muncaster, Ralph O. **101 Reasons You Can Believe**: *Why the Christian Faith Makes Sense.* Eugene, OR: Harvest House, 2004.

Pearson, Glenn. **That's a Great Question**: *What To Say When Your Faith Is Challenged.* Colorado Springs: Victor Books, 2007.

Powell, Doug. **Holman QuickSource Guide to Christian Apologetics**: *A Clear and Complete Overview*. Nashville: B&H Publishing, 2006.

Rhodes, Ron. **Answering the Objections of Atheists, Agnostics, and Skeptics**. Eugene, OR: Harvest House, 2006.

Strobel, Lee. **The Case for Faith**: *A Journalist Investigates the Toughest Objections to Christianity*. Grand Rapids: Zondervan, 2000.

Zacharias, Ravi, and Norman Geisler, eds. **Who Made God?** *And Answers to Over 100 Tough Questions of Faith*. Grand Rapids: Zondervan, 2003.

More Advanced Level

Boa, Kenneth, and Robert M. Bowman, Jr. **Faith Has Its Reasons**: *An Integrative Approach to Defending Christianity*. Second Edition. Waynesboro, GA: Authentic Publishing, 2001, 2005.

Campbell-Jack, W. C., and Gavin McGrath, eds. **New Dictionary of Christian Apologetics**. Downers Grove: InterVarsity Press, 2006.

Copan, Paul, and William Lane Craig, eds. **Come Let Us Reason**: *New Essays in Christian Apologetics*. Nashville: B&H Academic, 2012.

Craig, William L. **Reasonable Faith**: *Christian Truth and Apologetics* (a revised edition of *Apologetics: An Introduction*, Moody Press, 1984). Third Edition. Wheaton: Crossway Books/Good News Publishers, 1994, 2008.

Dembski, William, and Thomas Schirrrmacher, eds. **Tough-Minded Christianity**: *Honoring the Legacy of John Warwick Montgomery*. Nashville: B&H Academic, 2008.

Geisler, Norman L. **The Big Book of Christian Apologetics**: *An A to Z Guide* (abridged & adapted version of the *Baker Encyclopedia of Christian Apologetics*). Grand Rapids: Baker, 1999, 2012.

____. **Christian Apologetics**. 2nd Edition. Grand Rapids: Baker Academic, 1976, 2013.

____, and Paul K. Hoffman, eds. **Why I Am A Christian**: *Leading Thinkers Explain Why They Believe*. Revised Edition. Baker Books, 2001, 2006.

____, and Chad V. Meister, eds. **Reasons for Faith**: *Making a Case for the Christian Faith*. Wheaton: Crossway Books, 2007.

Groothuis, Douglas. **Christian Apologetics**: *A Comprehensive Case for Biblical Faith*. Downers Grove: IVP Academic, 2011.

House, H. Wayne, and Dennis W. Jowers. **Reasons for Our Hope**: *An Introduction to Christian Apologetics*. Nashville: B&H Academic, 2011.

McDowell, Joshua **Evidence for Christianity**: *Historical Evidences for the Christian Faith* (contains much of *Evidence That Demands a Verdict* and *New Evidence That Demands a Verdict*). Nashville: Thomas Nelson, 2006.

Schaeffer, Francis A. **The Complete Works of Francis A. Schaeffer**. 5 vols. Wheaton: Crossway Books, 1982.

Sproul, R. C. **Defending Your Faith**: *An Introduction to Apologetics*. Wheaton: Crossway Books, 2003.

Willard, Dallas, ed. **A Place for Truth**: *Leading Thinkers Explore Life's Hardest Questions*. Downers Grove: IVP Books, 2010.

Media

Foundations of Apologetics. A 12 volume DVD series. Norcross, GA: Ravi Zacharias International Ministries, 2007.

Mitchell, Chris. **Mere Christianity**: *A four-part video study guide*. Springfield, VA: C. S. Lewis Institute, 2010, www.cslewisinstitute.org.

Montgomery, John Warwick. **A Lawyer Examines the Case for Christianity**. Santa Barbara, CA: Veritas Forum-UCSB, 1999, www.veritas-uscb.org.

Keller, Timothy. **The Reason for God**: *Conversations on Faith and Life. A DVD Study*. Grand Rapids: Zondervan, 2010 (120 mins.).

The Search for Answers: *A Friendly Conversation* (1 CD). Ellicott City, MD: Search Ministries, Inc., 2009.

The Search for Meaning: *Two Friends Discuss Honest Questions about God* (6CDs). Ellicott City, MD: Search Ministries, Inc., 1999.

Strobel, Lee. **The Case for Faith**: *The Film*. La Mirada, CA: La Mirada Films, 2008 (79 mins.), www.leestrobel.com.

___. **Faith Under Fire**: *Vol. 1 – Faith & Jesus*. Grand Rapids: Zondervan, 2006 (60 mins.), www.zondervan.com.

___. **Faith Under Fire**: *Vol. 2 – Faith & Facts*. Grand Rapids: Zondervan, 2006 (60 mins.), www.zondervan.com.

___. **Faith Under Fire**: *Vol. 3 – Tough Faith Questions*. Grand Rapids: Zondervan, 2006 (60 mins.), www.zondervan.com.

___. **Faith Under Fire**: *Vol. 4 – A New Kind of Faith.*. Grand Rapids: Zondervan, 2006 (60 mins.), www.zondervan.com.

Relational Evangelism

Books

Aldrich, Joseph C. **LifeStyle Evangelism**: *Learning To Open Your Life to Those around You*. Colorado Springs: Multnomah Books, 1981, 1993.

Barrs, Jerram. **The Heart of Evangelism**. Wheaton: Crossway Books, 2001.

___. **Learning Evangelism from Jesus**. Wheaton: Crossway Books, 2009.

Bock, Darrell, and Mitch Glaser, eds. **To the Jew First**: *The Case for Jewish Evangelism in Scripture and History*. Grand Rapids: Kregel Publications, 2008.

Borthwick, Paul. Stop Witnessing...and Start Loving. Colorado Springs: NavPress, 2003.

Bowen, John P. **Evangelism for "Normal People"**: *Good News for Those Looking for a Fresh Approach*. Minneapolis: Augsburg Fortress, 2002.

Clegg, Tom, & Warren Bird. **Missing in America**: *Making an Eternal Difference in the World Next Door*. Loveland, CO: Group Publishing, 2007.

Coleman, Robert E. **The Heart of the Gospel**: *The Theology Behind the Master Plan of Evangelism*. Grand Rapids: Baker Books, 2011.

___. **The Master Plan of Evangelism**. Grand Rapids: Baker/Revell, 1963, 1993.

Dawson, Scott, ed. **The Complete Evangelism Guidebook**: *Expert Advice on Reaching Others for Christ*. Second Edition. Grand Rapids: Baker Books, 2006, 2008.

Downs, Tim. **Finding Common Ground:** *How To Communicate with Those Outside the Christian Community While We Still Can*. Chicago: Moody Press, 1999.

Earley, Dave, and David Wheeler. **Evangelism Is...**How To Share Jesus with Passion and Confidence. Nashville: B&H Academic, 2010.

Field Guide to Neighborhood Outreach. Loveland, CO: Group Publishing, 2007.

Fincher, Dale, and Jonalyn Fincher. **Coffee Shop Conversations**: *Making the Most of Spiritual Small Talk*. Grand Rapids: Zondervan, 2010.

Fischer, John. **Fearless Faith**: *Living Beyond the Walls of "Safe" Christianity*. Eugene, OR: Harvest House, 2002.

Geisler, Norman, and David Geisler. **Conversational Evangelism**: *How To Listen and Speak so You Can Be Heard*. Eugene, OR: Harvest House, 2009.

Green, Michael. **Sharing Your Faith with Friends and Family**: *Talking about Jesus without Offending*. Grand Rapids: Baker Books, 2005.

Harney, Kevin G. **Organic Outreach for Ordinary People**: *Sharing Good News Naturally*. Grand Rapids: Zondervan, 2009.

___. **Organic Outreach for Churches**: *Infusing Evangelistic Passion into Your Congregation*. Grand Rapids: Zondervan, 2011.

___, and Sherry Harney. **Organic Outreach for Families**: *Turning Your Home into a Lighthouse*. Grand Rapids: Zondervan, 2012.

Henderson, Jim. **Evangelism without Additives**: *What if Sharing Your Faith Meant Just Being Yourself?* (formerly, a.k.a. "Lost": *Discovering Ways To Connect with the People Jesus Misses Most*). Colorado Springs: WaterBrook Press, 2005, 2007.

Hybels, Bill. **Just Walk Across the Room**: *Simple Steps Pointing People to Faith*. Grand Rapids: Zondervan, 2006.

___, and Mark Mittelberg. **Becoming a Contagious Christian**. Grand Rapids: Zondervan, 1994.

Litfin, Duane. **Word Versus Deed**: *Resetting the Scales to a Biblical Balance*. Wheaton: Crossway, 2012.

Little, Paul E. **How To Give Away Your Faith**. Rev. Ed. Downers Grove: InterVarsity, 1966, 1988, 2006.

McDill, Wayne. **Making Friends for Christ**: *A Practical Approach to Relational Evangelism*. Second Ed. Maitland, FL: Xulon Press, 1979, 2010.

McGinnis, Alan Loy. **The Friendship Factor**: *How to Get Closer to the People You Care For*. 25th Anniversary Revised Edition. Minneapolis: Augsburg, 2004.

McRaney, Will Jr. **The Art of Personal Evangelism**: *Sharing Jesus in a Changing Culture*. Nashville: Broadman & Holman, 2003.

Medearis, Carl. **Speaking of Jesus**: *The Art of Not-Evangelism*. Colorado Springs: David C. Cook, 2011.

Meyer, Daniel. **Witness Essentials**: *Evangelism that Makes Disciples*. Downers Grove: IVP Connect, 2012.

Moreland, J. P., and Tim Muehlhoff. **The God Conversation**: *Using Stories and Illustrations To Explain Your Faith*. Downers Grove: InterVarsity Press, 2007.

Morgan, Elisa. **"I Can" Evangelism**: *Taking the "I Can't" Out of Sharing Your Faith* (formerly *Twinkle*). Grand Rapids: Revell, 2008.

Newman, Randy. **Bringing the Gospel Home**: *Witnessing to Family Members, Close Friends, and Others Who Know You Well*. Wheaton: Crossway, 2011.

___. **Corner Conversations**: *Engaging Dialogues About God and Life*. Grand Rapids: Kregel, 2006.

___. **Questioning Evangelism**: *Engaging People's Hearts the Way Jesus Did*. Grand Rapids: Kregel, 2004.

Nuenke, Doug. **Making Waves**: *Being an Influence for Jesus in Everyday Life*. Colorado Springs: NavPress, 2011.

Outreach Ministry in the 21st Century. *The Encyclopedia of Practical Ideas*. Loveland, CO: Group Publishing, 2007.

Pathak, Jay, and Dave Runyon. **The Art of Neighboring**: *Building Genuine Relationships Right Outside Your Door*. Grand Rapids: Baker Books, 2012.

Petersen, Jim. **Living Proof**. Colorado Springs: NavPress, 1989.

___, & Mike Shamy. **The Insider**: *Bringing the Kingdom of God into Your Everyday World*. Colorado Springs: NavPress, 2003.

Pippert, Rebecca M. **Out of the Saltshaker and into the World**: *Evangelism as a Way of Life*. Rev. Ed. Downers Grove: InterVarsity Press, 1979, 1999.

___. **Talking about Jesus without Sounding Religious**. Downers Grove: InterVarsity Press, 2003.

Pollock, Doug. **God Space**: *Where Spiritual Conversations Happen Naturally*. Loveland, CO: Group Publishing, 2009.

Reid, Alvin L **Evangelism Handbook**: *Biblical, Spiritual, Intentional, Missional*. Nashville: B & H Academic, 2009.

Richardson, Rick. **Evangelism Outside the Box**: *New Ways to Help People Experience the Good News*. Downers Grove: InterVarsity Press, 2000.

___. **Reimagining Evangelism**: *Inviting Friends on a Spiritual Journey.* Downers Grove: InterVarsity Press, 2006.

Root, Jerry, and Stan Guthrie. **The Sacrament of Evangelism**. Chicago: Moody Publishers, 2011.

Sjogren, Steve. **Conspiracy of Kindness**: *A Unique Approach to Sharing the Love of Jesus.* Third Edition. Ventura, CA: Regal Books/Gospel Light, 1993, 2003, 2007.

___, and Dave Ping. **Outflow**: *Outward-Focused Living in a Self-Focused World.* Loveland, CO: Group Publishing, 2006.

___, Dave Ping, and Doug Pollock. **Irresistible Evangelism**: *Natural Ways To Open Others to Jesus.* Loveland, CO: Group, 2004.

Sorensen, Stephen. **Like Your Neighbor?** *Doing Everyday Evangelism on Common Ground.* Downers Grove: InterVarsity, 2005.

Strobel, Lee, and Mark Mittelberg. **The Unexpected Adventure**: *Taking Everyday Risks To Talk with People about Jesus.* Grand Rapids: Zondervan, 2009.

Wretlind, Norm and Becky, with Jim Killam. **When God Is the Life of the Party**: *Reaching Neighbors through Creative Hospitality.* Colorado Springs: NavPress, 2003.

Video Training Resources

Eastman, Brett & Deanna, Todd & Denise Wendorff, and Karen Lee-Thorp. **Sharing Christ Together**. *Experiencing Christ Together Series.* Grand Rapids: Zondervan, 2005. 6 Session DVD. Study Guide also available.

___. **Sharing Your Life Mission Every Day**. *Doing Life Together Series.* Grand Rapids: Zondervan, 2005. 6 Session DVD. Study Guide also available.

Hybels, Bill. **Just Walk Across the Room**: *Simple Steps Pointing People to Faith.* Grand Rapids: Zondervan, 2006.

Mittelberg, Mark. **Building a Contagious Church**. Grand Rapids: Zondervan, 2000.

Sharp, Mary Jo. **Why Do You Believe That?** *A Faith Conversation.* Nashville: Lifeway Christian Resources, 2012.

Stanley, Andy. **Go Fish**: *Because of What's on the Line.* Colorado Springs: Multnomah Publishers, 2005.

THE AUTHORS

KENNETH BOA holds a B.S. from Case Institute of Technology, a Th.M. from Dallas Theological Seminary, a Ph.D. from New York University, and a D.Phil, from Oxford University, Oxford, England. He is the author or contributor to over 80 books.

Dr. Boa is in full-time ministry as President of Reflections Ministries, Inc., an organization that seeks to encourage, teach, and equip people to know Christ, follow him, become progressively conformed to his image, and reproduce his life in others. Ken and his wife Karen make their home in the Atlanta, Georgia, and have a daughter and son-in-law, Heather and Matthew Cottingham, and two grandchildren.

LARRY MOODY is a co-founder and former president of Search Ministries, Inc., a national organization based in Fort Worth, TX. Search's mission is "inviting people to take a next step toward God." Larry has a B.A. from King's College and a Th.M. from Dallas Theological Seminary. Larry has served on a variety of boards over his decades-long ministry career, including: Baltimore Colts Chaplain, PGA Tour Chaplain, Board of Regents at Dallas Theological Seminary and board member at EMF (K-LOVE and Air 1). He and his wife Ruth live in Ellicott City near their four adult children, their spouses and seven wonderful grandchildren.

Prior to their current roles, Ken and Larry worked together with New Life Ministries, Walk Thru the Bible, and Search Ministries.